Lost2bFound

B

Glenn Johnstone

Copyright © 2025 Glenn Johnstone

ISBN: 9781917778909

All rights reserved, including the right to reproduce this book, or portions thereof in any form. No part of this text may be reproduced, transmitted, downloaded, decompiled, reverse engineered, or stored, in any form or introduced into any information storage and retrieval system, in any form or by any means, whether electronic or mechanical without the express written permission of the author.

For Mam and Dad

Acknowledgments

It would be impossible for me to name and acknowledge each person who has been a part of my journey so far. Therefore, I'd like you to imagine a big, vibrant neon sign that simply says, "Thank you". It represents my heartfelt expression of gratitude, which is important to me. No one should feel overlooked for their kindness and support. Your contributions to my journey have provided me with purpose and inspiration.

Mam and Dad. You have been there alongside me to weather the storms, offering much needed support, protection, and strength when I needed it most. Your love and guidance have illuminated my path, allowing me to embrace the brighter moments with joy and gratitude.

My friends, work colleagues, and fellow adventurers, thank you for being there to share laughter, stories, and all those special moments. Moments that have meant so much. Your encouragement and kind words have made each challenge that much easier.

I owe a great debt of gratitude to the universe, not only for the many fortunate opportunities that have come my way, but also for the beautiful landscapes that speak to my soul, the gentle streams that murmur as they flow, the trees that whisper their welcome in the breeze, and the trails that offer me discovery and escape. I am thankful for the rolling hills, vibrant valleys, and all of the wonderful things that nature has been so kind to offer.

This book is also for all those fellow dreamers out there. I know all of our journeys can be tough at times but never give up on your dreams. Keep pushing forward, keep believing. Here's to gaining more knowledge, memories, and experiences from those adventures ahead!

Preface

"Sometimes in life, you have to be lost in order to be found."

Before I begin, I would like to offer a word of warning that this book contains some strong language, the majority of which was an expression to convey the deep emotions I was feeling during some very difficult times. Oh and the odd one to lighten a moment. As you will read if you decide to delve further into this book, you will discover I have a somewhat dark sense of humour. This has helped me get through some very challenging times and enabled me to see things in a different light. So I thought it would be best to give you a heads up from the start, as particular words are not there to cause any offence. It also got me thinking about "why" we tend to use what are maybe considered bad words, foul language, swear, curse, or profanities.

Yes, I could have replaced the odd "fuck" with a "dear me", however, this would not have expressed my true emotional state at particular times. Swearing can act as a release and a coping mechanism during immense stress, anger, frustration, or pain. I have learnt while working as a rehabilitation assistant, in which part of my role is to carry out speech and language therapy, that swear words are stored in our brains as "automatic" or "emotional" language.

Quite a number of the patients I am asked to carry out therapy with present with what is known as expressive or receptive "aphasia", sometimes referred to as dysphasia, "dys" being the Latin for bad, disordered, or difficult. Those patients with "expressive" dysphasia, depending on the level of their deficit, can really struggle with communication and finding the words they would like to say.

"Aphasia" is a disorder that affects a person's ability to communicate in a range of different ways, from speaking to understanding, reading to writing. "Automatic language" can be produced when no other words can be expressed, and quite often the automatic word is a swear word relaying a person's frustration, or in some cases anger at their situation. Is it wrong to say or produce those kind of words? No, it is merely an expression of an emotion.

As I have explained, my reasoning for the use of bad language within my book, I have also attempted to incorporate the use of the vernacular of the region in which I am from. This proved to be a lot more challenging than I anticipated. As although I can speak the lingo, typing it down, in order to properly convey the unique pronunciation patterns, vocabulary, and intonation took me sometime. I am sure there will be some errors, to my pit-village, broken dialect, so please forgive me. As you will see I have in certain places put an explanation, just in case you aren't from my neck of the woods. I mean I don't exactly speak Arapahoe, but some words and phrases may have you thinking "I haven't a clue what on earth he is on about."

I am not sure how I came up with the title for this book; it was just one of those thoughts that popped into my head, and then stubbornly refused to leave. The more I thought about it, the more fitting it became. After all, I have lost quite a bit in my life, less than some, perhaps more than others. Over the years, I have discovered a lot about myself, other people and the world around me. This is my story, and I will allow you, the reader, to decide whether I have managed to pull myself out of the deepest, darkest hole I could ever imagine, and if I have done things in my life worthy of a simple "He tried his best." At the end of the day, that is all any of us can do. I have no ambitions of becoming famous, nor do I want people to think of me as doing anything exceptional, in attempting to overcome the things that have occurred in my life. I believe we all have an inherent resilience, and that fight in us when life can go dramatically off course, suddenly surprising us in just what we can cope with and go on to do.

I always find it strange when people comment, "Oh, you have been through a lot; you are so brave." Well, yeah, I have probably had more than my fair share of stuff I would have preferred to have avoided. However, it has nothing to do with bravery. When everything falls apart, and you are placed in what feels like impossible situations, where there are no apparent good options, and you are forced to face whatever comes your way without a guidebook, what are you supposed to do? I'm just an ordinary bloke trying to get through life and avoid any catastrophes along the way.

So, where to begin? "Once upon a time" doesn't quite seem like a fitting start.

From a young age, I always felt different. It was as if I were on the outside looking in, on a world where I just didn't fit. I don't know where these feelings came from, even if I calm my mind today and ask myself, "Why?" I still can't give either you or myself an answer. Isn't it strange when we try to ask questions of ourselves, but then cannot come up with the answers we so desperately want or need? Maybe it's a form of self-preservation. For me my mind goes completely blank, a little bit like a computer rebooting. Things haven't really improved as I've gotten older; I've just become better at hiding the fact that I find it challenging to engage with people, and feel in order to do so, I have to pretend to be someone else.

I'm probably one of those annoying people who cover up discomfort by talking too much, using humour, overthinking, and reacting sensitively to situations, especially after being hurt by someone who never intended to hurt me in the first place. I guess I'm trying to give you a little background into the weird and wonderful things that go on inside my head. I believe it's relevant because what was about to happen would challenge me in ways I could never have imagined. For a time, I felt utterly alone and trapped in a living nightmare.

And so "my story", or as I like to call it, "my journey", is about my experiences both positive and negative that have shaped my life so far. Those experiences have taught me many new things and given me the strength and knowledge to hopefully find my way if ever I should become lost. It is not exactly a practical guide; however, it may give you some insight or room for thought into your own challenges. Even when you think you are shit out of options, you can still take some control of your destiny.

Introduction

Born and bred in Stanley County Durham, I had no real aspirations growing up. I would say I was bright at school; however, I tried to fly under the radar. I suffered some bullying and didn't particularly enjoy my time in, well, I'm not sure I would call it an education. I think I learnt more at the University of Life. Upon leaving school way back in 1984 at sixteen, I went on a Youth Training Scheme, trying to follow in my dad's footsteps as a motor mechanic. I would go to college for a few weeks at a time, then be on placement at the garage my dad was a partner in for a further few weeks. At that age, I was more interested in motorcycles and would tinker with the various small bikes I happened to get my hands on.

When I think back, being a mechanic wasn't really for me. I enjoyed the technical side of engineering, taking things apart and trying to put them back together without having any spare pieces remaining. However, I didn't particularly enjoy getting all oily and dirty. After I completed my Youth Training Scheme (YTS), I got a few useless qualifications, then pretty much went on another scheme, this time a Manpower Services Scheme, and began working down at Beamish Museum. I have to say I wasn't exactly sure what the job description would have been for this new role – maybe track technician. Apart from greasing the train and tram tracks, and doing the odd replacement of the rails, most of my time was spent messing around with the other lads, who were also on the same type of scheme. Hanging around in the compound was fun; it was where all the old-fashioned relics of yesteryear and days gone by were kept, and there was some interesting stuff. Oh, and when the weather was cold, we would hide out beneath the signal box, where there was always a nice warm open fire. The government created the schemes to improve employment figures and keep young people from signing on the dole. No one I ever knew got a permanent job after participating in these types of schemes. Following on from working down at Beamish Museum, I managed to get a temporary job working in a factory at Ever Ready. I absolutely hated it, and following being taken off the production line, and being placed on floor cleaning duties, I accidently broke the really expensive floor cleaning machine. I swear I didn't do it on purpose. I was then demoted to a bucket and mop. I eventually got the sack, after only three days, as I back chatted the supervisor, and it doesn't take too much imagination to guess where I told him to stick his mop.

Work was very hard to find during Maggie Thatcher's reign, which lasted from May 1979 to November 1990. The coal mines and local industries like shipbuilding and manufacturing were closing. The northeast was hit hard, and I'm not sure if the region has ever fully recovered. To this day, the area I live in is still classed as deprived. Following the Manpower Services Scheme I spent a couple of years on the dole, as it was known, claiming benefits. It pretty much felt like being on the scrap heap at only nineteen or so years of age. If my memory serves me right I was twenty-one when I managed to get a casual job, working at Royal Mail, and my local delivery office in Stanley. Following a good few months of proving that I was reliable, I was offered a permanent position along with a contract. I then became a "postie", complete with my very own badge number and uniform. At first, I didn't have my own set delivery, so I used to "float", meaning I completed other people's deliveries if they were off on annual leave or the sick. Over the years, I would go on to complete every delivery that the Derwentside Delivery Office had to offer.

Eventually, I became a delivery and collection driver. I remember those first few months as a van driver; it was a little stressful trying to remember the routes where all the post boxes were situated and being on time for the collections. Learning which key amongst a large bunch of other keys was a mission in itself. There were so many of them in different shapes and sizes; not all of them had the small round metal tags or numbers stamped onto them to identify which box they fit. There were large brass keys for the big red pillar boxes and small old bent keys, which fitted the Victorian boxes, which were set into some walls that had been there for years. As I would go to clear out some of the boxes, I would discover earwigs and other creepy crawlies inside and have to use the letters to fend them off.

Being a postman was probably my ideal job at the time, as I loved the outdoors, being out in the fresh air, and the fact that once I was out of the sorting office, I was on my own. I used to regularly jog around my deliveries, finding the job a breeze in those early years. I would go out with one light bag of mail, and for second deliveries, I would be lucky if I had seven or so letters. Things were to change as time went on, as more and more junk mail and heavier items got piled on. Towards the end of my time as a postman, it was so heavy. Each day it felt like being an overloaded donkey. I certainly don't envy the current men and women doing the job these days. People don't realise how much walking is involved, how many houses the posties have to go to, and the extent of the mail that has to be delivered. Walking duties are now six and a half hours long, and a postal worker can walk on average 10 miles per day.

I worked at Royal Mail for roughly six years, before what I can only describe as the catalyst to my roller coaster of a life was about to begin. That front seat of a car where I would desperately cling to the safety rail, my knuckles turning white. It felt like everything was totally out of my control, and the car I was in could leave the safety of the tracks at any moment. Telling this story, it feels strange for me to say "story", as it makes it sound like I've made things up, like in some children's fairy tale. Everything I am about to describe is true. My subconscious stubbornly refuses to let go of certain events. My mind has undoubtedly changed how I have perceived things over time, but that said, my memories feel as lucid in my mind today as when things happened.

I am not exactly starting my story from the beginning, but rather from a point in time that took me on a far different course than I ever imagined. Up until the age of twenty-seven, I had led a relatively unremarkable life, which then turned into a complex existence full of challenges and life-changing events. I'll try to explain them to the best of my recollection. You may find I jump in and out of time, moving between various years, as many things are interlinked, a mishmash of memories.

Chapter 1

Let me invite you to take a step back in time with me to April 1995. I was twenty-seven years old and in a relationship with a girl who lived on the new council estate, which was relatively close to my parents' house (with whom I lived). I had been visiting my now ex-girlfriend and came from her house to my parents at about 10:15 p.m. When I got home, my mam asked if I had eaten, and did I want anything, to which I replied, "Am okay thanks, am off to bed, a've got an early start in the mornin'."

I trotted upstairs and began to get ready for bed. My bedroom was the one facing the back street. I had just gotten into bed when I heard this commotion outside. With a heavy sigh, I impatiently threw off my duvet, got up, and stepped over to my window, taking a peek through the blinds. I could see what appeared at first glance to be two lads having some sort of an altercation, with lots of loud shouting. My first thought was, "Bloody drunks must have come down from the Buffs and are being dicks". The "Buffs", as it was called, used to be a club situated on Durham Road; it has since been demolished and replaced by a care home.

Only a few seconds passed by as I looked on. It was dark, and it took my eyes a little bit of time to adjust to the light. I noticed this guy with his back towards me was holding something in his hand. At first glance, I thought, and I know this might sound strange, but I remember thinking it nonetheless," He's holding a plastic pop bottle." The only illumination in the area was coming from an old flickering yellow streetlight. Suddenly, the guy who had his back to me swung at the other kid with whatever was in his hand, and as this other lad went to defend himself, he was struck on his extended arm. This blow appeared to injure his arm as he struggled to get it back up for the next vicious swing. The assailant moved forward and continued to strike this poor man, who desperately tried to back away and defend himself. The man being attacked was forced to the ground under a rain of heavy blows from what was now an apparent heavy object. The victim was now prone on the ground, desperately trying to defend himself and scramble away, but his attacker straddled him and began raining down blow after blow towards his head.

I then saw a neighbour from down the street come out of his yard and begin shouting at the assailant. I noticed he had a long thin pole, in his hands, it was a flimsy clothes prop. The neighbour's wife, wearing a dressing gown, was stood back in their yard, calling for the attacker to "Leave him alone." There was more shouting. "Get off him! He has had enough!" The assailant then took a few blows from the neighbour across his back, who was using this clothes prop. The neighbour obviously didn't want to get too close to this madman. The assailant briefly got up from his victim, who was now motionless and went threateningly towards the neighbour. This is when I saw that the assailant had some sort of a covering over his head and face; it was a balaclava. As the neighbour backed off, the assailant turned and resumed his attack on his fallen victim, striking him repeatedly until he was so exhausted from the assault that he could barely lift his arm, which was still holding the deadly weapon.

From that description of events, I know you may be thinking, "How long did you watch this terrible thing?" I can assure you it was seconds; it was as if time had stood still. I couldn't comprehend what was going on. However, when I had processed the information, and like I say, it was seconds rather than minutes, I immediately ran from my bedroom downstairs and as quickly as I could explain to my dad, told him, "Someone is being murdered outside, quick call the police". My dad could see I was fraught, so he immediately made the call. I quickly ran back upstairs, looking for some appropriate clothing, with the intention of going out to help the neighbour a few doors down, and try and get this assailant away from the guy he was attacking. I'm not sure what I was thinking; everything was going through my mind at a million miles per hour, "What could I do"? "How could I help"? "What could I use"? along with countless other thoughts. Unless you are in that situation, no one can say what they would do; it's real life and not like what you see in a movie or on television.

My dad joined me in my bedroom, having called 999 and asking for the police. As I was putting on my pants, we briefly looked out of the window, and as we did so saw that the assailant was making his way past our house. He was dressed in dark clothing, and as he passed by, he was tucking something under his jacket, which I later found out to be a hammer and a knife. Just as he got past our back gate, he removed his balaclava and also tucked this away. He continued walking quickly up towards the top of our street. My dad and I ran downstairs and headed outside towards our backyard. A police panda car came tearing around the corner of our street, its strobing blue lights illuminating the area; the police had already had reports of a serious incident. We began shouting, "That's him! That's him!", pointing in the direction of the attacker. The assailant went around the corner at the top of our street, and we ran through to the front garden of our house to see him running across the road. He then vanished somewhere into the housing estate on the opposite side.

My dad and I then went back through to the back street and down towards where this poor man was lying; he was motionless, in the gutter. It was evident that he was dead. There was so much blood spread across the pavement and running slowly down into a nearby drain. It was an ominous scene, as the faded yellow glow from an old streetlight intermingled with the police cars blue strobing lights, making the increasingly large pool of blood appear thick like oil. The man was unrecognisable, having sustained such a brutal and frenzied attack. It was the first time I had seen a dead body, let alone someone murdered.

At about 2:00 a.m. a detective came to our door, informing us that they had apprehended a suspect; the detective wanted to take a statement while it was fresh in our minds. Following giving my statement and the detective leaving, I couldn't sleep, the clock on our sitting room wall rhythmically ticking away as I sat on the couch, my head cupped between my hands. My thoughts weren't my own. I felt a sense of disassociation; it was like an old black and white movie was playing over and over in my mind. Waiting until it was time to go to work felt like an eternity.

I am not ashamed to say that when I was picked up for work by one of the delivery drivers, I was struggling to hold it together. I slowly climbed into the back of the van, greeted my work colleagues in a subdued manner, and then just sat silently in my own little world, hugging my postal bag tight to my chest. I didn't say anything about the events I had witnessed just hours earlier to the other lads in the van.

Bad news certainly spreads quick, as one of my colleagues almost immediately mentioned, "Did you hear about that murder last night?" Another of the postmen joined in the conversation and mentioned the name of the murdered man. It was then that I discovered that I knew the person. We weren't acquaintances, friends or anything; I just knew him from delivering his mail. He only lived down the street from me, on the new council estate. We used to chat in passing, and he always came across as a canny lad. I was later to find out that the murder was all over a lass. It was called a crime of passion. What a waste of life.

Following the murder, I couldn't face walking down our back street; if I had to go that way, I would take a detour and go out of our front gate or up and around the estate. I still live in the same house as I did all those years ago, and every time I pass that part of our street, I am transported back in my mind to that time and place, my thoughts returning to that moment. It is one of many memories embedded deep within my subconscious, a memory that although I know it makes no sense, I still feel guilty that I couldn't have done something to prevent that horrific crime. Thoughts of "If only I had been ten minutes later coming up from my girlfriend's, what could I have done?" "What would I have done?" Had I been in my car, would I have used it to knock the assailant over? But then, I might have been convicted of a crime myself and gone on to serve a prison sentence. I've learnt that you cannot live with regrets, but if I'm being totally honest, that's a lie, and I am a hypocrite.

Chapter 2

Let me try and explain. I have penned the words of this book as the recollections have come to me, and I am being honest in my accounts. Some things are very difficult for me to talk about. One of those things is to do with my children. I have two; they are, of course, all grown up now. My daughter, Kayleigh, is now thirty-three and has a daughter of her own, and my son, Kyle, is thirty-one. I split up with their mother just about the time when all this stuff started with my leg, when they were very young. After that, I didn't play a big part in my kids lives, only seeing them a couple of times a week. I couldn't do the everyday dad things, like having a knock around with a football, playing in the park, going swimming, or taking them on holidays. That said, I am not making excuses; at the end of the day, even though all this stuff was going on, I was a complete failure as a dad.

Over the years, I would say that I haven't had a strong relationship with my children. That is as much my fault as theirs. It hurts as all I ever wanted was to be like my mam and dad. You know to have a "normal family?" I have always been close to my parents and able to share anything. As you will read a little further on, both my dad and I were featured in a short documentary film called Meet the Local Hero, which portrayed part of my journey. In the film, my dad speaks openly to the camera, and upon viewing the film, I was taken aback by his words when he said, "I missed out a lot on our Glenn growing up because I was always working". That one sentence chokes me up. It's funny how history has repeated itself in some ways. I have the same regret about not being there for my kids, but for different reasons. At least I have had the opportunity to spend a lot of time with my dad over the years, especially following his retirement. Our relationship is something I am very proud of, and we are very close because we each make an effort.

I don't feel Kayleigh or Kyle have taken much interest in the things I have gone through or what I have achieved. Unfortunately, we have not got the same bond as I shared with my mother and father. Neither of my children have been there for appointments or when I have needed treatment, and generally, the only signs of concern are cursory messages, or if they want something. I would say our relationships have grown even further apart as they have gotten older and gone on to live their own lives. So, within my story, if I don't mention my children much, it is because I feel we have been absent from one another's lives. In a sense, we are like strangers. Maybe I should make more effort? I think I have built up incredibly high walls to protect myself in some regards.

The truth of the matter is I have been a terrible dad, and I am not sure if I hadn't taken ill, whether I would have been any better or worse after my relationship ended with their mother. I do know that going through what I did had a major effect not only on my physical, but also on my mental health. Looking back and reflecting as I write this, I think I was somewhere else in my head, a place that wasn't always reality. A big part of why things are the way they are now, is because my children grew up being used to me not being there and learning they didn't need me; I was broken. As time moved on and I became more withdrawn, this affected our future relationship to the point that I guess in my mind, they didn't particularly care about events in my life, whether positive or negative. I was disappointed that neither of them came to the screening of my film at Newcastle to offer even a little support; however, they will only know this if they read this book, as I have not mentioned anything to them. That bit was difficult to write and share.

Just after I wrote that previous part about Kayleigh and Kyle, I had the opportunity to talk with Kyle and get his honest opinion about whether he agreed with how I described some things; Kyle did agree with certain aspects and went on to share some of his memories from our time together when he was younger. One of those memories was of being scared when he was little, while a friend and I were watching *Resident Evil*; a zombie had jumped out from a cupboard. Kyle explained that this really scared him and stuck with him; he can still recall the fear. I think I can remember it vaguely. Kyle was only three or four at the time and most upset, crying his eyes out, bless him. It's amazing what memories stick with us in life. Oh, and don't take it that I was allowing Kyle to sit down with us and watch this horror movie at that age; he just happened to come in the room when it was on. Kyle then went on to describe all the hours we used to spend gaming together with Kayleigh, switching from the Sega video console to the PC and playing a game called *Wolfenstein-Enemy Territory*. I can remember building a computer for them, and how they had to share it. They would begrudgingly take turns; however, there were always arguments about how long each one had been on, and I would have to listen to them fighting, "It's my turn, it's my turn".

Kyle also reminded me that he occasionally joined me on some biking adventures when he was in his late teens. On one particular ride, I ended up falling off my bike and found myself upside down in some whiny bushes. I was clipped into my pedals, so stuck amongst all these vicious thorns. Kyle was laughing so much he struggled to help me out. I got my revenge though as a few weeks later, Kyle came off his bike and ended up in a huge nettle patch, much to my amusement. We had been taking some rather wobbly GoPro footage at the time of that adventure, and I just watched it back the other day. Man, I was creased up at Kyle, "Aghhh, it's not funny!", he was shouting, rubbing his arm and then pointing at the nettle patch. I of course edited the appropriate music to the video, "Everybody Hurts" by R.E.M. It seemed appropriate at the time. I'm pleased Kyle refreshed my memory and has some fond memories of his own; it made me smile and laugh.

Another very memorable memory was the time Kyle joined a few of my friends and I on our bikes, and we went wild camping with just bivvy bags for shelter. We all rode over to a place called Struthers Wood. The evening started off well with some good banter and a few laughs. Moving into the night, as we were all tucked in, the heavens opened up, and Kyle started to keep peering out from his bivvy bag. As the rain lashed down, it became clear we hadn't exactly picked a good spot; it was like lying in the middle of a stream. Inevitably, Kyle ended up getting soaked through and began complaining. In the end, I had to call my dad "The Ern" at about three o'clock in the morning. We then had to pack up our gear in the pitch-black darkness of the woods and attempt to push our bikes to the road where my dad could pick us up. By the time we had both gotten back to the car, we looked like a pair of drowned rats. Lesson learnt, be more prepared and check out the weather forecast.

Returning to those terrible events of April and the murder, I struggled to come to terms with what I had witnessed and had to take a few weeks off work. My head was all over the place; I was lost in a labyrinth within my mind, unable to escape. Upon my returning to work I was invited to what I can only describe as three debriefing sessions at Royal Mail in Newcastle. I was supposed to talk about what had happened, and how I was feeling, and then that was to be the end of it. It most definitely was not counselling, and I felt like it made things a whole lot worse. I desperately tried to put the past events out of my mind and just get on with my job. The whole situation caused me to become incredibly introverted; I just wanted to be left alone. In those days, there was no such thing as PTSD (Post Traumatic Stress Disorder); you were just expected to man up and have a stiff upper lip. How things have changed for the better regarding mental health and being able to talk without the attached stigma, though I do think there is a lot more that could be done in accessing help within the health service in a more timely manner.

As I continued to do my job, around May about a month after witnessing that horrible crime I started to limp. There was no real pain at first, however, now and again, without warning, my right leg would give way unexpectedly. I didn't give it much thought until one day when I was doing the Quaking Houses delivery, and this elderly lady stopped me and said, "Eee! Hinny you've been limp'in around all week, are ye alreet?" "Err, aye am okay, thanks," I replied. It was one of those automatic responses we all make when we are greeted and asked, "Are you okay?" However, was I really all right? Continuing with my delivery, I asked myself the question, "Do you think you're okay?", and my internal voice replied "No, not really." It was all the psychological and emotional stuff going on in my head that I couldn't process. I just wanted it to stop, to be able to go back to how things used to be. My leg felt like the least of my worries at the time. I was functioning on autopilot in a world that I no longer understood or recognised.

After finishing my shift that day and going home, I mentioned to my mam what the elderly lady had said and asked her if she could make me an appointment to see our GP about my leg. Within a few days, I had an appointment and attended the surgery to see what the doctor thought. The doctor examined my leg, looking at its range of movement around the knee area; however, he couldn't identify anything. I was then advised to get one of those support stockings, and he would arrange for me to have an X-ray.

A few days later, I was off for an X-ray at South Moor Community Hospital. I was informed that the results would probably take a week to come back and that my doctor would contact me if there was anything to report. Within two days, as I got in from work after completing the nighttime collections, my mam told me that the doctor had phoned and said he would stay back at the surgery because he wanted to see me. I had to go up at once. So off I went to the surgery. I can remember not being overly concerned about my leg. I was just totally numb, from a thoughts and processing point of view; it was a very strange feeling, like I was there going through the motions, however, not there in the real world. Everything felt "fuzzy." I didn't put two and two together, that this could potentially be bad news regarding the X-ray results.

Upon seeing my doctor, he informed me he had some rather bad news, explaining that the X-ray had shown something in my bone at the top of the tibia head. I looked at him rather perplexed and asked, "What does that mean?" "Well, you will have to have a biopsy," he said. "A what?" The doctor then explained what a biopsy was. A sample would need to be taken from my bone. This involved a minor surgical procedure, and this is when I started panicking. You see, I used to have an aversion to hospitals.

Let me now tell you a few tales, a look into some of my childhood and growing up, with stories that I hope you find amusing and lighten the mood.

Chapter 3

For starters, I blame my dad for my fear of anything to do with hospitals and whatnot. He used to have a real fear of needles, and the sight of blood made him queasy. My mam told me that when they first started courting, and for you young folks, courting means dating (Hey even dating might be a thing of the past; I am definitely not down with the kids). My son Kyle reliably informs me that when the younger generation now gets in a relationship, each party informs the other that they are "exclusive". I find that the older I get, the more complicated life becomes, what with political correctness and one thing and another. I even found myself Googling when doing some research for this book, as I was thinking, "Mmmmm, I wonder if I am allowed to say that". For me and many others, especially the older generation, people like my dad, it is very bad craic when they are told they shouldn't be using certain words, such as "Pet, Flower or Hinny", just in case it offends someone. Its like the world has gone totally mad. These words in the Northeast have always been known as a term of affection or endearment, never meant to cause offence or as an insult.

Anyway, returning to this tale, my mam and dad had gone to see this film called *The Tingler*. Obviously, Ern must not have been enjoying this flick; but he didn't want to come across as a big softie, so he made his excuses to head to the little boy's room. Upon leaving the picture hall, he had to go down some steps and ended up fainting, hitting the deck, splitting his chin open and snapping the thick signet ring he was wearing. One of the ushers had to go into the picture hall and try to find my mam then ask, "Did you come in with a young man, just he has had a bit of an accident on the steps outside?" My dad still has a scar hidden beneath his beard; I can remember it as a kid. I definitely think my dad's reactions to blood, needles, and all things, shall we say tingly, he passed down to me when I was a nipper.

That said, I am very proud of my dad; he still has a fear of needles. However, has been able to tolerate them as the years have progressed. I'd like to think it is because he knows how much I have gone through, and because I have helped him. I can remember some years ago, going along with him to our doctors as he needed blood taken. I went to reassure him and offer support. I tried teaching him a strategy that hopefully would help. As the nurse approached him with a needle, I just told him to look away, and then to try and think of his shopping list and what we needed that day. He then went on to quietly tell me some of the various items that he could think of on his list, and before he knew it, the procedure had been done. It may sound stupid, and I am not sure if my dad still uses a distraction technique, but he now attends the doctors for all his usual injections and whatnot alone, and while he doesn't like it, he is okay. I don't think anyone particularly enjoys needles, but at least now he can deal with them. Fear of needles? Yep! Back in the day, I stayed off school pretending to be ill when the BCGs were being done, so I didn't get mine; I have no scar. It's ironic that I have now become like a proverbial pincushion over the years.

Now then, what phobia could my mother have possibly passed on? Ah yes! My fear of wasps. I used to be afraid of bees too; however, that settled down somewhat when I saw the animated film *The Bee Movie*. I still do the wild thing around wasps, which I suppose to some, would be hilarious as I cannot run away, but I can hop pretty quickly while flapping my arms and doing the "Wild Thing". I remember I almost had my dad off the road on one occasion, when going to the Toon (Newcastle). A wasp had gotten into our car, and I was practically on his knee, as he was driving around this tight corner at Sunnyside, my dad shouting, "What the bloody hell are you doing man?", and me shouting, "Wasp, wasp!"

I was three when my mam and dad moved from Percy Terrace in New Kyo down to South Moor and Mitchell Street. At the end of our street was a huge pond, complete with newts, frogs, old tyres and rusty prams. When I was little, this pond would become part of my playground, where I would wear my wellies and go plodging, in search of said pet newts and frogs. Back in the day, as kids, we used to play in the "muck". I can't recall washing my hands all that often. I would quite happily come in and eat a sandwich with filthy hands and matching face and then go straight back out to play. Of course, if my mam saw me mucky, it would be out with the flannel, and that thing mothers used to do, so a scrub of my face and watch over me as I stood at the sink washing my hands, with me protesting to the effect of "Aww Ma!"

Funnily enough I rarely got colds or took ill. For those of you old enough to remember, I am sure if you were to think back, you would probably nod your head in agreement, and if you happen to be from the Northeast say "Eee Aye!" to my following statement. If a baby had a dummy in its mouth and the dummy accidentally fell out and landed on the floor, the mother would merely pick it up, pop it in her own mouth, give it a swift twirl and clean, then shove it straight back in the baby's gob. Omg! If that was done today people in hazmat suits would probably rock up, the whole area would be cordoned off and there would be a public inquiry.

Along with the pond there were these huge pit heaps, created by the spoils that had been brought from the local mines. Older kids would slide down the pit heaps on anything they could find, bits of lino and old tin baths. They also used to send tyres rolling down the steep bankside, watching them as they careered down, bouncing and crashing until they eventually stopped at the bottom. Allotments could be found at the base of the pit heaps and also following a path up towards Oxhill. There were all sorts of various small huts and sheds, some painted, with coloured stripes, these were pigeon crees. A popular hobby with many a working man. On their days off these men would spend hours in their respective fenced off allotments. A common sound of the day was of corn being rattled in containers, to call their birds, and then the sound of the birds themselves as they came home to roost. Another pastime was the growing of various vegetables, some of which would be entered into shows at the local working men's clubs. Most of the allotment's owners took great pride in their little plots, it was a place to relax, have a smoke and a kind of sanctuary from day-to-day stress.

A memory that comes to mind, probably from when my mother recounted it to me was from when I was around three years old, and I was playing out in the safety of our backyard. I got it in my head that I would go and visit my nana and grandad, who lived up in New Kyo, which was just over a mile away. I knew the way it was just up the Black Path, so called because it was black from all the coal dust from the nearby pit heaps. I would take my best friend, "Blackie," who was our Labrador; he used to follow me everywhere.

The first part of my adventure was figuring out how to get out of our backyard, as it had a high brick wall, and the gates latch was too high for me to reach. I eventually discovered that I could unhook the latch by using an old broom. Setting off up the street with my little red wheelbarrow, a spade, and of course wor Blackie. Up the Black Path, we headed, collecting small pieces of coal upon the way. We passed the "Three Stones". These were three concrete blocks, each side roughly about three feet across.

They were a kind of family meeting place at the top of the path. I then had to cross the railway line, which ferried the coal from the local mines. When the trains ran, they appeared to have an endless line of wagons, coming from as far up as the Tyne or heading down from the local collieries. Then, there was a little walk to nana and grandad's terraced house in Bell Terrace.

As I arrived at my grandparents' house I could see my grandad was having a shave near the back door, in the small kitchen. His galluses were dangling (braces), and he was wearing a string vest. His face was covered in shaving soap. "Eeh, what're ye'r deeing he'or, where's ye'r Ma?" To which I replied, "Oh, am a big lad, a:ve come up by meself.". "Howay, where's ye'r Ma?" Again, I repeated, "Am a big lad, a've come up by meself.". At that point my poor grandad almost had a fit, realising my mam was nowhere to be seen. He then instructed me to wait right there with nana, and he shot out of the door and began heading in the direction of the Black Path, his face still covered in soap. My mother who was by now frantic, having discovered her little boy was missing, was running up the opposite way. My mam and grandad caught sight of each other, and my mam worriedly shouted to my grandad, "Eeh! wor Glenn's gone missin!" Obviously my grandad attempted to reassure her that I was safe and sound up at his house, as quickly as he could get the words out. When they both arrived back, I knew I was properly in for it, when I saw my mother's face. I was then told the story about the man who lived in the pit heaps. "His name was Dicky Dark, and he went after naughty little boys who wandered off near the pit heaps". This was no Jackanory tale I can tell you. Needless to say, I never went back up the Black Path alone again. Now that I'm older, and I often ride my bikes over that way, whenever I get to the Black Path, it makes me smile to recall my mother and her stern words of warning. I do have to say, I still haven't seen Dicky Dark. Oh and the three stones are still there. They are a lot smaller now, as they have been weathered and worn away by time; they now sit on the other side of a barbed wire fence, overgrown by weeds.

Speaking of the Black Path, there used to be the "Charlie Brick Flats", these were at the top end of the path. I remember there was a big cooling tower which was locally known as "The Charlie". I wrote a poem about chimneys when I was very little, taking my inspiration from that large brick structure, and I'm sure it got published in a children's book; maybe that was the start of my poetry.

The brick flats were where they made brand new bricks. My dad would take Blackie for a walk every evening up the Black Path, and Blackie would retrieve a brick and happily carry it home. Where my dad would then place it in our outside shed. By the time Blackie was getting on in years, he practically had no teeth left; they were so worn from carrying all those bricks home. One day a man my dad knew came knocking at our door, informing my mother, "Oh your Ernie says you have some bricks I could have." It was to finish off a wall or an extension. My mam directed him to the shed, where all these new bricks were living, all collected by that big black lovable Labrador Blackie.

I should think myself lucky really in not becoming an amputee before I did, as on at least two occasions that come to mind, I have avoided the "chop" as it were. This first occasion I bet has happened to a lot of men, however they probably are to embarrassed to admit their traumatic experience. As this is an honest account, I thought I might as well be… well honest.

When we lived at Mitchell Street, which was a terraced house. One particular day while playing out in our backyard; I needed to go. I was just a little lad at the time and decided to use the old outside toilet, instead of having to go all the way indoors, and visiting the toilet which was located upstairs. The old outside toilet was adjoined to the brick shed in the corner of our yard. It was cold and damp, with spider's webs, and used to freak me out. The privy had a heavy wooden door and once it was closed the only light that crept in was from what came in around the door frame, beneath the door and a small vent at the top of the wall. Once inside I undid the zip to my pants and had a tinkle. Now I don't know if it was the dark setting, or my lack of concentration. However, when I pulled my zip up, I caught what I thought was my little pecker in the zip. At the time, I didn't know how to swear, or I might have said, "Arrgghh! Fuckin hell." Instead, I screamed a high-pitched scream, which is quite the theme it appears for me as a young child, and ran from the toilet with my little tinky winky stuck hanging out the front of my pants.

Running into our house my mam must have thought I was playing some sort of a naughty game, as I came in shouting about my little fella being stuck in my flies and then doing this little on the spot dance while tears streamed down my face. The sheer look of disbelief on my mam's face. She then had to jump into action. Actually, it wasn't my little pecker that was caught, it was my scrotum, but all the same, my little ball sack was trapped, stuck in a vice like grip between these vicious teeth of my zipper. My mam finally released my poor little bit of flesh, "Phew!" what a relief. Funnily enough ever since that day, I have always been extra cautious about tucking myself in correctly; a very valuable lesson was learnt that day.

The following tale I am recounting is from when I was about five or six when I visited my nana and grandad in New Kyo with my mam. I would sometimes play in the back street with the other local kids. In those days, children were always outside, "Out from beneath their mothers' feet", and it seemed safer than in current times. The streets were comprised of old, dingy, terraced houses that were near the colliery. The backs of the terraced houses faced one another. Set in the brick walls of each house along the street were two wooden doors; one was for the "Midden Man", who used to collect all the waste from the outside toilets back in the day, and the other was the coal bunker, where the coal man would tip that week's coal. It's funny how when I think of this memory, it comes to me like one of those old-fashioned photographs, in hues of brown with worn dog ears at the corners. I can recall the rag and bone man who would come up the street fairly regularly, not in a van or lorry mind you; no, it was like a scene from Steptoe and Son, as he had his old horse and cart and would come along the street, ringing his loud bell, and shouting "Any Ol'e Iron".

A little lad and I had discovered this old, discarded pram; we were taking great delight in using it as a toy. The little boy pushed me up and down the street while we made these car noises "Meeeeeeowwww". Now I know that when you read that, it probably sounded more like a cat in your head; however, I think you know what I mean. After a few blasts up and down the street, me holding on to the sides of this pram, I'm not sure exactly what happened next. However, I could have possibly become an amputee way before I did, with my leg. The pram which was one of those old metal framed collapsible ones, suddenly just collapsed, in a scissor like motion as I was sitting in it. As it did so, the tip of my left middle finger, well I think it was my left finger got caught, and I don't know how I didn't lose it. I ran screaming to my nana's house, where both my nana and mam were. There was blood dripping all over, coming from my damaged finger and nail. It took my poor mam a long time to calm me down; I was just little and in hysterics. Eventually, all cried out. I remember falling asleep, sobbing in my mam's arms in front of the warm flickering coal fire.

My finger ended up with a big bandage on it, and it would "putt, putt, putt". Eventually I would go on to wear a "finger poke", you know, like a protective cover tied in place. Not long after this accident, I went on a school trip to Washington Wildlife Park. I had a great time, but on the return home, my finger felt all kind of sweaty and wet. So there I was coming off the bus in floods of tears, holding my middle finger up to my mam, which in hindsight may have appeared like a rude gesture. I was wanting to look at it, however not wanting to look at it. All these years later, I don't have a scar on my finger; however, each of my middle fingers feels slightly different.

Isn't it strange the memories we have stored in our minds. I mean things that have been there years and years. While writing the previous recollection, yet another just popped into my mind. It is not particularly exciting; however, it is very prominent for some reason. I think what brought it to mind was the mention of the flickering coal fire. I used to spend a great deal of time with my nana and grandad Johnstone, over at Craghead, at their house in Holmside Terrace. One day while there, I was in my nana and grandad's kitchen, which back then was a very old-fashioned affair. The solid wood draws and cabinets, as I recall where painted a kind of baby blue, and they had small white knobs. There was one draw I remember that always used to stick, and this day I had wanted something from out of it. Anyway, once I had finished in the draw I went to push it back in, and I jammed a couple of fingers, which really hurt. All those years ago like I say, and I can still remember the tears and just how upset I was. However, the biggest part of my memory is of my nana cuddling me in on the sofa, in front of a blazing fire, that was mesmerising, as the flames licked the coals and the heat reached out and soothed me. I can also recall my grandad Ernie, sitting in his large chair at the side of the fire, puffing on his pipe with blueish smoke gently drifting upwards towards the ceiling, and the smell of the tobacco. To this day I love the sight of an open fire, how it relaxes me, and how when I stare into the embers, watching the flames dance, it can take me away.

My nana Dodd, my mam's mam would regularly babysit me on a weekend, as my parents enjoyed going to dancing lessons. Well, when I say enjoyed going to dancing lessons, my mother did, however, I can imagine my dad having two left feet and just going to keep my mother happy. Now for the older generation reading this, you will probably recall what "Spangles" were, and for those who don't, they were a square shaped, fruit flavoured, boiled sweet. This one particular evening, I just happened to have a packet of the after mentioned sweets. I don't know what possessed me to throw a sweet up in the air and try and catch it, but that is precisely what I attempted to do. It went straight into my gob, and then I proceeded to choke on the sweet as it got lodged in my throat. My poor nana was past herself, and in those days, people weren't exactly trained in first aid, so my nana's remedy was to pour her warm cup of tea down my throat and try and melt the obstruction. So, I was either going to choke or drown. Man, what a scary experience I can tell you; in fact, a good few years ago, I almost had a similar thing happen, when I choked on a piece of steak while in a restaurant. I was out with one of my friends at the time, and I thought, "Oh, that hasn't gone down right." I had a cough, then a splutter and tried to clear my air way. This soon turned to sheer panic; however, I was very fortunate to be able to hack the small piece of fatty obstruction up. It was just so stressful, as well as being extremely embarrassing, as I checked around to make sure no one had seen me. Thank goodness I didn't require any assistance, as I already felt like a complete numpty. I mean it's not exactly ideal trying to smile politely and give a thumbs up "Oh I am fine, as you are choking on something you probably should have been more careful with in the first place."

As I got a little older, my dad would take me to work with him; it would never be allowed these days, what with health and safety.

My dad was a self-employed motor mechanic working out of a garage over at Blackhill in Consett, at a place called "The Number One". One afternoon, a friend of his called in to discuss some work, and he had brought his son with him, who was about the same age as me. As my dad and his mate were chatting in the office, this little lad and I began playing "chasey", running around the garage, laughing and having a great time. As we were running around I ran between these two parked cars; little did I know that the pit boards had not been put over the rather deep inspection pit. I suddenly fell down the large hole, and as I did so smacked my chin on the edge of the pit, splitting the inside of my mouth wide open. I then began screaming the place down.

There I was in this big black hole which I couldn't get out of, my tongue probing what felt like this massive open wound in my mouth, alongside a horrible metallic taste, which I knew was blood; it was pouring from my mouth. My dad, hearing the commotion, ran over, leaned into the pit, and pulled me out. Mind you, no sympathy. No once out of the pit I got a stern telling off, a quick inspection of my mouth and then he said, "Ahh ye'll be alreet," then he went back to business with his friend. That is just how things were done in those days. Children were loved dearly; however, none of this mollycoddling palaver. I can remember having this huge swelling inside my mouth, with what felt like a massive lump of flesh just dangling, which I would constantly touch with my tongue. It lasted for weeks; all I ate was soup. I hated the feel of my mouth when I attempted to eat anything. I refused to go anywhere near a doctor or hospital; it would just heal itself, and I knew I wasn't allowed to whine on about it because of this. I can still feel the scar inside my mouth to this day. As I was writing about this incident and recalling what had happened all those years ago, I showed my dad the remaining scar inside my mouth, and he just said, "Stop whining," light heartedly mocking me.

I would now like you to imagine "Bonty Night", November the 5th and Guy Fawkes. We used to make a "Guy" with old clothes, stuffed with newspaper, and go out "Penny for the Guy'ing". It was one of those times of the year that was a special event on the calendar for us kids. Our parents didn't really have the money for fireworks or things like that. Kids would get together in local gangs, a good few months before November and go out in search of various stuff so that they could build as big a bonfire as possible. This is when "Bonty Raiding" was all the go. Each local gang would sneak into "Enemy Territory" and nick what the other gang had stashed. Looking back, all these kids must have looked like worker ants, carrying various bits and pieces from one place to another. How many times must one piece of wood or a tyre have been transported from here to there? No sooner had something been discovered than some other gang would have pilfered it.

I must have been about eight or nine, and all the big lads had built this "Geet Big Bonty" (a big bonfire). It was on the top field near the pond at the end of my street. The fire was started and took a good few hours to burn down, enough so that we could roast our "Tatties" (potatoes) on the embers. I began searching for the perfect stick to roast my potato on. I couldn't believe my luck when I found one. It was about eighteen inches long, and was made for the job, well apart from having this little bit of plastic attached towards one end. I took hold of the bit of plastic in one hand between my fingers and thumb, and with the other, I pulled. It didn't budge, so I tried again with a bit more force. Suddenly, the plastic came free and shot off the stick. Unfortunately, the stick wasn't made of wood at all; It was made out of fibreglass, and the fibreglass had splintered. I had now speared myself with this stick, and it was all the way through my left thumb. For a few seconds, I just stood there with my hand raised in front of my face dumbfounded, with what now looked like the shaft of an arrow completely through my wee thumb. Realisation and pain soon kicked in, becoming panic, and you guessed it, more screaming and tears as I ran home holding my hand out in front of me. I ran straight into our kitchen, which wasn't big enough to swing a cat in; my dad just happened to be nearby in the other room. He came to the kitchen wondering what all the noise was about. I couldn't explain to my dad what was wrong, as I was so freaked out. I just remember my right hand clasping my left wrist, and me holding my thumb up. Then my dad's expression as he must have been thinking, "What's he gone and done noo?"

My mam now entered the fray, as she had heard all the commotion, and when she saw me holding my thumb up realised my predicament, she also started panicking, saying "Eee Ernie, dee something". My grown-up brain would have said, "Yeah, dad for fucks sake, forget The Tingler, man up and pull this thing out. " Now, I would like you to imagine this as a dramatic cinematic scene from a movie, shot in slow motion. My little self-screaming" Aaghhhhh", my dad, the hero taking hold of my thumb with one hand while he pulled the piece of fibreglass, Errr! arrow out with the other hand, removing it from my poor little thumb. In reality it was all over in the blink of an eye and my mother immediately consoled me, and that was Bonty Night ruined, well at least until the following year. "Screw you tatty and that stupid stick." During recalling that memory it just gave me a twinge of phantom pain.

I have another recollection of bonfire night that was really funny, probably because it didn't happen to me. I was a little older and camping out with a couple of mates. We were gathered around the fire embers, and someone, "wasn't me" had thrown a paint aerosol can on to the fire. The can had been on the fire for a little while, then made a "Pffff" sound just before it exploded, the little ball contained within the can suddenly shot out with a loud "BANG" and one of the local lasses who was standing nearby the fire, got shot in the arse. She then went on to do this little on the spot dance, which reminded me somewhat of a rendition of river dance. She was jumping all around holding her arse and my friends and I just watched on. It was quite the show by all accounts and just needed some of that Irish fiddle music to really set the scene. The performance was short lived, and it was the girls turn to run home screaming and crying.

We were never particularly well off, even though my dad worked very hard, and my mam had various part time jobs throughout her life. That said, Christmases were always very special. In the grand scheme of things, I was spoiled, but not to the extent I was a brat. I always appreciated and looked after my things. I received everything from a Donny Osmond suit when I was small, "Donny who?" I hear you ask; you will have to go and Google him. The Bay City Rollers were also all the go around that period. I think we still have an old vinyl record in our loft from the Bay City Rollers. I am not making claim to buying it. I can recall the first record I ever bought. I would have been twelve and it was a 7-inch single, by Madness, "You're an Embarrassment", which I believe had "Crying Shame" on the B side.

One year, I received a NASA space suit complete with a helmet and an annoying sounding ray gun, which my dad later hid that Christmas evening. I got an Evel Knievel stunt bike, there were Action Men, and my dad made me a home-made garage to play with my many Corgi and Dinky cars. I have these very fond memories of my cousin David and I, where we would wait for our aunty Ann (My mam's youngest sister) to get off the bus when she had finished work and arrived home near Bell Terrace in New Kyo. Expecting her to go and buy us a toy car each. I spoke to my aunty Ann recently about this memory and she had me laughing as she recalled we would be there to meet her off the bus, not just on the odd occasion, but every night, thinking she would buy us a toy car each time.

I can remember the local newspaper shop that sold the toy cars, with its high dark brown wooden counters and matching shelves, newspapers all neatly folded lying on the top of the counter. Even now, I can recollect the smell and bring it to mind; it was a sort of dusty smell, that made me want to sneeze. We had to stand on our tiptoes, our little hands clamped on to the top of the counter, trying to peek over, to get a better view of all the cars placed on the shelves, along with the old-fashioned sweet jars. We would then point towards the cars and select which ones we would like to have a look at, eagerly awaiting the shopkeeper to pass them over. We would then carefully inspect the little toy cars, ensuring they were not ones we already had in our collections, before excitedly waiting for aunty Ann to pay for our new acquisitions. I would play for hours alone, just placing my cars in a long line at home and using the garage my dad had lovingly constructed for me.

Speaking to my uncle Dave and my cousin David just the other day, uncle Dave mentioned that apparently, I was quite the bully when I was younger, where our David was concerned. David was always a quiet kid, really placid. I asked him if he could remember the time when I must have particularly annoyed him, and he whacked me over the head with an Etcher Sketcher. The human mind is amazing in how much information it can store and how memories can suddenly resurface from years ago just by being triggered by a simple conversation.

Another year, I got this huge Scalextric track; parts of it were second hand, but I didn't mind. It was great fun fixing it up between our rather large dining and sitting room, then racing the cars around, as our Blackie tore around after them. "Hey, Blackie get off that Mk1 Escort!" That was my favourite car. I even went on to modify it, filling out the arches and fitting it with wider Porsche wheels. This may be where my modifying of cars first started.

When I think back I was always interested in, I suppose you would call it science. Both our David and myself had chemistry sets. Every week end our parents would take turns to visit one another, and they would play cards while David and I would be off in the kitchen making some sort of a concoction with various chemicals. Some of the stuff we used to make I guess would be proper dangerous by today standards and it used to stink. We used to turn on the oven and heat up small pieces of glass tubing that we used in our experiments. "Eee when a think back to some of the stuff we got up te." I must have been around eight or nine when I can recall having this old train set, and a friend and I deciding to do this experiment. Now don't ask me where we got the idea from, as back in those days there was no such thing as computers or the internet. So, no Googling on "How to make an electromagnet". We were up in my bedroom at Mitchell Street, and I had managed to get my hands on a large bolt. It was probably about four or five inches long. I had also found a large reel of copper wire. My friend and I wrapped the copper wire around and around the bolt, making a coil, leaving two ends, so that we could attach the negative and positive from the train sets transformer. Next we plugged the transformer in at the mains and switched it on. Within less than a second there was a buzzing sound, and we eagerly picked up the bolt to discover our experiment had worked, we now had an electromagnet, as it picked up a few nails and then proceeded to get stuck to an old biscuit tin. To remove the magnet, we had to switch it off, and then we tried it again. This time it was lying on the carpet of my bedroom floor, and we had it switched on a little longer, as we were excitedly playing. The buzzing then started getting louder and then suddenly I smelt and noticed smoke. "Turn it off, turn it off," I cried to my mate. Oh shit, I now had a big hole in my bedroom carpet, along with a somewhat scorched floorboard. The bolt was red hot. How my mam and dad didn't ever discover that big hole in my carpet I will never know. I think I used to hide it with a comic or some random toy. Obviously I wasn't going to "fess up", to carrying out really important scientific work being carried out in my bedroom, especially when it had gone slightly awry.

Every few years, I would get a new bike, and this one year, when I was probably around ten or eleven, I got a bright red shiny racer for Christmas. It was old school by today's standards, with the gear levers down on the frame. I was over the moon. Imagine my disappointment when I couldn't go out on the bike when we discovered it had a puncture. In those days, none of the shops were open during the holiday period, so I had to wait a few days until my dad could get a new tube and fix it. Man, I rode that bike miles. On one particular day, I had ridden all the way to Sunnyside and was coming back, riding on the road, heading home. I was flying down Crookgate Bank when a bus passed me on a sweeping bend; it felt really close, and the wind from the back of the bus made me veer off and hit the kerb. I flew off my bike, putting my hands out to try and save myself. It was super scary as I crashed, my head just missing one of those small concrete fire hydrant signs that was between the pavement and the grass verge. When I eventually pulled myself together, I realised how lucky I had been. No one wore protective gear in those days, like gloves or helmets.

My left palm was a mess; it was bleeding, and I had lots of gravel stuck to it. There was a little stone stuck deep in a wound, and I began to start crying as I picked my bike up and checked it over. By now, I was too scared to ride on the road, so I rode some and pushed the rest of the way on the footpath all the way to Tanfield, where my mam's aunty lived. She helped wash my hands, put some magic cream on, and dressed my poorly hand. I gave her my thanks, and rode sniffling all the way home. My left palm looked terrible, and I eventually had to give in and get it seen by a doctor. I still have a scar and the memory that came with it. It's funny how things stick with you; years later, I'm still cautious down banks and hills when riding my bikes.

When I was seventeen years old, my dad was asked to do a delivery job by a friend of his. The job involved delivering large polyurethane sacks to various pits around the country (coal mines). Apparently, they filled the sacks with concrete to make instant walls or something like that. Anyway, it was to be an adventure, and a lookout with my dad and one of my friends who was also coming along for the ride. As we got to the first drop, it was a freezing cold day; the ground was frozen solid beneath our feet as we jumped out from the lorry. Various vehicles had been driven through what must have been mud at the time, which had then set rock hard, causing uneven undulations in the ground. I gathered the first sack from the back of the lorry and took a few steps, then heard an enormous "CRACK!" as my ankle rolled on the uneven surface. I proceeded to hop around on one leg, shouting, "A've broke me leg!" Of course, I had no sympathy from my dad; he just said, "Stop skiving". I then had to hop to the wagon cab, and when I eventually managed to get in, and take my shoe off, my foot and ankle came up like a puddin! That was it no getting my shoe back on; my foot was now all floppy and wonky at the ankle.

A few more drops later, my dad had hit his tachograph time limit, so he suggested we take a break and have a nap in the back of the Luton wagon. Oh my God, it was Baltic! Even though I was wrapped up in some blankets that had been left in the back of the wagon, I was freezing, and my leg was throbbing with waves of pain, making me feel nauseous. Yep, my leg was definitely poorly. My dad figured he could take a detour and drive the short distance to Ollerton in Nottingham, as my uncle Eric and aunty Doris lived there, and we could rest up. As we got to the house, I had to hop up the path, which was excruciating. Upon hearing what had happened and looking at my ankle, my aunty Doris decided to collect some snow from her backyard, pop it into a bag and use it as an ice pack on my foot and ankle to try and get the swelling down; bless her. The plan was that we would wait for my cousin to come along, and she would invite her then boyfriend, now husband, who was at the time a student physio, to have a look at my leg.

Well, when said boyfriend arrived, he observed my leg as I lay on the settee and then must have thought it would be a good idea to try and realign my wonky foot. "FUCK ME," I almost hit the roof and thought I was going to pass out upon landing. The pain was unbelievable as I felt jagged broken bone scrape across jagged bone. I wouldn't go to hospital, and the drive home was absolute agony, as I tried to support my leg in the lorry, holding it with both hands under my knee, in a bent position with my foot wobbling like one of those bobble heads you pop upon the dash of your car. I went for a few days before I eventually knew I would have to visit hospital.

At the hospital, I was placed in a plaster cast, which was such a relief. The plasterer struggled to get my foot and ankle in the correct position; the pain was so bad upon each movement. A unique plaster cast which also went around my knee was put in place. It prevented any rotation of my lower leg when I stood up. It took months for the break of my fibula to heal, probably because I kept going out on my motorbike, and the cast kept breaking and falling off. The plasterer would ask why the cast had holes in the back near my heel. It was because I used the heel area to change gear, so he wasn't overly impressed. Yes, I know, what a plonker! Once the doctor said, "You might need surgery if this doesn't start healing," I took it more seriously and stayed in.

Funnily enough, six months later, while working at Beamish Museum on that Manpower Services Scheme I mentioned earlier, I was stupidly running about, being chased by one of my work colleagues as we fooled around. You would think I would have learnt my lesson about running around being chased. Well, I ended up getting a vice handle caught in the pocket of my Parker. I then pulled this rather large vice off the bench, and it landed on my foot, the opposite side this time. So that was another few months in a cast.

While we are here, and I have mentioned my uncle Eric and going to his house for, "Errr treatment,". I thought I would tell you a funny tale my mother told me about him. Eric was my mam's older brother; he was apparently a canny good footballer in his day and a lifelong "Toon" supporter. When my uncle Eric was little, he had been playing out with the "big lads", kids much older than himself; they had been over some local fields. Little Eric was late getting home and was being told off, "Where've ye been?" To which little Eric replied, "A've been ower' the fields with the big lads". "What a've ye been deeing ower' there?" "Oh, a've been te' see the hosses". (horses) "The hosses?" his mam and dad remarked. Little Eric replied, "Aye", going on to recount what he had seen. "There were some broon'uns, some black'uns, some grey'uns, and some fuckin' ones." He didn't understand bad language and the swearing that the other older kids must have been using, as he was a lot younger. However, he soon cottoned on when he got his arse tanned.

Chapter 4

I hope I haven't lost you off. If you recall, a little earlier, I mentioned having to go for a biopsy. I had to visit Shotley Bridge Hospital and the day surgery unit. Shotley Bridge has changed a lot from back in the day; a lot of the hospital's buildings have been demolished, and the land surrounding the hospital has been sold and redeveloped with new houses. I am going back to when the old hospital buildings, which people called "The Huts", were still in place. The huts used to be on a bank side. I always thought it was a stupid place to have the wards; when I say they were on a bank side, I mean it was really steep by all accounts. I am sure those who are familiar with the old layout and who are reading this will remember them. Imagine if the brakes came off a patient's wheelchair or trolley when they were at the top; well, they would definitely end up in hospital.

So, there I was on the day surgery unit, all nervous, having been prepped. An orthopaedic surgeon carried out the biopsy; it didn't take long at all. I awoke to discover only a minor dressing in place, and when I eventually got to look at the wound, it was small, with just a few old-fashioned stitches in place. However, it hurt like hell, as the surgeon had drilled into my bone, a few inches down from under my kneecap, more like the top of my shin.

About a week or so passed by, and I had word that I was to attend South Moor Community Hospital to get some results. The hospital was not far from where I lived, so I jumped in my car and drove over. My leg was still a wee bit sore at this point; however, the wound was healing up, and the stitches were due out. As I entered the consultant's small office, which resembled something from out of the '70s, he was there with his registrar, who was a small, friendly man of Indian descent. The registrar immediately made eye contact with me, and I noticed his slightly concerned look. I was invited to take a seat, and the consultant began explaining to me about this tumour in my leg. Going on to say while it was not cancerous and as such classed as being benign, it was a particularly aggressive tumour called a Giant Cell. "I thought of it as a bit like a giant flump in my leg, hungrily chomping away at my bone." It was a lot to take in at a time when I really couldn't process anything at all. I asked, "What does this mean?" "Like what happens next?" To which the consultant replied, "Well, it will have to be removed; the thing is, there is no one in the Northeast to carry out the surgery". Going on to inform me that it was quite a tricky procedure, requiring a very specialist surgeon. The consultant then went on to mention that there may be someone in Leeds or Glasgow and that they would start looking immediately.

In those days, I was a real home bird; I even got homesick when I went on a short trip to London with the school when I was around twelve or thirteen. Now, I don't know if this is a bizarre fact or just my childhood imagination being overactive. When we arrived in London and got to the hotel we were supposed to be staying at, well it was a proper dump, so we got moved to another hotel. The original hotel I am sure I remember as being at Cranley Gardens, you know? Where the infamous Dennis Nielson killed all those men. It's funny what you remember, or think you remember, and how at certain times, your mind can, and will deceive you or did it on this occasion?

So, getting back to this consultant review, there I was, and the extent of the whole situation was just not sinking in. I then asked what the worst-case scenario would be, to which I was informed, "Oh you will lose your leg". I was like, "Say what now?" There was me thinking I would get back to work at some point. Now, I had just been told in what came across as a nonchalant fashion that I may lose my leg. Without saying a word, I got up from the chair I had been sitting on, walked out of the office, and drove home. It just felt so surreal. As I got in my mother, who was in the kitchen and rather concerned, asked me what was said and how the appointment had gone. I repeated what I had been told in a somewhat stunned or possibly emotionless way, it's difficult to explain my emotional state at that moment in time. "Oh, he says I will lose me leg," to which my poor mam automatically replied, "Yer jokin'". I then lost my shit and shouted, "Dee ye think ah wid joke aboot something like that?" It was one of those moments I instantly regretted, speaking to my poor mother like that. She was just so worried.

For me, it just felt like this couldn't be happening; it was as if it was happening to someone else, and my head felt like it was going to explode. The phone began ringing, and my mam answered. It was the hospital wanting me to go back, as the consultation wasn't finished. I had just walked out. I returned to the hospital, however I can't for the life of me recall anything else that was said or agreed upon, or how I got back home. Following the consultation, what felt like months passed by. I was still working; however, my leg had become so painful and now had a large swelling at the side of my knee.

Continuing with my job I remember being out on delivery in one of the Ford Escort vans, up at East Stanley. It was a windy day, and I had opened the driver's door preparing to get out. As I reached over to the passenger seat to retrieve a packet, the wind caught the door, causing it to slam shut on my leg. I must have sat there for over half an hour just crying. My forehead was on the steering wheel, with my hands to either side just gripping the wheel, tears running down my face, a mixture of pain, turmoil and despair. Some weeks later, a friend asked if I could give him a hand to fit his dishwasher. He had had an accident on his motorbike, so he had an external fixator fitted, you know, one of those cage-like things, with pins that are inserted through the skin and into the bone to hold everything in place. As I knelt, resting on my knees to adjust the dishwasher, I experienced the most horrendous and nauseating pain; things were definitely not good.

June 6th, 1995, was my last day of work at Royal Mail. The staff had a whip round, and everyone gathered to bid farewell. I had been limping for months by now. My doctor began prescribing morphine as the pain was getting unbearable. I started popping pills, taking way more than I should. I just wanted relief from the pain and the thoughts in my head; I didn't care, I wanted to be out of it.

I can recall being alone at home one morning and needing to have a wee. I think I was on some other tablets at the time, and I am not sure if these were preventing me from being able to pass water. I was standing at the toilet and just couldn't go. I mean, I really wanted to. I had the urge, but nothing was happening. Suddenly, I was on the floor; my right leg had just given way from under me. The pain was excruciating; I thought my leg had snapped, all I was thinking was "Don't pass out, don't pass out." I had to crawl through to my mam and dad's bedroom, to try and get to the phone, there were no mobile phones in those days. To be honest I am not even sure how I managed to contact my mother, that bit is a blur. Upon speaking to my mam, she panicked and called for an ambulance; her friend Joan, who she was with, at the time immediately drove her home, and when I had been placed in the back of the ambulance, they followed it to the hospital.

I was taken to Shotley Bridge, and once there, a doctor examined me; he then went away to check X-rays and whatnot, and upon his return, he started going on about how serious this tumour was and mentioned amputation. I couldn't deal with that sort of shit, I didn't want to talk about it, I didn't want to hear it. I lost my temper and, in no uncertain terms told him where to go. I then angrily said to my mam, "Let's go, get me out of here now!" Borrowing a wheelchair my mam pushed me outside to where Joan had been patiently waiting, and she gave us a lift back home. Nothing could be done; my leg hadn't snapped or fallen off. It was just "Fucked" along with my head. By now, I was very hard to live with. I was always irritable and angry, and when I cried they felt like angry hot tears. I was frustrated, and my inner voice, or should I say voices, had become far louder; they were not at all helpful. I felt as if they were mocking, and criticising me, pulling me further down.

I hope you can understand and get a sense of the utter fear I felt at being what I thought was out of options. I know people go through some awful shit; for example, they may lose their job and then can't afford to pay their mortgage, resulting in them losing the home that they love. People may lose or have some possessions stolen that are dear to them, and it makes them angry and sad. The thing is, in the grand scheme of things, well life goes on. When it's something so terrifying related to your health everything else disappears, and you become consumed. You would gladly give up that prized material item if you could just return to how things were when you were okay. Every waking moment, and in some cases even when you are sleeping, it's like a dark shadow following you around. The shadow encompasses you, making you lose hope, as it drags you further and further down into its murky dark depths. It is like a heavy weight, so much so that finally you feel you have nothing left to give and life is over. It has such a profound effect; as I write this, I can feel my eyes welling up with a heavy sense of emotion. It is as if I am writing about someone else for whom I have the deepest empathy. I am so grateful that although I thought I had no options at the time, here I am, able to possibly give someone some hope to not give up. When you have hope, even the slightest bit, it acts as a small light in the darkness.

Finally, I learnt that a consultant orthopaedic surgeon had been found in the Northeast. He was a lovely gentleman, reminding me of Dustin Hoffman, you know the actor? Slightly small in stature, he had the most fantastic bedside manner. This new consultant invited me in for a review and explained exactly what kind of procedure he could do, and what was involved. A rather large incision would be made up the back of my right calf to allow access to my tibia. The tibia would be hollowed out, with the hope of removing all of the tumour, and once I was stitched up, I would have to wear a straight leg brace and not weight bear until the tibial bone reformed and became strong once again. It sounded like a traumatic yet good plan; I mean, as long as I had this thing removed, I could then get back on with life. I would be normal, well, as normal as I had ever been. I could then put all of this behind me and be thankful that I had had a lucky escape. Even my GP thought I would be back to work in, say six months. I was buoyed by the news even though I was really scared about the procedure; It was that little bright light of hope in what had been a very dark few months.

This was to be only the second time I had had an anaesthetic, the first being the biopsy. This procedure involved being under a lot longer. Some of my family visited following the surgery, and they informed me that I was canny amusing while recovering from the anaesthetic. I must have been watching some crime documentary before my op, and when I came around, I was worried that I had the Yorkshire Ripper's blood in my system. My poor cousin David, who just happens to be a doctor, got the brunt of my questioning, as I quizzed him on the effects of having some deranged killers blood coursing through my veins.

Following the surgery, I went on to wear a straight leg brace for seven months. I remained on painkillers, and my mood improved a little; however, as time went on, I began experiencing more and more pain around my knee, and it began to gradually swell in the same area as before. At first I just thought it was from the trauma of the surgery, but over the months, it got worse. I then had a trip on the stairs; this was probably six to seven months down the line, and I put weight through my leg. There was considerably more swelling, and my knee turned black and blue. A week or so later, I had an appointment to go back to the Freeman Hospital in Newcastle, where I had had my previous surgery.

Some X-rays were taken once again, and I had the most painful MRI; My leg was by now permanently fixed in position, with only a slight flex at the knee. During the MRI, they had to use a strap to pull my leg as straight as possible and keep it in place during the scan. More tears I am afraid, as it hurt so much. I was then invited to see the registrar, having been informed that my consultant was away working in America at that time. When I spoke to the registrar, he tried to politely fob me off, asking if I could wait until the consultant came back. I knew things weren't right, so I pressed him on what was going on, and he informed me that the scan had shown that the tumour had returned, and that it looked larger and more aggressive; plus, when I had put weight through my leg, I had crushed the top of the tibial head of the bone.

I was absolutely devastated; I pleaded with him to see if they could have another go at removing the tumour and fix my leg, maybe take a bit more out. However, the registrar said it wouldn't work. I just couldn't accept this and could feel myself having a meltdown in his office. "This can't be happening; what the fuck?" I can't describe the feelings that raced through my mind, sheer panic, base emotions, like when they talk about fight or flight. I was screwed on both counts. I was losing this fight with this poxy fucking tumour, which was eating my bone, and now I couldn't run away, as I was basically a cripple. What a sick ironic joke; my dark sense of whatever was starting to take shape. And this internal darkness was to get worse. The light I thought I had glimpsed was immediately snuffed out, like a weak flame from a candle. I soon discovered what the word "turmoil" meant, alongside that darkness.

A few more weeks went by, and upon my consultant's return, I had an appointment with him. Here I was to be provided with options, the first of which was amputation. "Fuck Me Amputation", how had it come to this. "Amputation", just hearing the word, made me freak out. It had only ever briefly been mentioned, and I had quickly eradicated the thought from my mind, building a huge wall of denial. "Amputation". The sound of the word, the feeling in the pit of my stomach, the terror, the nausea, and the panic. A full range of emotions that was like a sucker punch to my gut. I was totally unprepared. At that point it still wasn't an option in my head. "What are the other options?" I asked. To which I was informed "limb salvage". That didn't sound like a good option either. I was now stuck between a rock, a hard place, and it may as well of also been a huge drop off a fucking cliff just as s side bet.

I thought amputation was the end for me at that time; my life was over. I know that sounds dramatic; it's just such a difficult and terrifying thing to comprehend. I inquired about what limb salvage involved and was given an explanation of the procedure. The diseased bone would be removed, and an internal surgical steel prosthesis called a Kotz Prosthesis would be implanted into my leg, held in place with what was essentially the same stuff as what dentists use to keep teeth in place. I would be able to walk; however, I wouldn't be able to run due to the impact and the possibility of the prosthetic becoming loose. Basically, my leg would be glued in place with this massive chunk of metalwork, replacing my knee and parts of my bones. I didn't want this option either. I just wanted to close my eyes and wish everything back, to way before that horrible fucking murder.

I returned home with my poor mam and dad, who had both been along to support me. I had the most terrible feeling of anxiety and sadness. I now had to think over my options and then get back to the consultant with my decision as soon as possible. It is a dreadful feeling when all your choices appear to be negative ones. No one can make them for you. God knows I used to ask my mam and dad, "What should I do?" But I mean, what could they say? If they had chosen either one for me, in the long run, I would have somehow blamed them. Not because I didn't love them; it's just having someone to blame. I don't know, maybe it would have made things easier, as the decision would have been out of my hands.

It isn't easy trying to go back all those years and do some soul searching, reflecting on what was going through my head at the time. I wish I had had someone to talk to and guide me, to offer advice not someone to say, "Well I would do this, or I would do that." I have since spoken to people who have been in a similar situation to myself regarding the option of electing to have an amputation. Funnily enough, a gentleman just stopped me recently asking for advice, as he may have to decide on an elective amputation, due to an ongoing illness. He had seen me wandering around in my backyard while working on my car with The Ern (my dad). I was wearing my usual attire, typically shorts, with my prosthetic leg on show. All I can do is be honest and present people with information, and that information is not from a professional perspective as I am not trained in those things; no, it is from my own personal experience. I try to explain the positives and negatives that my experiences have taught me. Hopefully, armed with this information, people can make a very personal and informed choice for themselves. It has to be their own decision, and only then can they move forward.

I revisited my GP and explained that I was in severe pain; however, I didn't want to go back on morphine, having already struggled to come off it. I found it was very addictive, and it felt like I was never getting enough to combat the pain. My doctor suggested a new drug called Temgesic. These small tablets were to be placed under my tongue and allowed to dissolve, offering pain relief. Well, these turned out to be one of the worst drugs ever. They were very addictive and had some nasty side effects, which included depression, amongst many other things. I find it difficult to explain how these drugs made me feel; it was as if I always felt "dirty", not in the sense that I couldn't be bothered to get washed, no more a sense of being unclean from the inside, in a psychological sense. Again, the dose of meds didn't touch the pain, so I was taking them willy nilly to try and either knock myself out or take me away somewhere other than reality. I really didn't care about being part of this world. However, suicide had not entered my mind at this point.

As I took these drugs, I didn't know if they were working; I still had pain, however, would it have been even worse if I wasn't taking them? I didn't know if I was high. I didn't know if I was in the here and now or in some altered reality. Had the drugs affected me, or had I completely taken leave of my senses? Had all these events been too much for my mind? Endless questions just floated around in my head, which, in the grand scheme of things, didn't really matter. I was stuck and unable to make sense of anything anymore. I was just completely lost.

Finally, I made the decision to opt for limb salvage; I mean, I loved both of my legs, so it made sense to try and save this bad one. A few more months went by, and I counted down the days to my surgery. This was an incredibly stressful period. It was the knowing that I would never be the same, as well as the not knowing how this procedure would affect me moving forward. Stress is an integral part of our lives; however, to have it constantly, every moment of every day, can drive you to the edge.

Before going into hospital, aware that I would have a somewhat lengthy stay, I decided to go to the Metro Centre in Gateshead (The Metro Centre being a large shopping mall). I went with my dad, who very kindly drove me through, with the intention of visiting Waterstones to buy a big fat book. At that time, I could just about manage to walk around using elbow crutches. My plan was to buy a book to while away the hours while I was recovering in hospital. Now, I was not really an avid reader at that time. I think the only book that I wasn't forced to read as a kid was when I was off school; it was an old book that my dad had, I suppose from when he was a child. The book was called *The Atom Chasers*. I am gutted it has gone missing. I thought it was in our loft, But I haven't been able to find it.

Never mind. I ended up buying this fantasy trilogy book, *The Ice Wind Dale Trilogy*, written by R.A. Salvatore. I chose it because I liked the design of the front cover. Needless to say, this book got me hooked on the author, and on my return home from my stay in hospital, I began collecting his books, even moving on to special signed editions, and my collection grew and grew. During one of my many stays in hospital, I was waiting for a book to arrive from Barnes and Noble in the US. My dad had fired off an email asking when to expect its arrival, explaining it was for his son, and that I was currently in hospital going through some stuff. A lovely gentleman replied to my dad, and when I got out of the hospital I was blown away that this friendly man had written to me and explained that he had just had dinner with none other than R A Salvatore and another famous fantasy author Terry Brooks. My book was on its way, and this man had mentioned me to R.A. Salvatore. Imagine my surprise when about a week later I received a personal email from R.A. Salvatore. He sent his well wishes and hoped I had enjoyed his latest story. This message was followed up with a few more, where we told each other what we were currently up to. What a thoroughly lovely fellow, so down to earth.

I now enjoy reading and will pretty much read anything as long as it holds my attention. I have been known to have two or three books on the go at once, and there are books all over our house. Most are neatly placed on shelves; however, some are lying on the floor next to my bed. My dad has just come into my bedroom with a surprise as I write this. I've opened the Amazon cardboard packet and discovered that he has bought me a Penguin Cloth Bound Classic. A copy of George Orwell's *Nineteen Eighty-Four*. Books are such special gifts, and I cherish each one. I encourage everyone to pick up a book and let it carry them away to some distant land, to engage in some adventure or tale. Books can also provide you with helpful information and knowledge, some of which can help you going forward in life. As you read further, you will see that I have taken a lot from what I have read and interpreted it into my own way of thinking. I think there are books that stand the test of time, and I do have to say Alexandre Dumas's *The Count of Monte Cristo* is probably one of my current all-time favourites, along with Neville Goddard's "Feeling is The Secret", which I have read numerous times, and attempt to put his methodology into daily practice.

Chapter 5

The day of my surgery arrived. It was now August 1996, and the Euros were just about to start. At least I would have something to watch on TV during my stay in hospital, plus I had that thick fantasy book to get stuck into. I was all prepared for the surgery and that inevitable countdown, where you're given the anaesthetic, then feel yourself drift off into nothingness. Some twelve hours later, I awoke disorientated and in so much pain. I think I was in intensive care, in some recovery area; I am not entirely sure. The lights overhead were bright, and there was a lot of commotion, with nurses in blue scrubs performing their various duties. Monitors were beeping, along with the sounds of other various hospital equipment. I became aware of both a chemical taste in my mouth, and this smell as I breathed, it was the residuals from the anaesthetic. I could feel this horrible tube, that was stuck down my throat. As I came around nurses began speaking my name and reassuring me, "Glenn, Glenn it's OK; you have just come around from your procedure." I was then encouraged to cough up the tube. Man, it felt awful as they began pulling out this plastic tube. My thoughts being "Where the fuck is that tube?" Seriously it felt like they were pulling it from hell; my very soul was being drawn out of my body." The nursing staff then moved me from the patient trolley to a bed using a PAT slide, and as they slid me across I can recall crying out, as my leg was so painful, it didn't feel like it was my own or even attached.

I was taken on a patient bed along to one of the wards and placed into a cubicle, and once there experienced the most bizarre something or other. The room was small and dull, with a black and white TV on a bracket in the top corner near the ceiling. An old film was playing, something like Casablanca or an old gangster movie, complete with a lady resembling a gangster's moll. However, I can't remember any sound other than some monitor constantly beeping, and that of the oxygen filtering through the nasal cannula I had in place. Oh, and of course, myself groaning. Suddenly I had this sense I was floating, looking down directly from the ceiling; there I could see this poor bloke who was lying in a hospital bed, he didn't look good at all. He was all connected to various stuff, monitors and a drip. His head turned, and as our eyes met, there was a sudden realisation, "Fuckin Hell; Oh my God, that poor bloke is me." I blinked, through glazed eyes and that was the experience over as I drifted in and out of consciousness. It was like a total out of body experience. I had either died, and my soul wasn't quite ready to leave, or boy, these drugs were seriously doing some strange things to me; that said, I couldn't get enough of them. "Beep, beep, beep" went the machine as I pressed the small button to provide pain relief, it never felt like enough. I was itchy all the time, and everything just hurt. I didn't like the nasal cannula, and I can remember always pulling this out, as it made me feel dry and burned my nostrils.

Although I wanted the pain relief, and this memory has just returned to me as I have gone on to think back and edit this book. I can recall being so out of it on the morphine that I desperately wanted to tell someone, "I am in so much pain, it's unbearable." However, I couldn't speak. I was trapped inside my body, my mind screaming out. The very drug I had been given to alleviate the pain, was effectively silencing me to the outside world, and that recollection was very frightening.

My mam and dad were allowed to come and visit me, and I can remember telling them in no uncertain terms I would rather die, than ever go through something like that procedure again, and I meant it. The first time the nurses came to freshen me up, I think there were four of them, though I was on drugs, so it was a blur. They had come to change my bedding and give me a bed bath. I was in the buff under the bed sheets and couldn't string a sentence together so couldn't exactly comment on being, shall we say shy. Off with the sheets, and there I was, lying bollock naked while they were talking about holidays and the weather, "What have you brought for lunch?" You know, the usual small talk. A quick rub here, a quick rub there, a roll and a freshen up. I can remember the cold air as the fresh bed sheets were placed over me, and positioned in place, and then they were gone as quickly as they had arrived. Well, I might have felt a tad embarrassed, but I soon got used to no one particularly taking notice of me or my bits. Oh, and later in my stay, don't even get me started on how embarrassing it was to use a bedpan. I hated that poxy catheter too. It never felt like I was having a wee, just a constant wet feeling and drip, bloody drip.

This hospital stay was to last about a month. Every day, I asked, "Can I go home?" And I mean every day. I was then moved from the cubicle to a ward, and eventually, it was time to remove the dressing and the drain.

As I am on writing this story, many memories come to my mind, and some stick more than others; this is one of them. For some people, a memory may be brought on by a favourite song that carries them back in time, or a smell for instance, freshly cut grass, a scent or a fragrance. Spending time in a memorable place with all the sights and sounds on a warm day in the fresh air, alone or in good company, enjoying all that our senses can take in. This memory association I have in my mind must be a kinaesthetic one, something to do with feeling and sensation. I know all I have to do is take my mind back there, and it makes me feel all "queasy".

"The day the drain was to be removed" sounds like some big dramatic title. A young nurse came along and informed me that she would take me to a side room. This was to remove my dressings and this "small tube" that was in my leg, known as a drain. Once Transferred to a side room on a patient trolley, the nurse began removing the dressings, and revealed my now deformed leg, which had roughly fifty-six staples up the front, resembling a large zip. It was a multitude of colours, not quite as pretty as a rainbow, ranging from reds, with hues of purples, bits of black, and blues with shades of browns and yellows. Its appearance reminded me of a piece of discarded plastic; it just didn't look real. I now had Frankenstein's leg. I could still wiggle my toes, but I struggled to bend my knee, which was now a very odd shape. My knee felt stiff and clunky, and due to how the quadriceps tendon was stitched around a screw inside at the front, I wasn't allowed to attempt to bend my leg fully, just in case the tendon came loose, before it had had a chance to attach itself.

The dressings removed I could now see this thin tube inserted into my leg, and going somewhere under my skin. The drain had been collecting a fair bit of excess gunk, but it had become less and less as the days went by. "We have a plan," the nurse informed me. We'll count to three, and then I'll carefully remove the drain, nothing to it."

"OK, so we're going to count, you ready?"

"Oh, Okay. How bad can it be, right?"

"Okay, so... One, two."

And then she pulled it out quickly, and "FUCK ME!" I thought the tube down my throat was bad, but this was just horrendous. I felt the plastic tube deep under my skin being drawn out, along with the most nauseous feeling I have ever had. I almost passed out. The sensation was a combination of just plain weird and something that felt like it was crawling under my skin. This drain must have been in maybe four to six inches, I am not sure; what I did know was that it was "horrible, horrible, horrible". It wasn't just the feeling in my leg; the sensation somehow travelled up my body. I am trying to think of words to better describe the whole event, however I am at a loss, other than "Fucking Hell, it was bad".

Later, during my stay in hospital, I was to discover that the prosthesis once inserted into my leg, had made my leg about 3/4 to 1 inch shorter. This proved to make things difficult moving forward, as I struggled with the leg length discrepancy and the limited range of movement in my knee. As I slowly became stronger, I was encouraged to start getting out of bed, and with the help of elbow crutches, attempt to progress in my mobility. During surgery, I had to have an extensive blood transfusion, something like twenty-four units. I'm not sure if this was what was affecting me, but every time I stood up, I felt like all the blood rushed down to my big toe and then filled up my foot. From there, it crept up my shin and into my calf, and I felt like my leg would explode. I then would become dizzy and get the feeling that I was going to pass out. This sensation went on for weeks and weeks following the surgery. I used to have to plan where I was going. I would then try to get to wherever I was going as fast as I could, like some madman on elbow crutches, carrying a yellow bag of home brew; yes, I still had a catheter attached. Once I reached my chosen destination, I had to elevate my leg to relieve the pressure as quickly as I could.

Planning to go to the day room to watch the football was a mission in itself, always praying there would be somewhere available to sit down and put my leg up, as if there wasn't, I would have to make a double journey back to my bed, and I wasn't sure I could manage that. It was like bloody Russian Roulette. Oh, and one day, I thought I would try an excursion off the ward and take the lift downstairs, a change of scenery. Bad idea, I must have picked the slowest lift in the world, which visited every floor, and I almost passed out in the lift as I felt my head go light, and that awful sensation building up in my leg. I had to try to stand on my good leg and position Frankenstein's leg up on the handrail, while attempting to maintain my balance. If anyone had seen me, I would have resembled one of those ballerinas you see with their leg up on the rails completing their stretching exercises. My thought was, "Get your leg up, get your leg up, don't pass out, don't pass out".

As anyone who has been a patient in hospital can testify to, it can be very boring. The days and particularly the nights can feel endless. One day, during my stay while lying on my bed I found myself staring up at the ceiling. With nothing better to do, I began counting the holes in one of the suspended ceiling tiles. After calculating how many holes that single tile had, I went on to count how many tiles there were in the whole bay. Some of the tiles weren't quite whole ones, so I had to take these into account, and calculate just how many holes these had. I used a tissue box which had been sitting on my patient table along with a pen, to write down my findings, and then attempted to do the maths in my head and write down what I had discovered. I was never very good at maths, so the task was quite the challenge. My recollections, and I am going back here some years, tell me that there was something like two hundred and fifty-eight thousand holes in that ceiling.

August '96 was sweltering. I can remember my mam and dad borrowing a wheelchair; it had no support for my leg, so we also borrowed a bath board, and I sat on this while it supported my leg. It was so uncomfortable, but I was just happy to be outside in the beautiful sunshine. It's amazing all the small things that we just take for granted, the fresh air and all the pretty flowers. The blue sky and the birds chirping everything filled my senses. It's one of those memories where nothing exciting happened, a typical boring day on any other occasion. However, in my memory, it stands out. There with my mam and dad on a lovely hot day, out in the fresh air, my senses felt alive.

During my stay in hospital, I met and got along well with a fellow patient. He was in for a new hip and was in the bed opposite to me. This gentleman was a little older than I was, and an educated man. As I recall, he was a university lecturer, his field being engineering. This gentleman must have been religious, as he invited me to attend the hospital chapel one Sunday. There was nothing better to do, so I decided to allow myself to be pushed down to the hospital chapel and accompany my new friend for a Sunday service. It seemed like we were down there for ages. I forgot I hadn't had my medication, and this was the cause of my involuntary upsetedness, if that is even a word. I can tell you it wasn't a pretty sight.

As the service began, and went on I began crying, don't ask me why, it was totally involuntary. My underlying memory of it was lots of tears and snot. I didn't have a hanky, not good. I was trying to go unnoticed, wiping my nose on my sleeve as a hymn was being sung. It was that horrible stringy sort of snot, you know, the stuff that creates bubbles in children's noses; it just wouldn't stop. I'm sure the hymn that was being sung was *Lord Father of Mankind*. I don't know many hymns, but that one sticks in my mind. Oh, that and *Jerusalem*, which was penned as a poem by Sir William Blake in 1804, and then in 1916, Sir Hubert Parry wrote the music, and Blake's lyrics were put to it. I am a mind of useless information. Following my visit to the chapel I think I then went through a slightly off my head religious period, reading the bedside hospital Bible, and thinking I had seen the light. This didn't last long though, and I soon returned to my fantasy book.

After about a month of constant whining about going home. I make a terrible patient, I think the medical team caring for me got fed up and allowed me to escape. I wasn't feeling particularly well, and getting into my dad's small Citroen AX was a nightmare, as I had that damn straight leg brace back on. As soon as I got home, I had the Barry Whites, I had only gone and picked up a really nasty bug. I had to crawl up the stairs to get to the toilet and just felt drained and at a really low ebb.

Following the limb salvage procedure, I got it in my head that I would be okay and not need medication, so I stupidly threw out all the Temgesic tablets, figuring, "I don't need that shit anymore!" After a day or so, I just couldn't for the life of me figure out why, at about 9:45 a.m. every morning, I would just burst out crying. I could set a bloody alarm clock by it, and this went on for several weeks. I developed stomach cramps, was sweating, and just felt totally out of sorts. Obviously, it was withdrawals. You would think I was some sort of a junkie. I felt broken. After a month or so at home, I was invited to go for a physiotherapy session at the Freeman hospital. I was to get only one session. After the physio tried bending my leg, and I yelled out in pain so loud. No way was that leg going to bend to 90 degrees. I think the physio thought I had just had a run of the mill knee replacement and that I was overreacting.

Now, think again if you think things couldn't get any worse. My range of movement began to get less and less, and a small bump formed just below my kneecap. This was to be the start of twelve years of continuous pain, infections, stress, and depression. That little bump I mentioned ended up being like a mini volcano, just waiting to erupt. It looked like a blister, about one inch in circumference, and would grow and grow with horrible infectious fluid. It was causing me lots of pain. The community nurses would have to come out, to lance it and somewhat relieve the pressure. They would then try to drain it; however, within hours, it would fill up again. I had to return to hospital for a check-up, and following a swab, I was told that my leg had an infection, and I would require some antibiotics. Oral antibiotics wouldn't touch this thing. So, another surgical procedure would be necessary to try and clean out the area.

This was to become a running theme over the following years. I was in and out of hospital, having various procedures where my consultant would place things like Gentamicin beads or foam into my leg and then stitch me up. On one occasion, after my consultant had moved over to a different hospital, The Queen Elizabeth in Gateshead, I contracted MRSA. Nothing appeared to touch this, and I had a large open wound that was pouring out the foulest stuff. I ended up having to go for further surgery to cut out the infection, which required me to have a skin graft. The nurses would come with these terrible, freezing cold, luminous green second-generation antibiotic injections straight from out of the fridge. When they injected this stuff into me, I would get a dead arm, as the fluid was so cold. Going back a bit here, but I can recall this horror movie called *Reanimator*; well, it reminded me of that. Just the colour of the stuff in the syringes, it was practically glowing. The skin graft was taken from my right inner thigh, and I can remember it being sore and incredibly itchy as it healed. Apparently, they use something not too dissimilar to a cheese grater to obtain the skin from the site.

Even at this point, I was still trying to fight to save my misshapen, immobile, painful, and short leg. Dear me, if only I had chosen to have my leg amputated years earlier, I could have been in a much better place. However, that's the thing you think you're doing what is right at the time. I cannot even begin to explain my thoughts and emotions. My whole world was consumed by being stuck in this situation. "Limbo". I no longer led a life; it was purely an existence.

Chapter 6

As the years ticked by, my life became a routine series of visits from the community nurses, hospital appointments, admissions, and surgeries. The positives I took from my time being unwell were hard to find. However, upon reflection, I must say that all the NHS staff who looked after me were amazing.

I continued to have surgeries to remove infections, and it would be a few weeks or so before another returned. During a period where I felt reasonably well, even though my leg was still poorly and required constant attention with dressings. I decided to apply for a voluntary job. I needed to be doing something positive and worthwhile. I started volunteering at my local Citizens Advice Bureau between 2001 and 2002. I was training to become an adviser. I know it was sometime around 2002 because, at the time, I was completing training at home, and I have this dreadful underlying memory, and to this day I feel incredibly guilty, as I will explain a little later.

Around 2001, my mam complained of back pain; she put it down to her part time job at the newsagents where she worked, which required her to bring in the heavy bundles of newspapers from when they had been dropped off. Something that always sticks in my mind, as it will for many others, although for different reasons was the 9/11 Trade Towers Terrorist Attacks. I can recall watching it on the television and hearing the unbelievably terrible news alongside the footage. My mam was in the kitchen, and I called to her, to come and see. As she came in and stood to the side of our TV, standing near one of our armchairs, she had both her hands placed on her lower back and looked uncomfortable.

As time went on, my poor mam's pain and symptoms got progressively worse. She was in and out of the hospital, having various investigations, culminating in her being admitted to the University Hospital North Durham for two weeks, where she was diagnosed with pancreatic cancer. It is yet another one of those memories that resides deep in my mind, hearing the consultant's words as he issued that terrible news. Both my dad and myself sitting either side of my mother as we held her hands. As you can imagine our entire world just came crashing down. My mother just appeared unphased. I think she knew it was serious, and after all those months of being unwell, she had accepted her fate as it were. The consultant went on to offer my mam chemotherapy, which could have possibly prolonged her life; however, she refused; she just wanted to be at home.

Macmillan nurses and carers began providing support and were very kind and caring. My mams two sisters, aunty Claire and aunty Ann, would also come down and help out where they could. I helped nurse my mother at home for a further few months until she passed away quietly, my dad and I sitting on the bed beside her, again holding her hands. That final breath and the moment you realise you will never see this person who means so much to you again, words cannot describe it.

My mam always jested that she would be going to hell to be chief stoker. I don't think that would be the case, as she was such a lovely lady. I am not religious, and I don't know what happens after we are gone. That is why I think we should make the most of our time in the here and now, and say all the things we want to say to the living and show that we care. My dad removed my mother's wedding, engagement, and eternity rings, which all had small reducers fitted as my mam had lost so much weight, and they had been dropping off. I was then handed the rings, and for a little while, they lived on my bedside cabinet. I then placed them on my keyring, and they are there to this day. I never take my keys out with me; I would be devastated to lose those rings.

Getting back to my feelings of guilt that I mentioned earlier this is especially hard to put into words. My mother was in so much pain, and I can remember her constantly moaning in her bedroom. I was in my bedroom next door, trying to concentrate on completing these training modules. It is incredibly difficult trying to care for someone twenty-four hours per day. It got to the point where I couldn't stand it anymore. My internal voice shouted, "Will you please just shut up?" I had to go downstairs and try to sort myself out, with waves of guilt invading my thoughts. I then returned upstairs to try and reassure my poor, dear mother. At that point, I don't think she even knew I was there. I felt like I had failed her. This was because when she had been able to talk things through, pain was what she feared the most. I didn't want her so doped up that she was trapped inside her own body, unable to tell me she was in pain, like the experience I had had. But I also did not want her suffering. Those memories still bring an emotional response some twenty odd years later, as I ask myself "Could I have done anything more, or differently?" Over time, I can now also smile at some of the fond memories we shared, like when my mam who didn't often get tipsy, but when she did was hilarious, and would go on to make everyone around her laugh. Not long after we lost my mother, I quit the Citizens Advice. It was just too much trying to cope with the personal loss, and then also trying to help other people, while also dealing with this anchor that was weighing me down, my leg.

I was always closer to my mother than my father, not because I thought any less of my dad, but because he was always at work when I was little. My mam was very protective of me, probably overly so. I think it was because my parents didn't think they could have children. My mother had complications during my birth, and when I was born, I had a "twisted ankle", so my foot looked as if it was on back to front. Something had to be done, or I wouldn't know whether I was coming or going. It's very ironic to think now that I have a prosthetic leg, which has a rotator fitted at the ankle, that I can swivel my foot a whole 360 degrees.

I suppose I was mollycoddled as a nipper; Mam and Dad would spend hours massaging my wonky foot with warm olive oil upon an evening. This was to try and get it into proper alignment. As a young child, I was always with my mother. I'm no psychotherapist, but I think this somehow caused me to grow up introverted, and not a particularly good mixer in social situations. I spent a lot of time alone, happy in my own company. When I started nursery my poor mother had to literally drag me there kicking and screaming each morning. I absolutely hated nursery school with a passion, and didn't care much for the other children. When at school I preferred to sit at the back of the classroom on a rocking horse, all alone, while the other children would sit cross legged listening to the teacher reading a story.

Over time, I eventually got used to nursery and formed a crush on a teacher. I adored her and can remember inviting her to our house to see the twenty odd guinea pigs we had. Twenty odd you say. Well, that was my dad's fault. He thought he had two of the same sex wee pigs, obviously he was mistaken, and before we knew it, we had loads. I am sure they were like Gremlins, pop a bit of water on them, and another two or three appeared. My dad had to build an even bigger shed to accommodate them all. Getting back to the invite. I had told my mam, "Oh, the teacher's comin' to see wor guinea pigs the morra Ma.". Now, it either slipped her mind when she picked me up from nursery, or she simply didn't believe me.

The following day, after my mam had collected me from the nursery, she began sorting things out for washing. Various articles of clothing and things like bedding, towels, etc were strewn all over the floor and separated into appropriate piles. Now Imagine the scene, there was a knock at our door, and when my mam opened it, there was my teacher. I was all excited. However, my mother was mortified, and I got "The Look". Even though we didn't have much, my mam was incredibly house proud. Our washing machine, which was more akin to an old fashioned poss tub, must also have been just as excited to see my teacher, as it was dancing all over the floor, vibrating on full spin. My mother then rather embarrassingly invited my teacher in for a brief chat, before we all went outside to the shed so I could proudly show off my guinea pigs. Years later, my mam would retell this story to me and laugh about it, along with the other times I had embarrassed her.

There was a school event; I think it involved music and dancing, "Not my scene man" at the time. I was only about four or five, and the teacher I had a crush on was going to be there. I can remember being quite pleased with myself as I had the opportunity to sit beside her on one of the old school benches in the school's large hall. I was not best pleased though when this fella rocked up and sat down on the opposite side of the bench right next to my teacher, and they began chatting, and can you believe it even holding hands? I can remember having a right hump on, you know, the one where the face scowls, a loud huffing sound is made, and then a stamp of the feet while arms are crossed. It turned out okay though, as this guy blackmailed me with an ice cream and turned out to be a pretty nice man. I mean, when you are little, and it is a choice between a girl and a lovely ice cream with monkeys' blood and a flake, "No competition, right?"

Another tale to do with the guinea pigs, which we had now had for a good few years, and yes they had continued breeding. My poor dad remained attempting to keep on top of the situation by giving them away. Well as I've mentioned, I didn't really mix with other children, so I used to keep myself entertained. I would get my Action Men out and select a guinea pig to play along, sometimes popping one of my wee friends in Action Man's Jeep and then taking it for a bit of a spin. Mam told me my nana was coming down from New Kyo, so I had to put the guinea pig away because my nana was afraid of the little critters. Now, after tidying up the Action Man stuff, I am pretty sure I put the guinea pig away just as my nana arrived. After about half an hour, my mam suggested I go and check on the guinea pigs while she and nana were having a nice cup of tea. I went out to the shed and as I began counting, I got to eighteen, nineteen, twenty, and "Err hold on a minute," I suddenly realised number twenty-one was missing. I sheepishly returned to my mam and informed her, "Ma, one of the guinea pigs is missin'." She gave me one of those all too familiar looks and said, "Whatever you do, don't say anything to your nana."

Fortunately, a few minutes later, my nana got up to wash her teacup. She always liked to drink from a bone china teacup with a matching saucer. She reminded me of the Queen mother. I quickly took this opportunity to attempt to search for number twenty-one. Where could it be? I looked all over the place. Finally, I lifted one of the settee cushions and discovered a hyperventilating brown and white guinea pig; it was completely soaked through with sweat, following having been sat on for so long. My dear old nana must have been sitting on it for over an hour, and my nana, bless her was quite a rotund lady. Poor thing! I had to sneak it back into the shed and dry it off. I think that particular guinea pig's name was Lucky, and on this occasion, it certainly had been!

Over the years I was very fortunate that my mam and dad would allow me to have all sorts of pets. As I have already mentioned there was "Wor Blackie and the gang of guinea pigs". I also had everything from goldfish, which I won at the "Hoppins", which was a fair that used to come to the Town Moor in Newcastle. Mind you fish never lasted long. Then there was a large black rabbit whom I named Lefty, as it had a wonky ear. I bought it from Stanley Market without asking permission first and tried to pass it off as an Easter present to my mam. More work for The Ern, when he came in following a busy day at work as he had to start building a rabbit hutch. We also took in a stray collie I discovered wandering around the streets nearby, her name was Bess, and she was so adorable, what a lovely friendly dog. I had a couple of budgies that reminded me of Laurel and Hardie, one being really thin and always getting bullied by its fatter companion, and then there were the mice.

Now when I say mice, let me explain I only had one white mouse at a time, however it leads me into this tale. So my mam was away with the girls at Blackpool, leaving my dad to look after me. I had been whining on about wanting a pet mouse, and while my mother hated the little furry things, she had given in to my demands. That left my poor dad to take me to the pet shop and buy the said mouse along with a cage, the food, bedding etc. When I got my new little white and pink friend home I was so excited. I think at the time I was maybe eight or nine years old. My new best friend was in its cage, and I decided I was going to build it a Lego house. So, I began constructing this huge maze-like thing. I then took the mouse from its cage, it wasn't exactly tame and as I tried to wrangle this little ball of fur and place it next to its new play den, it ran away, going through the Lego maze, and shooting out of a side tunnel I had created, at warp factor nine. The mouse then proceeded to run under our sofa. Well, what to do? I went and got my dad and told him about the naughty mouse and that I had made this lovely house, and that the mouse was so unappreciative and had decided to "bugger off", where I thought it was now hiding in its new home, either under, or inside our sofa. Well, my dad was not best pleased, especially as it took him about an hour and a half to find the little devil. My dad had to tip the settee upside down, get a screwdriver and remove the mesh base. He then had his torch out trying to spot this little white and pink thing. Eventually, he caught sight of a wee tail poking out from one corner and made a grab. Next thing just like a magician he had this small mouse hanging upside down by its tail, while uttering under his breath "Gotcha you little bastard." I had never really heard my dad swear before, so I was a bit surprised, thinking if he was doing a magic trick, surely "Abracadabra" would have been a more appropriate choice of words in making a mouse reappear. My dad then proceeded to walk over to the mouses cage and put it back in. I then got a stern telling off "Diven't take it oot again." After my dad left the room, probably five or so minutes passed all instructions just fell out of my head. I opened the cage door and slipped my hand in, got the mouse out once again, thinking I'd take more care of it this time. I introduced the mouse to its Lego play area, and exactly the same thing happened, except this time I was quicker than the mouse. The only thing is in my attempt to capture it I inadvertently put too much weight down and, I ended up quite literally squashing, my new best friend. Oh my God! I was now a killer! I ran from the room to where my dad was, tears streaming down my face, with this little lifeless creature in the palm of my hand.

My dad, who I am sure just wanted to say, "What the fuck have you done now?", just looked at me with a puzzled expression. We had to have a mini burial service and later on in the evening when my dad spoke to my mother, on the phone as she was still in Blackpool, he explained what a nightmare of a day he had had and probably mentioned what a tit he had for a son, "The Mouse Killer". My mam was all "Aww, and dear me's", and then instructed my poor dad, "Well Ernie you will have to go out and get him another one tomorrow." So, the very next day we were off mouse shopping once again. I got yet another little white and pink mouse. This one was to last much longer, and I took ever such good care of, I'd like to say her. I named her "Pinky". She would get up on a morning as I got ready for school, and when I opened her cage door, come out on to my hand and just sit there as I gave her a little piece of toast. She would sit holding the tiny piece of toast in her ever so small paws, and even my mother took to her. After having Pinky for a year or so she developed a lump on her tail. My dad had to take her to the vet, and it was decided it was a nasty tumour, so the vet amputated half her tail. When my dad went to pick her up that evening, he said he had never been so embarrassed. You see it was Greyhound night, and all the blokes were in with their dogs getting seen. There on the counter was a shoe box, with large bold words stating, "Caution Mouse in Transit". I dearly loved that wee mouse, and I hope the one I squashed would have forgiven me for its untimely demise.

As I got a little older, my dad would allow me to accompany him on jobs. As I mentioned earlier, he was a motor mechanic. He would be fixing a car or a lorry, and I would hand him the relevant tools, from his rather disorganised toolbox. Things like the correct size socket or spanner. My dad worked outdoors in all weathers and never seemed to get cold. Me on the other hand, I can recall many times having to sit in some freezing cold old car we were running around in at the time. My dad, bless him, never owned a new car, not until he was pretty much due to retire. I can remember one old Datsun Cherry he used to own. It was black with a tinge of brown, the brown being rust. It used more oil than petrol and would leave huge plumes of blue smoke as it was driven along. It was a fairly entertaining car to ride in, as you could watch the road go by, not through the usual method of looking out the windows, but through the rather large hole in the passenger floor! Things haven't changed much as I've gotten older; my dad, who has just turned eighty-four in November, still pretty much makes me stand on the sidelines as he works and only allows me to pass him tools. Oh, and his current car, while it doesn't have holes in the floor, it does resemble a mobile skip!

Chapter 7

During the period when my mother was ill, my dad would agree he found it very difficult just to be still and be in the house. He would busy himself with going shopping or doing some chores and also continued to go to work as he had not yet retired. For me my experience was of being ill myself and listening to my mother in pain as she gradually got worse. I had this awful sense of feeling incredibly powerless and unable to help her. I did what I could, we would sit together, listening to some of her favourite music, or talk about memories from long ago. I would try to reassure her not to worry about how dad and I would get on with things once she was no longer around to keep us right. My mother had just celebrated her sixtieth birthday on May 16th, 2002; she passed away in the August of that year. I regret that my mam hasn't been able to see how far I've come, all that I've achieved and that I'm okay despite the various health issues and challenges I have faced. One thing I can be sure of is how proud she would have been of my dear old dad. He is everything, my best friend, my most loyal supporter, my car and bike mechanic, sometimes my personal shopper, and one of the most genuine and giving people I know. To have had such wonderful parents, I feel blessed despite all the negative things that have occurred in my life.

Life was just a blur from 2002 until about 2006. I always thought that if I wrote a book, it would start with a few interesting chapters. They may be sad, but they would hold the reader's attention, and then just as the reader turned to the next page, it would be blank. This would be the case pretty much until the final chapters. The reader would think, "What the hell kind of book is this?" Well, this is an analogy of how I felt my life had been up to a certain point. I had lived a somewhat average life with nothing anyone would really want to read about. I then had a few things going on, the majority of which were traumatic and negative, and then… nothing. It was as if I didn't exist. Every day was the same, pain, discomfort, numbness, depression, repeat. These were my blank pages, with nothing of note to write about. I could of course have filled those pages with dark scribbles and scary faces, an outcry of how cruel I felt life had been, and searching for someone to blame. So, with regards to 2002 until 2006. I am sat here trying to think of something either interesting or relevant to write about from those years, and it is as if someone has stolen a file from within a filing cabinet that exists within my mind; and that drawer is completely empty.

In 2006, I did have a period where I was free from infection, so my consultant suggested it might be a good time to remove my kneecap. You see I could feel the internal metalwork catching each time I attempted to bend my knee, and this was both painful as well as uncomfortable. A date was arranged for me to go in for the procedure, which wasn't supposed to be a big one. My right kneecap didn't really serve much purpose following having the metalwork inserted, and my Frankenstein leg was never going to win any beauty awards, so I wasn't concerned.

As far as I was aware, the surgery had been a success. I can't recall at what point I woke up. My underlying memory was that I came around and found myself sitting up in bed, the following morning, with the most horrendous headache. The back of my head was pounding away, reminding me of one of those old black and white Tarzan films, featuring Johnny Weissmuller, where the tribesman would be rhythmically banging on their drums. Breakfast had been brought along, and I was happily eating this when the consultant came in to see me. The first thing he said was, "I can't believe you're sitting up in bed." I was a bit confused, and then he explained that things hadn't gone exactly according to plan. My kneecap had been removed without incident, but when my leg had been bent in theatre to try and give me an improved range of movement, some blood vessels had gotten caught in the metalwork, and apparently, I had bled out. Oh, what a mess!

I think they had to call a vascular surgeon to stop the bleeding and stitch me up. The consultant went on to say, "We thought we'd almost lost you." I think that's what he said. I wasn't in the best frame of mind, my head pounding, probably from losing so much blood. When he made that comment, I thought he meant I had gotten lost on a patient trolley somewhere in the hospital, down some corridor or another, but it was more serious than that. It was touch and go with my life. I was then informed by my consultant that he wasn't prepared to do any other surgical procedures in the future, other than amputation. This news hit me like a tonne of bricks. I think deep down inside I had resigned myself to my current life of nothingness, however, my leg although useless and painful was still part of me. That horrible and terrifying word had now been mentioned yet again. I could feel myself building up the walls of denial inside my mind. It's mad to think, that I could try to convince myself, if I didn't think about it, it would all just go away.

I was allowed home after a day or so, with metal staples all down the front of my leg. The community nurses began coming to see me at home once again. Within a few days, the staples began tearing apart just below my knee. I now had a huge open gaping wound that was producing the most dreadful stuff. This continued to get worse and worse, and the nurses had to start coming more frequently. The remaining staples were removed not long after my return home. The wound wasn't healing and required multiple daily dressings. The nurses would pack the hole using sterile dressings containing silver. On occasion, a caustic stick would be used to burn over granulated flesh. The caustic sticks, if they dripped, burned like Fuck! It was like placing a red-hot cigar on the open wound and then pouring vinegar on it just to ensure I got the message.

When I returned to hospital for a check-up, it was decided I should be admitted, as my infected leg looked really bad. It was suggested a relatively new bit of technology at the time may help. This device was called a Vac's dressing. It was a small portable machine with a tube attached to a dressing that would be placed over an affected area. The machine was supposed to suck up the bad infectious wet material, and help keep the area dry, so that it had a chance to heal. As I recall, they used the Vac's machine for about six weeks, and I was on a sort of day release. I was allowed home during the day but had to return each night and spend it in the hospital. This six-week period wasn't too bad. I think it was because going in and out of the hospital was a change of scenery, and I got to interact with the nurses one of whom I had a crush on, so it became a bit of a social thing, you know, seeing new faces and engaging in brief conversations. Whereas being at home was isolating and lonely. In the end, the Vac's dressing was unsuccessful in helping clear up the infection, and heal the large hole in my leg, which just continued to grow in size.

Over the years, I garnered new friends. These friends were always there. The first one was that dark sense of humour I acquired; and when I say dark, I mean very dark. The other friend, which sounds even more out there, was pain. I became so used to pain, that in a way, I welcomed it. The pain was reality. I became lost; I retreated into my own dark little world. The hole in my leg was so big and deep that I could look in and see the metalwork. The infection was so bad that somehow, it was pressing on what felt like my sciatic nerve, and I was in constant agonising pain.

I was back at home, being cared for by the community nurses. They began coming four times a day, seven days a week. Each day, I became more and more withdrawn. Gradually, it began where I wouldn't speak much. I was struggling to sleep and felt awake 24 hours a day, frozen in time in a meaningless world. I wasn't eating, and things got so bad that one evening, a nurse had to be called out to administer Midazolam as I was in so much pain. I desperately just needed to relax and sleep. I wouldn't have cared if I had never woke up at that point. In fact, I welcomed death. It was so sweet to drift off into that total blackness, with no thoughts, no pain, no worries, just nothingness. It was short lived, and I returned to my living nightmare. My mind, which I think many people would consider fragile by now, was in actual fact, trying to protect me. By attempting to take me away from the pain and creating this impenetrable wall, however, in doing so, it was also cutting me off from the real world.

One of the supervising nurses became very concerned about my well-being and spoke with my dad. A voluntary section was even discussed and considered. I was now in limbo, and dark thoughts began forming in my mind. Deep, dark and bottomless chasms, evil intent. The wind at my back pushing me towards my impending doom. Being attacked from the inside, destruction, loss of hope. I have underlying memories of standing on the edge of this vast black hole, and if I fell in, I knew I would be completely lost, my mind would snap, and I would be forever broken. I would never return. I had the most vivid thoughts. It's strange because I've gone on to use this dark period in my life creatively, writing poetry and lyrics to music alongside a newfound passion for learning to play the guitar. But more on that later.

I thought I was beyond salvaging; it was too late. It felt like I was being punished, made to suffer for as long as possible by some unknown entity with malicious intent. I longed to go to sleep and never wake up. One of the supervising nurses who had spoken with my dad, came to see me. She sat beside me and spoke in a friendly voice. saying, "Do you know why most people get down and feel depressed?" I think it was a rhetorical question, as I certainly didn't reply. The nurse answered her own question, "It's because people tend to look too far into the past or too far into the future. You have to learn to live for today, in the moment. Your life is passing you by," She continued, "You know your leg is never going to be right." "It's now your enemy." "You cannot continue as you are, give yourself a chance at having a life". "I know losing your leg is a huge and scary thing but having an amputation could help you move on". "Yes, you may still have pain, but you may discover that everything changes, and you can go out and start doing things, and living life".

I am not entirely sure how those words reached me, or why they had such a profound effect, but it was like an epiphany, one of those cartoon light bulb moments where the bulb lights up above your head with a "Ding!" Within days, I had contacted my consultant's secretary to arrange an appointment. When I saw my consultant, I explained that I wanted to have my leg off as soon as possible. "How about next week?" I asked. To which my consultant replied "No, no we can't just get you in and do a procedure like that". I was told it couldn't and wouldn't be done that quickly, as I needed time to process the decision and ensure it was the right one for me. After a few more weeks, a preliminary date was set for my surgery and amputation; it was about three months down the line. I now had a date, and strangely enough it felt good, exciting even. I could see myself being proactive and moving forward. The calendar on our wall became a countdown, and I would place a tick on it each day. I still had enormous pain. However, my mind now had something else to focus on.

I sold my beloved Mini Cooper S, and with the money, my dad bought an automatic Honda Jazz that we could share. I also went out and bought an expensive top drawer Carbon Mountain Bike, an Ibis Mojo SL. That was my inspiration. My mindset was "I would ride a bike again". I had always had bikes as a youngster and had moved on to motorbikes at the age of sixteen. I wanted to get back into cycling, so I set myself the challenge and began researching riding as an amputee.

Finally, the day of my amputation September 11th, 2007, came around. I know it's hard to believe, but I was not afraid at all; I was excited. I said farewell to my leg, which hadn't really been mine for years, and I was all ready to be placed under the anaesthetic. When I woke up, the first thing I did was try to sit up, and I almost knocked myself out as this stump came flying up from under the bed covers to greet me. Man, my wee leg was so light. I inspected it through the bandages; it felt weird. I can remember, while I was in hospital, the registrar came along to see me; she was a really pretty lady from Greece. That first time she redressed my stump using a tight elastic bandage, I almost jumped off the bed as I got this sudden shooting pain. I think the bandage had pressed on my sciatic nerve. I can't recall how long I was in hospital, not very long and then I was off home.

About eight weeks after having my leg off, I was fitted for a prosthetic leg over at the Disablement Services Centre in Newcastle. I remember the first time I was shown around the facility; it had been while I was waiting to go in for my amputation. A consultant introduced himself, and I was shown a prosthetic limb, which was standing in the corner of his office. It was fitted with horrible looking foam resembling the shape of a leg and covered with the same stuff as ladies' tights to mimic skin. It had a horrible old fashioned black shoe on its foot, and this constrictive looking kind of strap that I assumed was to keep it in place. The leg looked more like it should be back where I used to work, Beamish Museum. I'm not ashamed to admit I cried; it was nothing like what I had seen online. I hated my first and second prosthetic legs; the hydraulic knees were challenging to get the hang of, and at times, could be unstable. Plus, that God awful belt that kept the socket in place was just so restrictive and uncomfortable. I broke my first knee within a few months, so I had to be provided with a sturdier version. Eventually, I got used to the limb over time, though it was never comfortable.

Speaking of comfort, any seasoned amputee will tell you this, you can have thousands of pounds worth of high-tech equipment; however, if your socket is uncomfortable, it is one of the most frustrating things to deal with. A poorly fitting socket can cause a whole range of problems, both physically and mentally. It can be too tight or too loose, and it can cause blisters and sores. You can bottom out and sit on what is known as your residual bone, which is the bone that has been cut through. I have experienced this when my socket has been too big for me. I then get a pain at the end of my femur that I can only describe as being similar to a toothache like pain. It radiates, pulses, and gnaws away.

The mental side of things can be very difficult if your limb is not fitting correctly, as you lose a great deal of your independence. Depending on if you are able to work, you may have to take time off, and other things like hobbies or interests may have to be put on hold. This is why I am so grateful for those days when my limb is fitting, and I can just get on with things. Although I have a limb loss, it is more or less second nature after all these years, and as for putting on a fake cover to try to make it appear more like a normal leg no way. To be perfectly honest, I am proud to wear my prosthetic, with shorts in its bare-naked form. This is part of who I am now. I have gone through the five stages of grief to get to this point, and I am comfortable in myself. I figure that if other people can't deal with my missing leg, well, that is on them.

Following my amputation, I would have recurring lucid dreams which all revolved around running. I would run everywhere and never appear to get tired. I just loved running. Imagine my disappointment when I would wake up and realise I could no longer run; even the stairs were a challenge. To this day, one of my pet hates is not so much coming downstairs as I can do this quite well with my current micro processed knee, which is an Ossur Rheo XC; however, going up one step at a time makes me feel inferior. The knee has the ability to go up foot over foot, but it just takes so much extra energy, and I am always worried I may kick someone behind me when I have to flick the knee through.

In the early days after becoming an amputee, I used to notice, like when I was out shopping, that I would get these funny looks, people looking, however, trying to hide the fact they were. It used to really annoy me, so I would play the same game with them and follow them around, let's say, a store, giving them peculiar looks, "Hey look, you have two heads?" Then I became used to being different and understood that people generally don't intend to be mean; they are either interested but maybe too shy to ask, or they are unfortunately just ignorant. I think the worst reactions are when little kids are fascinated by my, "Robot Leg", as I have heard it called, and tell their parents, only to be ushered away. If you are reading this, allow your kids to ask questions and educate them. We are all different in various ways, and it's okay.

Chapter 8

Following my amputation, I didn't have anyone to talk to about day-to-day stuff involving prosthetics and whatnot, so I set up a Facebook group and aptly named it Facebook Amputees; I know original, right? I had been experimenting with how to ride my new bike, and I will admit, at certain points, through sheer frustration, I was ready to quit before I even began. I just couldn't get my head around how to get on the damn thing and push off. The fact I had to place my prosthetic foot up on to the pedal, and as I went to complete a revolution of the cranks it would then fall off, did my head in. Oh, and getting the correct seat height, too high, and I couldn't get on the bike, and too low, and my socket would hit the back of my prosthetic knee, causing my foot to bounce off. You would think I had Tourette's, as on many occasions, my skin would get nipped between the socket and my saddle, and I would then go on to swear and get really pissed off.

The first day I attempted a proper ride was on the Millennium Green, over by the Font. The Font or Bloemfontein, which is its correct name, is a little way along from where I lived. My dad took me and my bike over by car, so that I could have my first actual practice on some grass. It was a Tuesday, as I recall, and after removing the bike from our car, I managed to mount the bike and temporarily secure my prosthetic foot in place with a fudged together kind of toe strap. I pushed off, and I was away. A little, no a lot of wobbles, but I did it. After a bit of practice doing some loops on the flat, oh, and by the way, I never turned right, as I would lose my balance, as this was my missing leg side, I rode counterclockwise around and around. Then I took great delight in riding up and around Teletubby Hill, which is just a small round hill on the green. I was soon out of breath after never having ridden a bike for so long. However, it was also so much fun after all those years.

The next day, I gathered my gear and set off from home towards the coast. Some fifteen miles later, and you have to consider that I hadn't been on a bike for about thirteen years, well, I was overjoyed. The sense of achievement, being out in the fresh air and being independent. I was also thoroughly knackered and sore. I had ridden some of the way, and on the bigger hills, pushed some of the way. I had managed to fall off several times as my stupid brain still thought I had a leg. My stupid brain couldn't get it into its stupid mind that my right leg was no longer there. So, I would stop, go to put my leg out, and in comedy fashion, just keel over "Do'h"! It took a long time to relearn how to get on and off and maintain my balance on a bike. As I said, I was tired following that first long ride, so I got my phone out and called my dad. "Can you come doon and pick me up please?" He answered and asked where I was "Oh at Richard Hardie's." To which he replied, "So at Newfield"? I then informed him, "No, doon at Sunderland." He then said, "How've ye got doon there"? And I was so proud to tell him "On me bike".

With the Facebook group formed, I was soon in contact with lots of fellow amputees and other people in the know, like clinicians. I was getting valuable information and being able to hand out some newly discovered tips for cycling and advice I had garnered as a new amputee. Quite out of the blue, a South African prosthetist asked how I was getting on with my cycling. This gentleman's name was Johan Snyder's. Johan was a prosthetist and had happened to come across my Facebook group. He went on to contact me and asked if I could provide some tips for a patient he was treating who was about to have an amputation. I was only too happy to try and help, and this is when I was asked if I was having any challenges or difficulties with my prosthetic components. I replied "Yes," going on to tell Johan that I was having some challenges. The biggest of which was my socket. It felt like it was sitting a little high up on my thigh, causing it to continuously nip away at my upper leg. Johan then informed me that he might know someone who could help, and he very kindly put me in touch with a prosthetist in the UK, named Jamie Gillespie. Jamie worked for a clinic named Pace Rehabilitation, and this is really where my cycling proper took off, and I rediscovered my passion. I have so many people to thank upon my journey for their kindness and support. It is incredible how life works out at times and how one person's simple offer of help can lead you on a whole different path. So, a huge thank you to Johan and Jamie, who are two of the most friendly and dedicated people. They were the springboard I needed at the start and have played a huge role in all my following adventures.

Soon, I was out on my bike almost every day. My fitness went from strength to strength. I was still riding around cursing and muttering, as that damn socket would nip me, and at the time, "dropper seat posts", which are a fantastic bit of kit, had not been invented. Now, I set myself a challenge, to ride all the big hills and banks in my local area. To complete my own personal challenge. My rule was, I had to ride up each of my chosen routes without stopping. I was ecstatic when I completed Lanchester Bank; my dad had driven over to watch me on the final climb and to take some photos for posterity. To motivate me in my climbs when my good leg and little stump were burning, and I thought I could go no further, I would pick a target, say a lamppost, a sign, or a tree, then think to myself, "just get to the next one." I would imagine my mam cheering me on, and then once I got to my target, repeat the process, "Just get to the next one." I was very proud of my achievements. One day, I recounted all the banks and hills I had done, telling one of my friend's dads about Lanchester Bank. He then said, "The old'un or the new'un?" I was like, "what, whad'ye mean?" He then repeated himself, going on to inform me that the old bank was named the "Peth". "It's the one that comes oot by the vets, next te' the church", he said. "Oh Ah haven't tried that one." To which he then replied, "Ahh well ye haven't done a bank until ye've done the Peth." Right, that was it. Challenge accepted; the very next day, I rode all the way down the bank into Lanchester. "Wheeeeeeeee"! And I started up the old bank, the Peth, which was more of a "Urgghhhhhhh", while trying to catch my breath. The first tight bend was so steep I was struggling to keep my front wheel down. I did it though and completed the bank without stopping. I immediately rang my dad to tell him, well when I say immediately, I had to catch my breath as my lungs, leg and little leg were burning.

 Not too long following my amputation, when I felt I was at a fairly good fitness, and of course balance level. I was on a quest to challenge myself. It was as if I had something to prove. So I decided to raise funds by doing my own charity bicycle ride. I was very proud to represent the charities Help for Heroes and Cancer Research, and raised a few thousand quid, which I then gave half to each of my chosen causes. It was a very special moment.

 As mentioned, I had been researching various prosthetic knees, none of which would allow me to do what I wanted, and that was to ride a mountain bike out of the saddle over jumps and rougher trails. You see, by now, I was getting bored of just sitting on the saddle; I wanted more. Then, while I was checking out YouTube, I came across a guy in the US who had purposely designed an extreme sports knee, named the Bartlett Tendon. I tried to contact the designer of the knee, a gentleman named Brian Bartlett; however, at first, I was unsuccessful. Moving on with continued research, I discovered that Brian had sponsored one of his friends, a guy named Jason Lalla. Jason was a Paralympian Gold medallist skier, a keen mountain biker, plus he was also a prosthetist. I was fortunate enough to find that I could contact Jason via email, and following some brief correspondence, Jason very kindly invited me to phone him at home. So, one evening, I made the call, and I soon discovered what a lovely gentleman Jason was; he was only too happy to discuss Brian and his unique knee design. We must have been on the phone for forty-five minutes to an hour, and it just felt like talking to an old friend.

Jason informed me that Brian had to go in for a revision of his amputated leg, and was in recovery, going on to say that he would put a call into Brian on my behalf. A few weeks passed, and then I was over the moon to get a response from Brian, who informed me that his knee design wasn't quite in production yet; however, as soon as it was, he would let me know. As the weeks went by, we kept in touch, and eventually, I received a message saying the first batch of Bartlett Tendon knees were going into production. Brian had designed and self-funded the knees and built each one individually in his house's basement workshop. This was around the end of 2008, and I was still a very new amputee.

I was invited to visit Jamie at Pace Rehabilitations Amersham clinic. While there, he introduced me to a friendly chap named Ollie Smith. Ollie worked for Ossur, a major manufacturer and supplier of prosthetic equipment. Ollie very kindly provided me with a much better way of keeping my leg attached; this was a seal in liner instead of that horrible waist belt. Both Jamie and Ollie set about measuring and casting me for a unique cycling specific socket. The socket was fitted to a Total Knee 2100 hydraulic knee, and my riding then went one step further again as I was finally comfortable. This was to be the start of Pace Rehabilitation's fantastic support of me in my endeavours. I owe Pace and everyone involved a huge debt of gratitude for their friendship and support over the years.

A few more months down the line, I had already excitedly told Jamie all about Brian and his awesome prosthetic knee design. Jamie was very interested, as it is a prosthetist's job to get the best out of equipment and enable their clients/patients to achieve their goals. Jamie asked me to see if Brian would be interested in coming to the UK to do a presentation; this would be sometime the following year, 2009. Strathclyde University was going to be arranging a conference, which had various guest speakers. There was to be a two-day series of presentations to be arranged at a venue in Scotland. I contacted Brian, and he thought this would be an excellent opportunity to showcase his knee, so things were set in motion.

I continued cycling, using it as an outlet to help me with my mood and any phantom pain I encountered. Speaking of phantom pain, this was a new and somewhat bizarre experience to me at the time, and something even to this day I am not sure I fully understand. All I know is that it bloody well hurts. I discovered there was nothing like suffering from bad phantom pain and just heading down to my local woods, screaming, shouting, and swearing as I tore around the local trails, trying to relieve my frustration and pain as well as attempting to improve my mindset. Riding helped me feel like I had achieved something, and I was winning in this personal challenge. I had an absolute blast cycling in 2008 through to the end of that year, even though I used an ordinary hydraulic knee and had to sit on the saddle.

One day, while out for a walk with Mr Hinks. Mr Hinks being the English bull Terrier I had at the time, my old school friend Carl came past me in his little Suzuki Jimny. Then seeing me he turned around and pulled over to have a chat and a catch up. We must have been there for ages because when Carl went to pull away, his car battery was flat. He had inadvertently left his sidelights on. I rang my dad, and he came to rescue Carl, popping a set of jump leads from one car to another; then Carl was on his way. Following this reconnection, we started going out regularly on bike jaunts. Carl being even more of a bike fanatic than myself. It was great fun. Carl was very supportive of me and would happily ride at my pace; he's a cracking mate.

Approaching the end of 2008, while cycling towards Beamish with Carl, I developed a horrible stomach cramp and didn't feel well at all. I let Carl know I wasn't feeling great and that I was going to take a shortcut up by No Place, (yes, it's an actual place) and head home. My stomach settled somewhat over the course of the next few weeks, and I thought no more about it. A couple of weeks later, Carl and I had arranged a ride up to Kielder Forest for an all-day adventure. The weather was lovely; it was a glorious day. We rode from the morning well into the evening as it started to get dark. As we rode back to where the car was parked to pack up our things, my new bike felt a bit off and wasn't riding right. I stopped and got off, and upon closer inspection, I saw that the rear triangle was twisted and the frame around the bottom bracket was broken. I was most disappointed, to say the least, and had a few choice words.

After getting home, the following day I arranged to take the bike back down to Stif Mountain Bikes in Leeds, where I had purchased it. I was gutted as the frame had to be returned to America, and a replacement needed to be ordered. Waiting the 6 weeks or so for the return of the new frame and the rebuilding of the whole bike, felt like forever. Upon getting word to head back down to Stif and pick up my bike, I couldn't wait to get back in the saddle.

Going down to Stif to pick up my bike, I had arranged to meet a lovely couple I had met via my Facebook amputee group, this was Julian and Trudi. Julian used to be an active guy who enjoyed cycling and climbing; however, he had been diagnosed with an osteosarcoma in his left arm, which resulted in him having to have his arm amputated further than expected, the surgeon having to go through his shoulder. When my dad and I met Julian and Trudi, we knew they were "our kind of people", so warm and friendly. I admired Julian and Trudi's positivity; they began telling us about how Julian was going to attempt to ride a bike again. Sharing their ideas for making some sort of a prosthetic to help with this. As we kept in touch on Facebook, I followed Julian's progress, and they did indeed MacGyver a prosthetic that assisted Julian in riding his bike. Julian and Trudi were such good sports; they would post pictures and videos of themselves, some of which were of Julian falling off his bike and of course, getting back up. Julian never gave up right until the last, when that horrible disease took him. I didn't know him long or well; however, Julian and Trudi left an impression on me after that single meeting never to give up. I just messaged Trudi to make sure I could share this story and that I had the details correct, as it was such a long time ago. Trudi really touched me by saying, "Thank you for keeping Julian's memory alive." I told Trudi, "I still have Julian's phone number stored in my phone", to which she replied, "Me too".

After our lovely meeting with that most awesome couple and spending a long time looking around Stif at all their "bike porn". Ern and I headed back home with my newly built bike in the back of our car. On the way back, I began feeling poorly with my stomach. It was similar to the last time but much worse, so much so that I was doubled up in the passenger seat. My dad decided to take me straight to hospital, and we went to the Queen Elizabeth in Gateshead, where I had had my leg amputated. I was seen quickly, blood was taken, and then the usual observations and examinations were done. After a few hours at the hospital, the doctor returned and informed me he didn't think there was anything to worry about; however, he wanted me to see a haematologist over in Durham, as he had discovered a small node in my neck near my collarbone. We drove home, and over the next few weeks, I had the odd upset stomach, but nothing too serious. I wasn't overly concerned about this "little lump". Truth be told, when I tried to feel it, I could barely find it.

I awaited the appointment and, when it arrived, went to see a lovely Scottish doctor who I instantly liked. She sounded a little bit like Mrs Doubtfire and had a somewhat dry sense of humour. I asked her what was going on, and she replied in her Mrs Doubtfire like voice. In all truth, I expected her to start with, "Well, Dear,", Just like in the movie.
"Well, I have some good news, and I have some bad news".
"Err, okay, what's the bad news?" I asked.
"You have cancer," she replied.
"What!!!" I exclaimed.
I then asked, "Well, what's the good news?"
"It's the best one you can get" she said. She went on to explain that I had non-Hodgkin's follicular lymphoma. It was classed as low grade, so it was a slow-moving cancer. I would probably die from old age before the non-Hodgkin's would become an issue. Admittedly, I had a minor freak out over this news; however, as the months went by and I just had to go for what they call "Watch and wait", I didn't really give the non-Hodgkin's much thought. I mean, isn't life basically watching and waiting anyway? Plus, the cancer specialist nurses I was seeing were wonderful. They

always took the time to reassure me, offer support and were just at the end of the phone and would return my calls if ever I had queries or issues.

Carl and I continued our regular rides for several years, generally on a Friday evening. We would choose some local loop and head off, chatting, having fun, and enjoying each other's company talking about "bike porn" and the good old days. Like many people, we never fell out; I guess life just got in the way. Our rides became less regular, and I returned to heading out alone with my mp3 player for company. I love going out into nature on some quiet trail and just being in the moment. I don't particularly enjoy riding on the roads, as there are too many drivers who are not exactly fans of cyclists and some who are just plain dangerous, with no consideration for other road users.

I just bumped into Carl's dad and sister the other day in Stanley, and they informed me that Carl had not been very well. So, as soon as I got home, I messaged him to check in. Carl messaged back immediately, saying he hadn't been well but wasn't complaining. This was because he said, "You've been through a lot worse." Typical Carl. I replied, "Everyone's own problems are the worst because it's happening to them." Carl is such a nice fella, and I miss our time riding together.

I've just been WhatsApp'ing Carl again, going over some old memories, and he reminded me of a few from when we were at school. We were around twelve years old, and Carl's brother Lee, who is a little older and would have been about fourteen or fifteen at the time, was with us. It had been snowing heavily, enough to build an igloo type construction up against the wall in my backyard. We were happily on constructing it, and having a jolly good time, when the sky turned very heavy, with a misty fog. The sky was becoming darker and darker with large snowflakes slowly falling. There was an orange yellow glow cast from a nearby old-fashioned streetlight. Besides this streetlight, there was a large, thick wooden pole with a big transformer attached to it at the top. Some years earlier, a large horse, scared by a lightning storm, had broken loose and ran from the top field down our back street. The horse had slipped and collided with the pole, and ever since whenever it rained or, in this case snowed, the transformer would crackle, and on some occasions you could see electrical sparks. We were in our element, hoping it would snow even more, maybe the boiler would break at school, and we could get time off. Suddenly, there was a huge blueish white flash and an almighty bang. An old metal bucket, which had been sitting in our yard and was only about ten feet away from us, suddenly flew into the air and shot across the yard, one side of its handle blown off. When it landed, we all took a double take at one another and this destroyed bucket. I just said, "Right, I'm going in." I was off indoors. Just before I went in, I could see Carl and his brother running out of our backyard and heading down the back street, trying to get home as quickly as possible through all the deep snow. It had been a huge bolt of lightning that had struck the bucket. It was so scary yet rather exciting at the same time. It was one of those childhood memories we often reminisced about, like, "Do you remember the time?"

Carl and I have always had a passion for bikes. One Christmas, Carl got a Raleigh Super Burner with upgraded Skyway Tuff 2's, "the first love of my life" Carl reliably informed me. I got a Peugeot something or other BMX. We would spend hours playing on those bikes, and along with other local kids, we'd hang around Stanley, either riding up the front street or in what used to be the Fine Fare car park. We would construct ramps from old pallets and then ride and jump off them. We also took over an old area called the "Gas Works" near the local police station, at the bottom end of Stanley. We would tear down one side of the embankment, fly up the other, and take off jumping over obstacles, seeing who could get the highest and furthest.

We thought we were awesome, attempting jumps and tricks and playing "tuggy" (tag) on the bikes. Back then, there were no helmets or protective gear, and bike lights were massive Ever Ready contraptions with huge batteries; they ruined our street cred, so we rarely fitted the lights. As Carl says, "We were the kings of the kerbs, and we thought we owned the streets." We were good kids though, and rarely got into trouble, probably because we knew we would get a clip around the ear, and another from our parents if they found out we had been up to no good. I think the most daring and naughtiest thing I ever did as a kid on the odd occasion, was when I camped out and would go, "Garden

Raiding" over the local allotments. Looking back, it was a stupid thing to do, and more about the thrill of evading detection and being caught, rather than nicking a few snaggers or tatties (turnips/potatoes). Of course, I never used to go on to vandalise the allotments or destroy the owner's property. Definitely not like a lot of today's generation who carry knives and show no respect.

Carl and I petitioned our local council to build a BMX track. We were around thirteen years old at the time. After school, we'd collect signatures and eventually presented them to a local councillor. There was an area of wasteland we had in mind where the Iceland store is now situated, so we suggested this as the site. I recall that the area in question was probably some sort of an "ash pit". Years ago, I would dig there as a kid in search of old bottles like pop alleys and those thick coloured glass bottles from days gone by. Imagine both Carl and my surprise when the council took our petition seriously and approved our idea. Even asking us how we would like the BMX track designed. Absolutely amazing! The diggers showed up not long after, and the track of our dreams became a reality.

Chapter 9

As 2009 arrived, I was super excited when Jamie got in touch, informing me that Strathclyde University had chosen Hampden Park, the International Football stadium in Glasgow Scotland as their venue to hold their conference. We would finally get to meet Brian and have the opportunity to view his unique sporting knee, the Bartlett Tendon. I counted down the days on my calendar in excited anticipation of this huge event. When the day eventually arrived to head off up to Scotland I had everything prepared, including my bike, which my dad had given me a hand put in the back of our car. I was taking my bike so that Brian could demonstrate his knee in action. By my standards the drive from my home in Stanley and Co Durham, up to Glasgow was huge, however I pretty much managed to follow the sat nav without too many problems. Upon arriving at Hampden Park, I had butterflies due to how excited I was. I can only describe it as a bit like when you are a kid, and you have the opportunity to meet one of your childhood heroes. That first meeting with Brian and his lovely partner Laurie, who had accompanied him on his trip, was such a very special occasion for me, one I will never forget. This meeting was to become such a huge and integral part of my journey. Following our initial introduction, Brian offered to give Jamie and myself a demo of his knee; he asked if he could borrow my bike and then proceeded to jump aboard and set off cycling indoors Hampden Park. I don't think the security guard was too impressed when he shot down the two flights of stairs towards the exit at the front of the ground.

    Over the two days, I was at Hampden Park, there were some fantastic presentations, each one very interesting; however, the whole reason I was there was to hear from Brian, and I was engrossed in what he had to say as he demonstrated his knee. When all the presentations had concluded, including some remarkable guest speakers recounting their personal stories and experiences, we arranged to go for something to eat at an Indian restaurant. Brian, Laurie, Jamie, and I sat down in the restaurant and enjoyed a meal, some interesting conversation, and a chance to get to know one another a little better. Following this, Jamie and Brian negotiated a deal that would suit both parties. This was a one-year exclusive contract for the sale and provision of the Bartlett Tendon here in the UK through Pace Rehabilitation. At the end of the conversation Brian added that he would like me to be the first person in the UK to trial the new knee, "Wow! What an honour," I was thrilled.

It was time for me to head back home and funnily enough this proved to be a little more challenging than when I had drove up to Glasgow. The sat nav must have decided to have a bit of a laugh with me, as I ended up in some rough looking housing estate. If anyone had seen me they would think I was a little mental, as I was having this argument with what would have appeared to be no one. In reality I was letting the sat nav, which was one of those small stand-alone devices that you mount on the dash or attach to the windscreen, know exactly what I thought of it. I can't tell you how close that little device was to being chucked out of the window as I decided to try and navigate my own way home.

Following my visit at the conference Jamie informed me that he would be in touch about the redesigning of my socket, as it would require artificial tendon receivers to be fitted. The artificial tendons and receivers were an important part of how the Bartlett Tendon worked. We also had to wait for Brian to return home and then send out one of his knees to Pace. It wasn't long before I was off for another fitting with Jamie. My dad, ever the trusty supporter, drove me back down to Pace's Amersham clinic. My socket was fitted with the required receivers, and the whole knee was prepared and set up. I took my bike along with my turbo trainer so that I could have a go on the new prosthetic limb. Brian had made using the knee look easy, being able to move about on the bike and pedal out of the saddle, foot over foot at will. When I attempted to ride out of the saddle on the turbo trainer, imagine my disappointment when I couldn't do it. I was left disheartened and felt as if I had failed. Jamie, ever the optimist, reassured me and suggested I take the whole prosthetic home and practice, so that's exactly what I did.

The next day, when I was back at home, I decided to go on a long ride and didn't manage to pedal while out of the saddle once. Upon returning home, my face tripping me up, I explained my frustrations to my dad, and he gave me a great piece of advice.

"Diven't gan for geet lang rides; just practice aroon the block and try te change ye'r position on the bike". So off I headed once more. At first, there was nothing, not even one pedal stroke, but then I somehow managed a pedal stroke while out of the saddle before quickly finding myself sitting back down. I then recalled what Brian had said to me, "There is a sweet spot". " That's it" I thought. I then had another go, changing my position slightly, and I got two, three and then four complete pedal strokes and started to figure out a lot of the technique was indeed in the positioning of my hands on the bars, slightly leaning forward and the position of my hips to gain resistance from the tendons and carry the stroke through. The feeling on the bike was pure joy, and I instantly fell in love with the knee. I excitedly got in touch with Jamie to share the good news.

While all this was happening, I was attending the pain clinic at Bensham under the Gateshead Trust. Funnily enough, the specialist nurse I was to see knew me from school. She was a couple of years older than me, and what a lovely friendly and supportive person she was. The nurse was trying to sort out my pain management. At the same time, I was also seeing a friendly psychologist at the hospital, and she was trying to help me with a lot of my mental anxieties, and in moving forward dealing with my amputation. I received some much need advice about "doing too much". As I have mentioned I was on this kind of mission to prove myself, and ultimately burned myself out, so had to take a step back somewhat, which really frustrated me.

I had encountered this thing called phantom sensation, as well as phantom pain. They are two completely different feelings. The phantom sensation I found was beneficial, as it let me know where my missing foot was supposed to be, which helped when I was walking. I still had the occasional trip and stumble, which generally happened when I was not concentrating or on an uneven surface, plus when I was tired. Inclines and descents could be challenging to negotiate due to how the prosthetic knee operated. There are so many things you don't take into consideration as a normal person, like your proprioception, or in layperson's terms, where your limbs are in relation to your body in space. When you have a prosthetic limb, it can be very challenging at first to become accustomed to how you move and your new body mechanics.

I found it difficult trying to explain the next few paragraphs, as I wasn't sure whether to write in past tense or present. You see I have pretty much experienced the phantom pain and sensations ever since my amputation. So, bear in mind everything I am about to describe is ongoing.

The phantom pain, which, fortunately, I didn't get all the time, was horrendous. It is hard trying to explain to someone just how bad the pain could be. People don't understand how something can be so painful when the limb was no longer there. I could experience a range of different sensations when the pain started. I know if it travelled from my toes up towards my ankle and then anywhere above, I was in for a prolonged period of pain. Try to imagine a clear glass vase in the shape of a foot and an ankle, moving up to a shin and calf. Then imagine filling this up slowly with water, which is either coloured blue to represent cold or red to represent heat. As the water slowly rises, that is the equivalent of the level where I could feel the different sensations. My foot could be like it was in a freezing cold block of ice, going all tingly, moving to cramp in my toes, particularly my big toe, with an awful sensation right under my toenails; then, as it progressed, it would move across and into the sole of my foot. Finally, a throbbing numbness enveloped the bottom half of my leg, with an additional sensation of being crushed. It could also feel like something creeping and crawling under my skin.

If it was the red colour, this was more like a painful cramp with electric shocks, as if someone was using a cattle prod; it is called stump jump. My whole body would go rigid. I could not relax and would start to pre-empt the pain, causing me to tense up before the jolt, and when I say tense up, it was not just my stump or residual limb as it's called, it was my whole core, up to my shoulders and my neck. I would grit my teeth and clench my fists. I experienced burning sensations, which made me feel like I was on fire. Then there was the old pliers, as if someone had taken hold of my toenails and they were slowly peeling each one of them off; add a vice to the mix, and yet more of a crushing sensation, becoming tighter and tighter; how about someone driving a nail into your foot. Oh, and that personal favourite, that ex that didn't particularly like me, and had her Voodoo doll out, taking great delight in sticking needles into my various toes, or the sole of my foot.

Thinking of the here and now, the pain for me tends to come in measured intervals and waves. I just think it has subsided, then a build-up in the form of a wave starting small and rising to a nausea inducing crescendo before fading, then waiting for the next one. All the pain relief I have ever tried over the years has never been effective, well apart from the Midazolam, but I mean that wouldn't be an option for long term pain management. I was placed on Gabapentin, the maximum dose and also had a period on Pregabalin. Then there was Amitriptyline, which made me feel like a complete zombie, all monged out. I just couldn't give a fuck when I was on that stuff. I couldn't function from one day to the next. It was like having a permanent foggy hangover all the time. Both the Gabapentin and Pregabalin seriously did some weird things to my thought process. I mean, my mind probably wasn't in the best shape mentally anyway, before starting these medications, but the thoughts that were popping into my head were like, "Oh my God, who the fuck said that?", then "what?", That's definitely not me thinking that?" and a whole barrage of other thoughts that would just creep in and scare the hell out of me. You should seriously know you are in trouble when you start having conversations with yourself and it's not just one voice or personality that is involved.

I did one of my usual stupid tricks around December of 2009/2010 and just stopped taking my Gabapentin, or was it Pregabalin? All I can say is I think I broke something inside my head, as although I had suffered depression in the past, now it was a totally different feeling, and to be honest, I am not sure I ever fully recovered. I can't explain it; all I can say is that something had changed. Gabapentin was initially used to treat partial seizures in people with epilepsy. Pregabalin is also used for epilepsy and anxiety. I am not a chemist, and I don't want to bore you with a researched chemistry lesson, but as far as I understand, Gabapentin and Pregabalin are similar in how they work by blocking a pain signal to your neuro receptors. All I know is I wanted to be drug free. I had had enough of painkillers and antibiotics.

Chapter 10

In 2009/2010, I was still unemployed. Scott the P.R. Guru from Pace whom I had met while attending my prosthetic fitting sessions with Jamie, happened to mention this thing called "Casualty Simulation", and would I be interested in taking part? I thought, "Why not give it a go?" So, I got in touch with the agency and was invited to attend an interview, followed by a day's introductory training session. Not long after, I began taking part in what was to become a very exciting year or so. The "Cas Sim" was a great gig, and I met some truly wonderful people. I got to play the role of all sorts of different characters, from injured hostages and soldiers, to even on one occasion a Taliban warlord, "Derka Derk", complete with a turban and my leg blown off, with loads of fake blood squirting everywhere. I was a bit like an extreme Mr Benn, if you can recall the TV programme from years ago, complete with my various costumes. On one occasion, while I was taking part in a scenario with soldiers from the Territorial Army, I was introduced to the Duke of Westminster. The exercise was taking place on his land, and he came walking along with his two dogs. He showed great interest in what was going on and began chatting to everyone who was there. Of course, I didn't recognise him at the time, it wasn't until he had walked off and I asked one of the ranking soldiers "Who was that?" and he informed me "Oh that is the Major General of our regiment", going on to say, "You will probably know him better as the Duke of Westminster, he owns the land we are on".

Having the opportunity to work with the emergency services and the armed forces during training was very rewarding. After all the knocks I had experienced, it really brought me out of my shell. Helping to train troops on how to deal with casualties in preparation for Afghanistan was an interesting experience, and being part of the exercises, which felt so real, was thrilling. One of my most exciting experiences was when I was working at Otterburn and took part in a scenario dressed as a wounded soldier. Following being triaged, I was airlifted by a Merlin helicopter as part of the simulation. I was assisted in making sure I was securely strapped in, then the pilot took off and flew over the moors, carrying out what felt like low flight manoeuvres. It was so exhilarating, as I looked out of the open doors of the helicopter as it twisted and turned over the landscape. This was to be my first time flying, let alone in a helicopter.

I also took part in a hostage situation that lasted all day in Bradford, which was equally as exciting. It was late in the evening when the armed police stormed the building, complete with flash bangs. One officer was dressed in a bomb disposal outfit, others entered with dogs, and yet more officers with weapons drawn; it felt like complete chaos. I was literally dragged from the building by two officers wearing black balaclavas and then placed on a stretcher. From there, I was triaged while remaining under close guard of armed officers. When you are involved in something like that, it really brings home that although this was a simulation, this is what would happen in "Real Life", and it's scary.

Ooh! Another scenario I took part in was in Scotland. This particular job was terrifying, as it involved a dirty bomb. As I recall, it took place on an old NHS hospital site, and all of the emergency services were involved. Hundreds of students played the roles of those affected within the blast zone. What was scary was that the emergency service personnel were not allowed to attend the blast area for about four hours, and when they did arrive, they were wearing hazmat suits, complete with breathing apparatus. Man, I lay there for hours before finally being discovered amongst all the other people who were playing their parts of having been involved in this frightening incident. I can recall having to get stripped off and going through several tents, almost naked and getting washed off with large brushes and disinfectant. I felt like one of those cows you see being herded into a pen. These types of jobs really did give me room for thought in the roles of all the various emergency services and our armed forces.

I also spent a week at Thetford in the ten-million-pound purpose-built Afghan village, where troops were trained and made ready for deployment to Afghanistan. In this one scenario, Gurkhas were taking the part of Taliban fighters, and what a fantastic group of lads they were. They were so very friendly. I remember it being scorching hot during the week I was there. I was playing the role of a Taliban warlord, complete with my outfit. I had my leg blown off as part of the simulation, when the compound I was in had been under attack. As the soldiers stormed the compound, I tried to make it as authentic as possible by being as thoroughly agitated and angry as I could be. I was shouting, "Derka, Derk" taking my cue for the Afghan lingo after having watched the comedy film "Team America". I really got stuck into the role, and as a female soldier approached me and went to bend down to inspect my wounds, then treat me, I saw an opportunity to make a grab for her rifle, and thought "Ooh, this may make the scenario a bit more lifelike". The next thing I knew, I had this rather large soldier jump on me and pin me down. I was winded, so no more "Derka Derk's from me". After the scenario ended, I was left alone in the compound for a while until the transport came to pick me up. It was so hot that I crawled under this small table that was in the corner of the compound to get into the shade. I then fell asleep. It felt like I was there for ages; some soldiers arrived back, and they helped me to an area where I would await with the rest of the troops who had by now completed their training for that day, to get transport back to the base. As I was sitting there, this rather large soldier approached me. He had a velvet bag in his hand and was handing out sweets. As I shielded my eyes from the sun and peered up from where I was sitting on the ground, I recognised him. It was the same guy who had jumped on me; he was now wearing a dog collar; he was the regiments pastor. What a lovely, jovial fella he was.

At the time, I had not noticed, but I had been bitten or stung by something on the back of my left hand. It just started with a red area; however, by the time I got home, it looked terribly infected, so I had to go to hospital to get an injection, and a dressing put on. Fortunately, after a couple of weeks or so, it started clearing up. I'm not sure what caused the nasty looking swelling and infection; I'm just pleased I didn't end up with something more serious.

My riding continued from 2010 into 2011; by this time, I had amassed quite a collection of bikes. I had been off them for so long that I now figured I needed a different bike for each occasion and the type of riding I intended on doing. At one point, I owned ten bikes. Around this time, I purchased my first GoPro and started shooting some pretty naff videos of me riding. Never mind, I had real fun on my adventures and enjoyed trying to be creative. It's something I have continued with, and I'm always trying to improve my photography and video skills, both in shooting and editing, as well as attempting to write interesting and engaging content for my blog, which you can find over at kotz68.blogspot.com

For some reason, I got it in my head that I wanted to try downhill mountain biking, so after saving up, my dad and I hand built a downhill bike from the frame up. The frame was from a German company called Propain, and I really enjoyed researching the various parts, ordering them, then fitting the bits and bobs, and working alongside my dad to make this bespoke creation. I had a few rides out in the local woods and took the bike to Hamsterley a few times, practising on the 4X track. I started experiencing some issues with my Bartlett Tendon, where the tendons would pop out from the receivers, and I became paranoid that if I attempted a drop or jump and the tendons detached, I'd have no support and could possibly end up having a serious accident. Plus, I began reconsidering why did I even want to do downhill? I mean, I wasn't exactly a spring chicken, so attempting to tear down a downhill course at my age was just plain daft. Upon reflection, I think I was trying to prove something to no one other than myself.

I decided to put the bike up for sale and to go for a more leisurely style of riding. So, I reinvested in a fat bike and bought a Sandman Hogger from Belgium. The people at Sandman Bikes were brilliant. When I first saw the bike online, I approached the company with a friendly email, asking if they'd be interested in sponsoring me. Bikes like prosthetics can be very expensive, and the model I liked had a titanium frame and upside-down forks, so yeah it was pricey. I was invited to become an ambassador for Sandman Bikes; what an honour. I mean, I wasn't a professional rider, more just like an ordinary "Joe Bloggs", yet these lovely people were willing to put a great deal of faith in me, and I aimed to do them proud. I endeavoured to write and post content to represent the company and promote them where I could. I still have the bike, and I love it.

I attended a few meets with fellow fat bike riders, all of whom were very welcoming. The fat bike scene is somewhat niche, with people who are genuinely obsessed with their bikes. They would talk about tyre pressures, riding on beaches or snow, and looking forward to bad winters with lots of snowfall, as they could still ride their bikes.

I discovered an important lesson when I approached Sandman Bikes. If you put yourself out there, there are opportunities to grab. I began to realise that I had something unique to offer. There's an old saying here in the Northeast, "Shy bairns get nee broth," which essentially means if you don't ask or take action, you get nothing. Now, I'm not talking about "freebies". Over the years, I've received a lot of support from various people and organisations. However, it's been a two-way street. I would never feel comfortable just taking. When I approached anyone, I made sure to write exactly what I thought I had to offer, and then I did my utmost to follow through in ways which were beneficial to that person or organisation.

Chapter 11

Around 2011/2012, A small black dog appeared in my life; it would go on to get larger, as did its shadow; the bigger the dog grew the bigger and darker its shadow. Of course, this wasn't an actual physical dog that had by chance followed me home; no, this was an analogy to describe my depression. I first came across this symbolic representation after reading some book or another. Apparently, Winston Churchill coined the term to describe his own depression. It can encapsulate a range of complexities relating to depression and highlight its sometimes-misunderstood nature. My darkness had no form before reading about the black dog and understanding what it represented; it just was! Oh, and I think if you have your own black dog, you should never name it, as you then give it power. I had encountered depression throughout my life; this was even before all this other stuff started way back in 1995 when I was twenty-seven. When I was younger, I suppose I had appeared outwardly like an ordinary kid. However, there was always a certain melancholy within me. Even when I had just come out of my late teens and into my early twenties, I couldn't put a name on what you would call this darkness that would follow me around. Don't get me wrong, it wasn't there all the time; I have some wonderful memories, with feelings of joy and exhilaration growing up. I just always knew that there was this other "Thing" that could creep up on me at any time.

When I was around twenty-one, I was unhappy, so I decided, for some inexplicable reason, to begin taking paracetamol and drinking. I am not sure I realised the seriousness of my stupidity. However, before I knew it, I developed severe pain in my kidneys, and I was rushed into hospital with the most horrendous pain in my side. I was given this stuff to drink, which inevitably made me puke up. I was then told that I had to remain in the hospital overnight and a psychologist would speak to me the following morning. In the morning, the psychologist arrived and began asking me questions, questions I had no real answers to. I couldn't explain why I had been so stupid or what the hell I was thinking. Looking back, I think, "What an idiot", what a total waste of resources for the busy hospital doctors and nurses". I am unsure if it was a cry for help, as I can't explain what was happening in my mind. Now I think, what must I have put my poor mam and dad through? Their only child, and there I was, potentially trying to end my life.

Of course, this wasn't the last time I would do something stupid. A few years later, I bought this Astra GTE. It was my pride and joy; I was a complete hooligan in the car and ended up writing it off after only six months of ownership. Well, for some reason, again, these feelings gradually crept up on me. I was feeling down, so I decided to head down to our local woods in my car in the middle of the night, having nicked the long extendible pipe off my mam's hoover, and gas myself. There I was, sitting in the car with the engine running, listening to some tunes of the era, either Bon Jovi or Guns and Roses. Then, suddenly, this thought popped into my head. It was a thought that didn't belong to me. It just said, "You do know you have filled the car up with unleaded petrol?" I began laughing to myself as I thought, "Oh am not sure this'll work", and at that point, I got out of the car, removed the pipe, popped it in the boot, and then got back in and drove home, replacing my mams hoover pipe, as I knew I would get bollocked if she discovered it missing. I often think back on that memory and the dark humour involved in that thought that potentially saved my life. Obviously, there was another side of me that wanted to remain in this world. It's strange to think that when I took ill at twenty-seven, I probably had more cause not to want to be here, yet I fought so much harder.

Moving to the present, I am not going to lie; I have had to fight hard against those inner demons that whisper to me, telling me things would be so much easier if I just gave up. I think what draws me back is the fact that life is so unpredictable. One minute, we can be leading the most boring, painful, traumatic, depressing and stressful existence, and then magically, something comes along, and everything changes. I don't want to miss out on the possibilities. I mean, I am going to be dead one day, so why not just hang in and take advantage of all of life's experiences? As I was writing this chapter, a kind of phrase or quote, if you like, came into mind. It expresses a sentiment about resilience. It's not particularly eloquent. However, I hope you can understand its meaning and where it comes from.

"Illness, disease or old age may take me. However, if I give into my demons, I will have failed".

By now, I had a good understanding of when I was feeling down. It seemed ironic that I could have a part of my body cut off to try and solve a problem, and yet here I was with a somewhat broken mind. Over the years, I had become good at "swapping heads". Outside, I could be the most upbeat and positive person, meeting and greeting people, striving to promote positivity and discussing disability issues. However, once I was home and alone, I would chuck my positive head into a darkened cupboard, and I would resort to wearing this other head that I didn't particularly like. It was negative, ugly, and basically didn't want to do "Fuck all". All those years fighting, and for what? I had to try and get some help. I approached my doctor and was invited to attend some cognitive behavioural therapy (CBT). I am a big believer in trying stuff. You can't say you don't like something if you haven't first given it a go. So, I went to this CBT and met with the therapist. After the first session, I discovered I didn't particularly like the therapist. Maybe it was because she was challenging me. I have to think this through before I write about why I possibly didn't like her.

Do you think we all have a little OCD, Obsessive Compulsive Disorder in us? Or are we all on "The Spectrum?" I do, and well, maybe it was down to this. The therapist, I felt was trying to change some of my core behaviours, and I didn't like this. I am not good with change, which my work colleagues will testify to. It takes me a long time to get my head around stuff. I am a big believer in that old saying, "If it ain't broke, don't fuck around and try and fix it". I guess I am a typical Aries and can be as stubborn as hell. If I'm being honest, I can come across as being moody. When I say I come across as being moody, I may as well face facts and admit I can be a right pain in the arse. I struggle with inner conflict every day, and it's very tiring trying to quieten my inner voice to get on with tasks I am not particularly enamoured by. I had written "Voices" plural, but then thought "Mmmmm, anyone reading this by now is going to think I have schizophrenia". So, let's just pretend it is only the one voice. Plus, I don't want you to think that this voice or voices are always negative; sometimes, they can help me brainstorm and problem solve, and sometimes, we get on really well. I don't know what goes on in other people's heads, so this is just a little snapshot of mine; maybe you can relate; maybe you think, "This guy's nuts".

Going back to the therapist, she asked what hobbies and interests I had, and I explained my love of cycling, being out in nature, taking photos, shooting videos, and then posting them on my blog as stories of my adventures. She then delved into this a little more, asking why I had to post everything I did on the same day and why I couldn't go a few days, weeks or months before posting about my adventures. I informed her that it didn't feel as real to me if I didn't write a story or post the images on the same day. The memories would fade, and I would forget the experience. The therapist decided I was searching for gratification through my blog and its posts, and this was causing me to have highs and lows in my mood. She wanted me to stop posting and leave my adventures for a few days, a week or even more, and then post a little story later on. I was unhappy about this but agreed to give it a go. The plan somewhat backfired though, as I stopped going out on my bike, ceased taking pictures and I didn't go out and make any videos. "Hello isolation, my old friend". I became miserable; I wasn't searching for gratification and a buzz, well, not in my mind. After all I had been through I couldn't give a fuck who checked out my blog; no, for me, the gratification and buzz came from documenting adventures, as I called them and being able to relive them through the stories and images for myself, a reminder of my achievements if you like. It would be great if anyone else wanted to look at them and comment. However, that was not my end goal. Being told to hold back on something I enjoyed doing, well, let's just say although I was polite to the therapist's face, internally, I was in a lot of conflict and had some choice words floating around in my head.

Fortunately, this lady had to go off on some course or another, and she got replaced by this other therapist, who had a whole different approach. I got on well with him, and he asked if I would like to go on a six-week meditation course in Durham. I thought, "Why not?" So, I started attending these mindfulness sessions. The man who led the course would use a Tibetan bell that would be rung at the start of a session, and then at the end. I never thought I would be able to relax so much in a group of strangers. I am not particularly comfortable in groups, and there was no rocking horse to climb aboard to escape. I found myself lying in an unfamiliar building on a thin mat, listening to this man, and you know what? It was just so relaxing. I thought I had fallen asleep as time went by so quickly. However, I know I was just in an altered state of consciousness; it was like drifting, my body as light as a feather. I enjoyed my short time spent there, and this is when I first discovered the concept of mindfulness.

Nearing the end of my CBT sessions, I heard about a volunteer job that I had applied for, which you will read about in the next part of my story. I can't say whether it was down to the CBT, the mindfulness, or this good news that helped me move on and finally make the black dog disappear for a time. As for changing my heads, which you will understand is also an analogy of my personalities, I don't have a range of heads hidden in my wardrobe. I still struggle at times with who I am, and who I want to be. Over the years, I have found it incredibly difficult to accept praise or positive comments. I tend to think, "Surely they cannot be talking about me; who is this person?"

In late 2011/2012, my love of cycling brought another friend into my life, John. I had a few issues with the Department of Work and Pensions (DWP). I needed some advice, so I called into the Citizens Advice Bureau. A gentleman a bit younger than myself kindly assisted me in completing some forms, and as we got chatting, I discovered that I had worked with his sister when I was at the CAB. Following John's assistance a few weeks later, while I was out on my bike, I just happened to bump into him as we were both riding home; we got talking, and it was like fate had brought us together; we arranged to head out for a ride later that week, and the rest is history. That chance meeting when I went to get some help led to a long friendship, which is still going strong and has been filled with lots of fun adventures.

As you will now all be aware, I had been out of work for some time through some pretty serious health concerns. I had been on a long-term sickness benefit called incapacity benefit; however, around 2011, a reassessment programme was commenced by the government to get claimants onto a new type of sickness benefit called employment and support allowance. The forms John had tried to assist me with were for this claim, and after a few weeks, I got a reply saying I was no longer entitled to sickness benefits. I appealed this decision and had to wait a few months before attending a tribunal in Durham. I was again turned down at the tribunal, so a week later, I had to visit the local job centre to discuss what options were available. My dad went along with me to the appointment, assisting me in carrying my paperwork and providing moral support. You see, at the time, I couldn't wear my prosthetic limb as it wasn't fitting, and I had some major sores, so I was forced to get around on my elbow crutches.

Once at the job centre, we didn't have to wait too long before one of the advisers invited us into a ground floor room. My dad and I took a seat, and almost immediately, my dad angrily spouted out, "You know this is ridiculous, that Iain Duncan Smith (who happened to be the minister for work and pensions at the time) must think his bloody leg is going to grow back." This jobcentre adviser then looked up from his paperwork and said, in a quizzical voice, "Oh, will it?" I then incredulously turned to look at my dad. He, in return, with the same expression, looked at me before returning to look at this man, where he then said, "No seriously will it grow back?" Unbelievable! I just replied back to the adviser in a rather sarcastic tone of voice "Errrr… NO!" I mean, did this guy think that if I stood in a bucket of manure and watered my leg each day, it would start growing back? When the interview came to an end, I was no further forward, and as I got outside with my dad, I said, "Oh my God! I can't fucking believe that".

A few more weeks passed, and I was again invited to attend the job centre. I was still on my elbow crutches and was asked if I could use the stairs to attend my interview in a room on the upper floor. "It may take me a little time, and I may struggle", I replied. I was then escorted by one of the Gestapo like security guards to a small lift, and I was taken upstairs. Here, I was introduced to an adviser, who explained that I could no longer apply for sickness benefits; I would have to go onto Job Seekers allowance. I informed him, "But my doctor says I am not fit for work". Is there anything else I can claim to help me get by?" The adviser then replied, "No, nothing other than a crisis loan". I was then informed that if I went ahead with claiming Job Seekers allowance, I would have to sign a binding contract to say that I was fit for work and that I would actively look for employment. Again, I reiterated, "But I am not fit for work at the moment. I have had my leg amputated, and I'm having ongoing problems". "Also, I have been diagnosed with non-Hodgkin's lymphoma". I was very stressed over the whole situation, which wasn't helping my mental state. Again, the adviser just suggested that I agree to go on the Job Seekers allowance. Ultimately this appeared to be my only option, and the adviser started explaining what Job Seekers was, and what my commitments would be.

Firstly, the adviser informed me, while gesturing with "air quotes", "There is no such thing as a disability", you have a condition, and as such, there are certain criteria involved in how far you have to travel, and how many jobs you are expected to look for each week". As the interview went on, every time this adviser mentioned disability…Err! I mean condition, in conversation and the relaying of instructions about Job Seekers allowance, he would use the "air quotes" gesture. A thought popped into my head as I was sitting there, by now zoned out; I just wanted to grab his fingers, break his air quotes and give him a fucking condition. Following my interview with the DWP, I became a volunteer at the Royal Victoria Infirmary. Even then, the DWP got involved, informing me that my Job Seekers allowance would stop if I volunteered more than sixteen hours per week, as then I would be considered as not actively looking for work.

So how I started at the Royal Victoria Infirmary. I was invited to a volunteer day, and when I had my interview, I was asked where I would like to work. I was given options like the Medi Cinema, Charlie Bear, or MacMillan Cancer. "Oh no" I replied, "I would like to work on a ward and meet patients. Maybe I can make them cups of tea or do some administrative type of work". My way of thinking was that while I had no clinical experience or qualifications, I did have heaps of life experience. I wanted to help by chatting with people who might been going through similar things to what I had. At the time, I was told "Oh, I don't know if we've ever had volunteers on the ward before we will have to get back to you". I mentioned that I thought I would be best suited to volunteer somewhere related to orthopaedics, as I had spent so much time with my own health concerns related in this field. A few weeks later, a lovely physiotherapist rang me, saying, "Glenn, we have an opportunity for you to come and volunteer in the hospital; it's on our stroke unit, how do you feel about that?" There was no pressure, and I thought, "Mmmm! I don't know the first thing about strokes, but why not give it a go". So, we arranged a time and date to start my volunteering, and that was that.

On my first day, I was met at the Leazes entrance by this tall, 6'6" Kiwi. "G'day, I'm Dan". Dan was the senior physiotherapist on the stroke unit. He was laid back and super easy to get along with, plus he had this wicked sense of humour. Dan also had a wealth of knowledge, and I felt very fortunate that he took me under his wing from day one. Dan led me onto the stroke unit, introduced me to a few people, and showed me around. Over the next few months, I would work closely with him, learning the ropes, and having a jolly good laugh at Dan. As mentioned he had this great sense of humour, and when visiting patients, he would use various, and I have to say terrible accents, including I am not sure if it was German where he would say "Ya, it is good". He would also attempt to get patients to carry out their resisted therapy exercises by saying "Go on poooosh, pretend you don't like me", which to me sounded like his variation of a Scottish accent. From day one, I discovered that I wouldn't just be making cups of tea and doing paperwork. No, I was pretty much thrown in at the deep end and I don't mean that in a negative way. I thrived in this new role, and before long, I began staying longer each day at work, gaining more experience and knowledge working alongside both Dan and another lovely, friendly physio named Becci.

My first day working alongside Becci, we went to see this elderly gentleman. He was sitting in a tilt in space chair and was just a small dot of a man. I had been observing Becci, and she asked me to go and get some blankets for the gentleman, along with a glass of milk. So off I went, and when I returned, I placed a blanket over this old fella's knees and a one around his shoulders and tucked him in all neat and cosy, before handing him the glass of milk. As I went to make sure he was comfortable, I said "There ye gan, are ye alreet?" To which he replied in a gravelly voice, holding a long tone, "Fuck Off". I just stepped back and said, "Fair enough". Becci was still in the bay and had overhead our interaction and was trying to hide the fact that she was in stitches, laughing away. When we came out of the bay, and Becci had composed herself, she very kindly said, "That was so funny; your response was brilliant". As I have gained experience over the years on the unit, I have encountered all sorts of different people and learnt lots of valuable lessons in being non-judgemental, learning to listen, and being patient, understanding and compassionate. It is important to try to discover what someone is going through, and their way of thinking, while also being as friendly, supportive and caring as possible.

Following working on the ward for about five to six months as a volunteer, I was encouraged to apply for a part time job that had become available. This was as a part time physiotherapy assistant. As I recall, there were 240 applicants, so imagine my surprise when I was shortlisted. Later, that same day, I found out I had got the position, and this was a huge confidence boost for me. I began working eighteen and a half hours per week. It was good to get back into paid work, especially as I found the job very rewarding. Finally, I could give something back, and I felt accepted for being me, which in turn really helped me accept myself.

Reflecting back, being able to turn a lot of my negatives into positives, from my own personal experiences as a patient to help others, helped me feel all those years had not been completely wasted. I discovered I had a certain empathy with the patients in my care, and it helped me relate to them. I have now been working for just over twelve years on the same ward, which is now a Hyper Acute Stroke Unit. After some years as a physio assistant, I applied for another role and became a rehabilitation assistant. This meant I would be working across three different therapies, physio, occupational, and speech & language therapy. In 2023, my colleagues nominated me for a Care & Compassion award. They are a tremendous team of people, so dedicated, compassionate, and caring, not only toward the patients but also towards one another, and of course towards me. I often get teased at work, because for some reason they comment that I am always the one patients remember, when they have been on our ward. I think its just because people can remember I am an amputee, which makes me a little different. Maybe it is also my pretty broad "Durhamite mining accent". I suppose it also has a lot to do with how I engage with my patients. I always maintain a professional approach; however, I have a somewhat unique bedside manner and tend to try and use a lot of positivity and humour, dependent on the situation of course.

When I started volunteering in 2012, I wore a hydraulic Ossur Total Knee 2100. I was adept at using the knee. However, I can recall many an unsettled night, worrying about my knee "breaking", by that I mean "bending" without warning if I hadn't correctly positioned myself. On several occasions, when I thought the knee was stable and under me, I would go down like a tonne of bricks in the blink of an eye. There was nothing I could do to prevent it, which used to stress me out to no end. I wasn't so worried about myself, more so the patients in my care. When treating patients, especially while mobilising, I often walked sideways so that my prosthetic knee was always locked out.

Safety has always been paramount, and I'm pleased to say that I have only had a few unexpected accidents at work. Hold on while I reach out to touch a piece of wood for luck. Once, I fell off a bed after safely assisting a patient down as he fainted. On another occasion, I concussed myself as I bent down to move a cable which was on the floor. I didn't see the patient locker hidden behind the curtain and cracked my head near my eye on the corner of the locker, so I can't really blame my leg for that one. I ended up with a right shiner for a couple of weeks. Oh, and I had a hilarious fall while in the gym with one of the other rehabilitation assistants I used to work with. The plinth was positioned low behind me; my prosthetic knee must have just say been barely touching the plinth, causing it to bend ever so slightly. As I went to take a step, my prosthetic knee gave way, and I fell backwards, doing a flip and ending up flat on my back. At first, my colleague didn't know what to do and was very concerned; it all happened so quickly. However, when she saw I was in fits of laughter, as I was lying on the floor, she then couldn't help me up for laughing herself. Being a lower limb amputee, trips, stumbles, and falls are all just an occupational hazard. I won't even go into detail about what it's like trying to walk in the snow or on ice, imagine Bambi on that frozen pond, and that will give you a good idea.

In 2012 I ended the Facebook amputee group. Things just got ridiculous. My dad and a few friends were helping as admins of the group. Everything had been going well; the group had approximately 2,500 members worldwide. Then things started to go wrong. People began posting inappropriate things, and some strange characters, known as devotees, started sneaking into the group. These were dangerous people with weird and wonderful notions about amputees. Then, certain people started bullying others, something I couldn't get my head around. There was also the issue of people competing over the extent of their amputations as if it were some sort of contest. "Oh, I've had a leg off,". " I've had two legs off," "Me, I've had two legs, an arm, and half my head", I mean, come on! This one bloke said he identified as an octopus and that he'd had all his tentacles cut off. Really? No! I just made that up. But imagine he would win, tentacles down! One day, I came in from work, and my poor dad was ever so stressed over the group. "Reet, that's it! a've had enough", I told him. I discovered a programme online, downloaded it, set it up, and left it running overnight, deleting everyone. By the morning, everyone had been deleted. I just needed to remove myself, and that was it the group was gone.

I was angry and upset, as I had put a lot of time and effort into the group and tried to make it a safe and informative place where people like myself could find support. I felt I had failed those people who needed it most, but I was done with selfish, bullying, spiteful people. The group had brought me a lot of contacts and positive opportunities. I wanted it to be for everyone, to give everyone valued information, advice and opportunities, not just for what it brought me. That's when I looked into how to set up a blog, which I named Post Amp Adventures. I could write and post whatever I wanted (within reason). I could tell my own stories and hopefully still help people. I could have people guest post with interesting stories of their own, share information, and not have the headache of policing the site.

And so, my blog has been going since May 2012. It doesn't get all that much traffic, but I don't really mind. The blog is a way for me to reflect, and it is pretty cathartic to write a post and get things out of my head. I don't just post about everything being sunshine and rainbows, or about how many Jaffa cakes I've eaten on a particular day, or even whether a Jaffa cake is considered a cake or a biscuit. If I have some valuable piece of information, even if it's about a personal negative experience, I'll share it. I might do little reviews of things I have purchased or share good tips or pieces of advice, anything really. I enjoy writing about my various adventures, my cars, bikes, guitars, nature, books and people I meet along the way. I am never afraid to share my dreams or insights. There are no rules and no specifics. I'm not a professional writer, as you can probably tell from the way I write. Ideally, in sharing parts of my life, I would like to think that if even one person enjoys a tale I tell, or I can possibly help make someone feel a little better if they are facing something unknown, well that is good enough for me.

More exciting news came in 2012, including being sponsored by Brian Bartlett on a new Bartlett Tendon; this took the burden off me trying to fund a knee myself. Prosthetic equipment is very expensive; and like anything mechanical (including parts of the human body), they can wear out. Around this time, I was also invited to Pace Rehabilitation's Manchester clinic, which was much nearer to home for me. There, I met a fantastic team of people, including the founder of Pace Rehabilitation, Toby Carlsson. Both my dad and I couldn't have asked to meet a friendlier man. Toby became my prosthetist and took over where Jamie had left off, discussing my riding needs, designing sockets, and offering support for many years to come.

I don't know how it came about, possibly through Scott Richardson, Paces P.R. guru. I was contacted to take part in my first live interview and TV appearance. It was with BBC Look North. I was also to be featured in a local newspaper, the *Northern Echo*. My first thought was, "Wow, surely people wouldn't be interested in anything I'm doing". The constant fact remained in my head that I was just an ordinary bloke who had been through a set of unfortunate circumstances. However, I had been given a second chance in a way.

The interview was to be based on the revolutionary new sports knee I was using, the Bartlett Tendon, and the support I was receiving from both Brian and Pace Rehabilitation. When the reporter and his cameraman arrived at our house, we had a chat to cover the story, and it was funny when the cameraman said, "Okay, can we go somewhere local and get some footage for the news feature?" I replied, "Yes, of course; however, I also have some of my own GoPro footage you may like to use". The cameraman said, "Oh I think we may be better off getting our own, no offence but some of the homemade videos we see don't come across well on television". I persisted and said, "It's really not too bad", and invited both the cameraman and the reporter to watch a short clip on our TV. After viewing the clip for a few minutes, the cameraman changed his mind and said, "This is brilliant!" Then he asked, "Can we take it and include it as part of the news segment?" Of course, I agreed. I was very happy with myself and my achievement. We then headed down to Beamish Woods, to a quiet area where I did a little riding and was filmed.

The interview took place with no second takes and a bit of adlibbing. Waiting for the piece to appear on the evening news broadcast was so exciting. After watching it, I had mixed emotions; on the one hand, the piece came across very well, and on the other, well, I thought I sounded like a complete muppet. In hindsight, I was very proud. Following the TV interview, I did the piece for the *Northern Echo* and got my name and picture in the paper. I am not the most photogenic person, but for me, it was more about getting a message out there to say thank you for your support, and in raising awareness around disability and what you can achieve.

It was all go after this. I got invited to do a live interview on BBC Radio Tees. Everyone at BBC Radio Tees, from the security personnel to the lady at the front desk and the radio hosts were absolutely brilliant, making my dad and myself feel at ease and very welcome. This was another first for me, speaking on live radio, and I have to say I was very nervous. In my head, I was trying to stop myself from saying "Err, and Mmmm" in response to questions, which is very difficult to do as these pauses are used to give yourself time to think. There was no need to be anxious as the radio presenter supported me throughout the interview, and I soon just went with the flow.

I continued to ride my various bikes throughout 2012, and the weeks turned into months. Then, 2013 came around, and I was invited to do another live BBC Radio Tees interview. I jumped at the chance, as I had enjoyed the last one, and it had been successful with the audience. Things were going well for me, health wise and prosthetics wise. Yes, I had the non-Hodgkin's in the back of my mind, not knowing exactly what to expect with that, but I was taking it one day at a time. I was enjoying my cycling adventures, and I had now been working for approximately a year in a job I loved.

In 2013, Pace Rehabilitation organised and held a conference in London. It was to be held at the Royal College of Physicians, and I was invited to participate in one of the presentations. My train tickets there and back were all sorted by Pace, and I was very kindly offered a room to stay in for the night at the Royal College. The room was named after one of the famous physicians and was extremely posh. My role was to ride through some doors into the auditorium, then come down the stairs and up onto the stage, demonstrating my Bartlett Tendon Knee. Now, the week earlier, I had fitted some new parts to my Sandman fat bike. One of these new parts just happened to be a pair of wider handlebars. So, Imagine the scene, Scott was standing at the doors to the auditorium; I rode towards the doors and, just as I was going through, caught my handlebars on the edge of the door frame and almost fell off. Everyone turned and looked in my direction. I could feel their eyes boring into me. "Aww crap what should I do?" I thought. I had lost all momentum and was now just standing there like a complete imbecile. In a loud voice I shouted, "Err just hold on a minute", as I tried to back my bike out of the doorway, using one leg. Eventually, I got out into the foyer and told Scott to hold both the doors open, and I gave it another go, successfully riding my bike while out of the saddle, with both my knees flexed and my body positioned over the back wheel as I shot down the stairs and came to a dramatic stop on the stage, to a huge round of applause. What a buzz of adrenaline. Thank God I didn't have a talking role.

I was still getting to know people within the hospital, especially from other departments and wards, when I was invited to go out for a meal and some drinks. This would be an excellent opportunity to meet people. Dan was going. However, he made it clear he would only be out until 10:00 to 10:30 p.m. as he was a family man, and late nights out weren't his thing. On the night in question, my dad dropped me off in the Toon (Newcastle), and I met up with Dan. Dan and I then proceeded to this Spanish tapas restaurant, where we had arranged to meet some other people. Once inside, I was introduced to a few new faces, most of whom were girls. I went on to enjoy a lovely meal and a few drinks. I have never been a big drinker; I'm not too fond of the taste, so on this occasion, I just had a few small bottles of cider, which I could at least tolerate. Following the meal, it was agreed that we would visit another local place and headed to this nearby pub. When we arrived at the pub, I sat down with Dan, and we began chatting about nothing in particular, just enjoying the pleasure of everyone's company and the relaxed atmosphere. I ordered a JD and coke and sat there sipping this until Dan mentioned it was time he was heading home, as it was around 10:30 p.m. The next thing I knew, some of the girls came over and said they were going to the bar downstairs in the pub, and did I want to come along and join them. Now, at this point, I should have declined and said, "No, I am going to call my dad and get him to come and pick me up". However, I thought, "Meh, why not hang with these lasses? I mean, they were sensible professionals, right?" "Err I couldn't have been more wrong". You know the phrase "Letting your hair down"? Well, I was about to experience a night that I don't know if I can fully remember, but here goes I will try and give you what I can vaguely recall.

We went downstairs into the bar; it was dark, with loud music playing and lights flashing. One of the girls shouted in my ear "Do you want a drink?", and before I knew it, I had a glass of something or other placed in my hand. Apparently, it was something called a Jaeger Bomb. This was to continue into the night, and I lost count of how many of these drinks I had, along with all my senses. I can't tell you how long we were in the bar; time seemed to go by quickly. I was then informed, "Oh, we are off too!" It was someone's house I didn't know. By that point, I was completely out of my tree and just went along with whatever, so I found myself being bundled into a taxi with all these girls heading to some unknown destination to continue whatever this was.

When we got to this lass's house and all piled in, it must have been about 3:30 in the morning, and we were all pretty inebriated. The girl in question, whose house it was, hadn't told her boyfriend she was bringing all these people back, so obviously, he wasn't best pleased, and basically we all got ejected. I had stepped outside as I wasn't feeling particularly well, and I mean it didn't seem polite to vomit all over someone's carpet, saying that it was not much better to do it on the neighbour's pavement. Following hurling up, I walked, or should I say staggered, back towards the house but couldn't remember which one it was. There I was, wandering up and down the street lost; fortunately, I saw a few of the girls come out of the gate to the house. They had booked various taxis and were off home, but I think they had by now forgotten about me. I was now in a place I didn't know, and my sense of direction is shocking at the best of times. I returned to the house and asked the girl who lived there where we were, as I called my dad. I then attempted to relay directions, going back and forth between this lass and my dad. By now, it was probably getting on for 4:00 a.m. With slurred speech, I tried to explain where I was. "I'm at such and such an address". "Where is that though?" he asked. So, I asked the girl, "Where is that? and she told me Forrest Hall. I relayed this information, "Am in Forrest Hall", to which he replied, "Forrest Hall?, where the bloody hell is that?" My poor dad then said, "Look just wait there, am on me way". Well, I must have waited all of 2 minutes and thought, "Oh that is long enough", so I decided to whip out my phone and use Google Maps to find my way home. It is probably the only time I have used Google Maps, and I've thought, "Ooh it's worked" … "Thought" being the operative word. Well, that is what drink will do for you. So my new best friend and I were off. I followed the directions given by the friendly lady's voice coming from my phone, I mean I was only twenty odd miles away from home.

About an hour into walking, a car pulled up. It was my dad. "Where the bloody hell have ye'r been?" he said sternly. "I've been lookin' all ow'er for y'er, up and doon this road". Obviously, the sat nav woman had led me slightly astray. I'm sure at one point I walked over the same pedestrian bridge twice, if there is even a pedestrian bridge in Forrest Hall. "A thought I'd just walk yem". I said, to which an annoyed and very disappointed father said, "Just get in." On the way back, as we got onto the Causey Arch Road, I informed my dad "Urgggghhh, I diven't feel well", he wasn't about to stop, so I wound my window down and proceeded to throw up and it went all down the side of our car. It must have been a terrible sight, as the previous night's tapas, cider, JD & coke, plus, let's not forget countless Jaeger Bombs, came out of me like a scene from some horror film, thank God there was no blowback from the wind as we were travelling down the road, and no one was behind us.

When we arrived home in the wee hours of the morning, I could hardly stand; however, my first thought was, "I must clean the car." So, there I was in our kitchen, trying to fill the kettle up with water and then heading outside to wash all these chunks off the side of the car. Once I thought I had it all off, I returned indoors and headed upstairs to bed. I couldn't get to sleep though, as my room wouldn't stay still and kept spinning. I felt ill. No word of a lie I had a hangover for about a week.

These girls had broken me, and following this, I pretty much didn't drink alcohol again, well, apart from when I visited America, which is in the following part of my story.

Chapter 12

I mentioned earlier that I had always considered myself a "home bird". My mam and dad didn't have an adventurous bone in their bodies and never wanted to travel so I guessed I would just follow suit. However, all those years of isolation, and being unable to do stuff, must have had an impact on me as I started thinking about travelling, and broadening my horizons. I mentioned my thoughts to one of my work colleagues, with whom I had become friends, and she said, "Okay Glenn, I'm off on annual leave for a few weeks as I'm getting married". "By the time I get back, I expect you have booked some tickets and are going away somewhere". At this point, I'm not even sure if I had a passport. Needless to say, by the time my friend returned, I had sorted a three-week trip away to America.

I was to fly from Newcastle to Schiphol, and from Schiphol, I would visit my first destination in America, Seattle. Here I would meet my friend Brian and stay with him for a short while. This was to be my first ever flight on an aeroplane. My only other experience of flying was the exciting ride I had on that helicopter. As I flew from Newcastle and arrived in Schiphol, I went through the most extensive search by the customs personnel. Alongside what felt like a quick fire round of questioning, a little like being a contestant on Mastermind.

The flight from Schiphol to Seattle was around ten hours long, and when I arrived at the airport, I was totally bemused that I would have to ride a subway train to get out of the airport, and to the car park where Brian would meet me. I can remember just standing there looking around after having collected my suitcase and thinking, "Where the hell do I go? This place is massive!" Fortunately, there was a friendly lady who directed me to the shuttle like train, and not long after, I found myself getting off alongside the other passengers. I was able to discover the car park relatively easily. It was such a relief to see Brian waiting nearby, and after placing my case in his car, we were soon off on the journey to his house.

Once at Brian's house, I was given a brief tour and allowed to settle in. Then Brian suggested we head out for a bite to eat and a few drinks, going to a local favourite place of his. It was only a short ride to Jak's Grill. It was great catching up over a steak and a few drinks, talking about how my riding had been going, and telling Brian about my new job and all the lovely people I had met. Returning to Brian's place, it was a pretty warm evening, so he suggested we could have a few more drinks while we relaxed in his hot tub. Brian returned with a couple of glasses and handed one to me, explaining that this was one of his favourite drinks on special occasions. It was a bourbon called Makers Mark. Now, I usually wouldn't drink anything like this, so I am not sure if it was the whole atmosphere of being in a strange new country while relaxing in a hot tub, and just going with the flow, but that drink certainly went down real smooth, and I enjoyed the taste, so much so when offered a few more how could I refuse? It's funny I have never drank Makers Mark since, and I am not sure if I did; I would even enjoy the taste. In my mind, there is just this associated memory of the sights, sounds, smells and of course tastes of a happy time, that although distant I can recall, and it makes me smile. That is what good memories are made up of, and why we should strive to make as many as we can.

As Brian and I chatted and enjoyed our drinks in the hot tub, it began to rain lightly. This soon turned to heavier rainfall, and the sound of loud rumbles of thunder could be heard off in the distance, becoming increasingly louder. Suddenly, there was a loud crack of lightning, and the night sky was lit up. It just felt so surreal. There I was drinking bourbon, while chilling in a hot tub during a thunderstorm, enjoying the great company of my friend who was also so inspirational to me.

The following morning, Brian and I took a ride through the city on road bikes. One of Seattle's nicknames is the Emerald City; this is due to its year-round greenery. It is a beautiful place, very busy, with lots of hustle and bustle and things going on wherever you look. There are, as you would imagine, lots of pedestrian crossings, so riding was very much stop start. Brian had the right of way at one crossing; he was already halfway over it, as the lights notified pedestrians not to cross.

Suddenly this lady just stepped out and almost collided with Brian. We were both clipped in; and it's impossible to unclip your prosthetic foot unless you are stationary with your good foot down. As we rode to the next pedestrian crossing, this guy who had been following us on his bike started having a go at Brian about not giving way to the pedestrian. Brian politely explained he had the right of way and couldn't stop as he couldn't unclip on that side in time. We rode on, and this guy was still having a go by the time we reached the next crossing. This continued for two more crossings until Brian stopped, dismounted his bike and said to the guy, "Look, do you want to go?" This fella then got the message and rode off, eventually leaving Brian alone, who was by now thoroughly pissed off. So much so that he set off and continued up the hill we were on, forgetting about me. A traffic light had turned red, so I had to stop as he continued way on ahead up the hill. I then lost sight of him, and I panicked! I didn't have my phone, nor did I know Brian's home address or even how to get back to his place. All I could do was pedal like the clappers up the hill and try and find where he had gone. Fortunately for me, Brian had only gone up the hill a short distance and pulled off around a corner to wait for me, what a relief. As we took a moment and commented on what a complete jerk the other cyclist had been, Brian became much more relaxed, and mentioned we were near this famous market that he thought I might enjoy having a look around. Off we headed, and it didn't take too long before we arrived at the Pike's Place Market. The market is one of the oldest farmer's markets in the whole of the United States. We dismounted our bikes, and pushed them between the various stalls, then arrived at what is known as the "Famous flying fish" market stall. This is where fishmongers throw fish back and forth to one another as they sell them to customers. It was very entertaining listening to the banter of the fishmongers and seeing all these fish flying through the air.

Seattle is such an iconic city with lots of history; it is the birthplace of Starbucks Coffee and where the grunge music scene began, way back in the 80s and 90s with groups such as Nirvana, Pearl Jam and Soundgarden. I got to see the Space Needle from afar, but didn't have the opportunity to visit. The Space Needle is Seattle's most iconic landmark, built in 1962 for the World's Fair; it stands 605 feet, has three observation decks, and looks very futuristic. There just wasn't enough time to fit everything in. I would have loved the opportunity to spend more time exploring both the city and further afield; it is such a beautiful and interesting place.

Brian had a real treat in store the following day. He put a couple of his mountain bikes on his car and drove what felt like miles to the Clinton Mukilteo ferry, the direct route from the Seattle area and Tacoma. We then took the ferry over to Whidbey Island, where we would go on to ride these amazing forest trails on mountain bikes alongside Brian's two dogs, Bear and Scout. Bear was a seasoned trail dog, while Scout was just learning. As I recall, we only saw two people all day in the forest. The trails were flowing, and it was a beautiful sunny day. I was in my element. A memory of that day that was very special for me was when Brian and I stopped to have a drink of water. Brian turned to me and commented on how well I had adapted to his knee design, saying, "You're probably riding better than I am at the moment". It was such a huge compliment and one I was very proud to accept. A few years back, I would never have imagined I would ever be able to ride a bike again, let alone riding a bike in some other country, in the most amazing setting, and add to that with a friend who had inspired me so much.

More fantastic memories made, it was almost time for the next part of my adventure and to say farewell, but before I left, Brian took me to a very friendly Mexican restaurant to try some authentic dishes. I sampled some proper Margaritas in glasses, which were like goldfish bowls. Oh, and we returned to Jak's Grill and shared the biggest steak I had ever seen in my life; it was a whopping 18 ounces. One more surprise before I left, Brian treated me to a ticket to a baseball game, and we watched the Seattle Mariners, this is where I sampled my first ever "corn dog". The weather was warm, so I necked a large bottle of this really strong beer. This also helped wash down the rather salty monkey nuts I had begun munching on. Well, I was on my jollies, so was grabbing every opportunity to try things and savouring each moment.

Just before the final day with Brian, I borrowed his computer and arranged an internal flight. I was off to stay with one of my other friends who I had met on Facebook. This was Mark, an awesome dude who shared my love of cycling and all things to do with bicycles. When I had told Mark about my plans to visit America, he immediately invited me to visit him and stay at his house. Mark is such a lovely giving guy and now long-time friend; I wish we lived closer, as he's one of those people you have so much fun hanging out with.

Mark picked me up from Salt Lake City airport, and we headed to his hometown, about 40 minutes away in Ogden, Utah. He had arranged for me to borrow a mountain bike from a very friendly local bike shop, named The Bike Shoppe. When we arrived at the shop I was introduced to the owner, Matt again a lovely fella. Matt loaned me a Trek Stache for my stay, which enabled me to head out on some epic trails in the foothills of the mountains alongside Mark and some of his friends, whom he had introduced me to. Each and every one of them was so welcoming and friendly. The bike I loaned had a dropper seat post, and this made a huge difference to how I could get on and off the bike, so in the back of my mind, I immediately knew this would be one of my first investments when I returned home.

Riding pretty much commenced as soon as I had gotten unpacked at Mark's. I had brought along a very special gift for Mark and presented him with a "Newcastle Broon Ale" cycling jersey. Mark immediately popped the top on and would go on to wear it for our ride out. Following a quick swap over of my knees, Mark, two of his friends, and I were off exploring the local trails. On my first ride with the guys, I was going uphill to reach the foothills of the mountains, and it never occurred to me why I was so out of breath. I mean, at the time, I thought I was in pretty good shape. However, I was to learn that we were riding at an increased altitude, so the air was a little thinner, making the exertion a bit more difficult. Reaching the top of the trail, it was almost time for the best part, the ride back down, but before doing this we took the opportunity to get some photos of the occasion. Mark led the way down the trail, which had a lot of twists and turns. On the very first switchback, I almost came a cropper, as unbeknownst to me; those damn Yanks have their brakes set up the opposite way around to us Brits, so I grabbed the front brake instead of the back and almost washed out. I flew through the rough tumbleweed at the side of the trail. The following day, Mark relayed the story of my adventure through the undergrowth to his dad, Cliff, who then said "Glenn, you do know there are snakes in dem' dare hills", and we all laughed. I am so pleased I didn't encounter any of those critters.

As Mark had to work for a few days, his mom and dad very kindly offered to show me around and keep me entertained. They took me to visit the Hill Air Force Museum, which was so interesting. After four hours of walking around, I still hadn't seen everything. One of the highlights was looking around a Lockheed SR-71, also known as the Blackbird. The following day, we visited the Browning Museum, which again was very interesting; there were some fantastic old cars there, as well as all the various guns. Mark's mom and dad, Sandy and Cliff, were simply the most welcoming and wonderful people. It brought home how much I missed my mam, as within a few days of knowing these people, they felt like they were family. Mark's mother, Sandy, was very kind in saying she would love to adopt me. Sandy would go on to send me regular handwritten birthday and Christmas cards each year. Handwritten notes are such a lost art. I loved receiving them; it is proper old school and so special to take the time to write thoughtful words. Everyone and their dog appear to send text messages these days. This family holds a very special place in my heart.

Awakening early one morning while Mark was still asleep, I decided to head out for a walk. Mark's house wasn't too far from the foothills of the mountains and various trails leading up. I selected one and began hiking upwards. After a good few miles of venturing up the trail I stopped to look back at where I had come from. I could see all the houses below me in the distance; the view was spectacular as the early morning sunshine lit up the surrounding area. After taking in the scene, I turned and began the descent back down, choosing a different route. As I began coming down the trail, I am sure I saw a tarantula, or at least it was its shed skin. I wasn't going to get too close and start nosing around. Finally, I was back down at the bottom of the trailhead, complete with its signposts. However, I was now in a different place from where I had initially set off up the trail. This meant I had to try and figure out which road to go down to get back to

Mark's house. As I walked along the various pavements and streets, I encountered people who were out in their yards, and each and every one of them was polite and said "hello" as I passed by. Eventually I managed to find my way back to Mark's, who was by now up, and asked where I had been. "Oh, just out for a walk up one of the trails". "What a place to live with a mountain practically on your doorstep and the most beautiful views once you are up there". I am still not too sure about all the spiders and snakes. However, Mark mentioned although he has lived in Utah all his life, he has only ever seen a snake once. They tend to keep themselves to themselves.

During my short stay with Mark, he took me on quite a few scenic cycling adventures, and I only fell off once, which was good going for me. It happened when I attempted to ride a steep trail with a tight turn to my right. I had to stop, and when I went to push off from a nearby tree, I missed the tree with my hand and proceeded to fall to my amputated side.. Mark was straight there to help me up. Neither myself nor the borrowed bike I was riding was hurt, so we shared a laugh; that is, after all what cycling and being with your friends is all about. Just being in the moment and having fun, even when things don't go according to plan.

On two separate days, Mark kindly popped our bikes on the back of his Jeep and drove us to two amazing places. The first destination was Snow Basin Resort, which has a base elevation of 6316 feet above sea level. Mount Ogden summit then rises to an elevation of 9570 feet. In 2002 the Winter Olympics were hosted, at Snow Basin and they included the downhill, super-G, and combined races. A few of Mark's friends met us at the resort, and I got to ride in a cable car to the top of the mountain, along with Mark, his friends and of course our bikes. We then tore down the mountainside on a trail that wound its way down with tight turns and a vicious descent. It was so good we took the bikes back up in the cable car and did it all over again. Due to the small sharp rocks, my bike got two pinch flats on the way down. Fortunately, one of Mark's friends was able to repair them for me on both occasions. What a fantastic and very memorable experience. The following day and the second trip was a real surprise. Mark drove the almost forty-eight miles from Ogden, Utah, to Logan Utah, where we would meet another friend of Mark's and a gentleman I briefly had met, again on Facebook. He was yet another keen fat biker. While out with Mark's mom and dad, I had purchased a GoPro, and Mark suggested attaching it to his bike so that he could ride behind, and get some footage of us all riding, and then we would have something to remember the day. Boy, what a ride this turned out to be.

Mark's friend took us along a trail that ran beside a river, and then we turned right and on to a trail that climbed and climbed, heading up the side of a mountain. I found the tight switchbacks very challenging. It wasn't easy trying to keep momentum and then also turn where required, especially if a turn was to my right. It had taken me quite a while to learn how to maintain my balance, and as I turned right, I had to ensure my prosthetic knee didn't catch my handlebars. As we levelled off on one section of the trail and stopped for a breather and to have a drink, Mark's friend described the next section of the trail, saying, "OK, this bit we are coming to now; if you are going to fall off, make sure you fall to your right side, where you will be close to the mountainside, whatever you do don't fall off on the left, as no one is coming to get you". I was to discover what Mark's friend meant. As we rode along this narrow section of the trail, the mountainside was within touching distance on my right; however, there was a considerable drop to my left. Don't get me wrong, it wasn't a sheer drop. However, it was enough to make me think, "Jeez, diven't fall off Glenn", that's a canny way doon like". Approaching the top of the trail we stopped for another rest, and here we saw some hikers and asked if they wouldn't mind taking a few photographs of us as a lovely memento of our adventure. We then got back on our bikes, and the ride down this mountain trail was so exhilarating. What an absolutely amazing experience, what with all the beautiful scenery and spending time with these two very friendly people.

Time to say farewell to Mark as he dropped me off at Salt Lake City and the airport so that I could catch my next internal flight and visit my friend Shannon. I had met Shannon through my Facebook amputee group some years earlier. She was an amputee, having lost her leg in a terrible car accident. Man, the flight from Salt Lake City to Dallas was a scary one. I was a very inexperienced traveller, and this was my first time experiencing turbulence as we flew over some mountains. I think these would have been the Rocky Mountains range. I am sure the plane I was on stopped in Phoenix as a connecting flight, some passengers got off while others got on. I'm not sure I can claim I have been to Phoenix, as my feet never touched the ground; I just sat and waited for the aircraft to take off once more.

When Shannon picked me up from Fort Worth International Airport, she told me we would be staying with some of her close friends. The ride to Shannon's friends didn't take too long, and we caught up with one another on the journey. Soon, we arrived at this very big ranch style house with a rather large swimming pool, and I was introduced to Shannon's friend, her husband, and their family. The family had a huge Maine Coon cat, which I was told was very independent. That first night, while in the sitting room, the cat came over and made friends with me, padding up and down on my leg. Then that was it, I never saw it again until my last night, and it entered the bedroom I was staying in. The cat slept at the bottom of the bed next to my one good foot, and come the morning it just got up, and left without even a parting "Meow".

One very hot day, Shannon's friends invited us to take a dip in their swimming pool, which was just to the side of their house, but before we could go in, we would have to check for water moccasins. I thought, "Water moccasins, what the hell are we looking for slippers for?" I was then informed that a water moccasin is a venomous snake. So, it was a case of "Errr, yes, definitely check for those". I later looked up what a water moccasin was, and Google told me it was also known as a cotton mouth. There definitely are some dangerous critters in Texas. Here in the UK the only venomous snake we have is the adder, whereas in the US of A and the state of Texas they have fifteen potentially dangerous snake species or subspecies.

Now, I have never smoked. However, I was asked if I would like to partake in a quick sample of this long and fat, what do you call it? "Joint, Weed, Grass, Pot, Mary Jane, Ganja or Reefer, but to name a few". I thought, "Meh! I'm on holiday, why not?" It was such a mellow feeling, and everything just appeared happier and somewhat brighter. The lights around the pool became hazy, and began to flare in soft colourful patterns, it was sooooo! relaxing just floating, feeling the warm sensation of the water against my skin. My mind just drifted off into some very pleasant dream like state, with a huge sigh as I calmly released my breath, everything just became right in the world. Now at this point, I must make it clear I haven't smoked wacky backy since. I'm all for trying new experiences, and I can tick that one off my list.

While in Texas, I had the opportunity to visit Dallas and the Texas School Book Depository. This is where Lee Harvey Oswald was to have allegedly shot JFK. No way man, I've been on the grassy knoll, and I have seen where Lee Harvey Oswald was supposed to have fired those three shots. I got to wear a cowboy hat, hold a six shooter, and have my photo taken below the Book Depository in a gift shop. Oh, and I got to sample more delicious Mexican food at a fantastic restaurant.

From Texas, I booked a flight to New York, where I would spend an evening, get up the following morning, and head to New York for my biggest challenge yet. On the flight from Dallas, I got talking to a fellow passenger who I was sat next to. She was a lovely lady, and I shared what I had been up to on my travels. In return, the lady went on to tell me about her family relocating from Long Island to Dallas, as her husband had gotten a job there. This lady was so kind, when we got to JFK, she helped me with directions; it's such a huge airport. Once I had collected my suitcase, I somehow found the airport hotel bus, which took me to my hotel to check in. Once I was settled in my room, I quickly checked my phone and got directions to this nearby fried chicken restaurant, so I walked for about 10 minutes and got myself a meal to go. I then returned to the hotel and settled in for the night. The following morning, bright and early, I made my way by the hopper bus back to JFK, got a ticket for the Air Train and then took the subway into New York City.

I managed to get to the Empire State Building; however, I was slightly surprised as I thought it would be a stand-alone building. So there I was, walking down the street looking for a tall building, and I almost walked past it. It was in the street. Who knew? I asked the attendant if I could take the stairs, which I thought would be a good challenge; however, he informed me this wasn't allowed, telling me that the stairs were only open one day per year and this was for a race up or down the stairs. So I had to take the elevator to the upper floor. I got some cool pictures from different angles on top of the Empire State. I could see for miles and was able to spot a good deal of the famous landmarks, like Brooklyn Bridge and The Statue of Liberty, over on Liberty Island.

Following getting the elevator back down from the Empire State Building, I got lost trying to find Ground Zero. I was pretty much walking around blind, not sure which way to go and found myself on Broadway, according to the street sign. I approached a friendly New York policeman, and asked for some directions, and he very kindly pointed me the correct way. My sense of direction is abysmal, and I had no map. Because all the buildings were so tall, it wasn't much use just looking up to try and identify a building to give me an idea of which way to go. I can recall stopping at an ice cream truck, getting a huge ice cream, and taking a selfie. It wasn't until I got home that I realised the sign for Ground Zero was right behind me. By now, I had spotted the Freedom Tower, which appeared to be made out of shiny mirrors and glistened in the sunshine.

Eventually I found my way to Ground Zero, which was a weird experience at first, as I just didn't get it. In my head, I was thinking, "This is supposed to be a memorial". It was so loud and busy with lots of people. I had thought it would be more serene. There were these dark marble walls, constructed in a square, built on the same footprints as where the towers had originally stood. On top of these walls were all the names of the victims engraved in gold. Inside the walls, water cascaded down like mini waterfalls. I recall there being a solitary red rose placed on one of the walls. Possibly brought by a family member or friend of one of the victims or placed there by someone who just wanted to pay their respects. It wasn't until I was leaving, when I turned around for one last look, that I finally understood what the memorials represented. This place was so alive before the attacks, so it was only fitting that those dreadful events did not change the makeup of New York and its people. The loss of life is celebrated through continuation and not willing to give in to terrorism.

Believe it or not, I had been wandering around for some 8 hours, so I didn't get to go to Liberty Island or visit the Statue of Liberty; I only saw these and the Brookland Bridge as described from my vantage point on top of the Empire State Building. New York was interesting. However, I'm not sure it was me. It reminded me of a huge Blackpool, with all its tourist shops, T-shirts, and souvenirs. I didn't see any Kiss Me Quick hats, though there were lots of large apples on things.

During my American adventure I had been wandering around, wearing my cycling socket with my everyday knee. You see, logistically, taking two legs, my cycling, plus my every day leg wasn't feasible. I just took two different knees and would swap them out depending on what I was intending doing, either walking or cycling. My cycling socket, which I thought was the best fit at the time was not exactly designed for walking around all day, and boy, was I sore. One of the most challenging moments in New York was figuring out how to get back to the airport hotel where I was staying. I knew I had to catch the subway and then the Air Train back; however, my mobile phone's battery had gone flat, and I didn't have a map. There I was, alone in a huge city, without a clue about where to go. I can't believe how incredibly calm I was. I just thought to myself, "Hey, you're in a country that speaks English; just go and ask someone for directions", and so that is what I did. I first asked at a shop where I had bought some much needed water and got some basic directions to head to a particular subway entrance. Once at the subway, I asked a lady at one of the kiosks. It was funny as I was on the platform, and she was on her Tannoy. She pointed in the general direction I was to go and, in a somewhat annoyed New York accent, was shouting, "Just keep going", she must have been thinking, "Who the Hell is this strange speaking alien?"

Once on the train, I met a friendly guy who assisted me in which stop to get off at; he must have noticed I was somewhat lost. I had to travel something like nineteen stops before I arrived at the one for the JFK Air Train. I then took the Air Train back to the airport. Once at JFK, I found the free hopper bus to take me back to the hotel I was staying in and had the most relaxing bath before falling asleep exhausted. I awoke the following morning, checked out and again jumped on the hopper to head back to the airport for the final time. As I have already mentioned, JFK airport is vast, so finding my way around was yet another challenge. However, I took it in my stride, which is funny as even thinking about it now freaks me out; how did I manage to do this? It's like it is a world away in my memory. All in all, I spent three weeks in the United States. Wow! What a baptism of fire for someone who gets lost at the end of their own street. That adventure gave me new confidence, changed my perception of myself, and was a fantastic experience.

Chapter 13

In 2014, the friendly people at Pace Rehabilitation, put me in contact with a fantastic organisation called the Arctic One Foundation. Arctic One is a charitable organisation, and what I admired most from the start was their ethos and transparency. The Arctic One Foundation exists to help both non-disabled individuals, and those with disabilities in their sporting endeavours; it has a grant system called "The Forward Motion Grant". Individuals or groups are invited to apply for funding, which can then be used to assist in their sporting activities.

I was excited to meet the people running the Foundation, and to be presented with some new challenges, working alongside Arctic One, helping to create awareness while also, trying to raise funds through various sponsored activities. My first challenge was at Hawridge, a duathlon, where I met Matt Kirby and would later meet Bex Stubbings. They are the co-founders of Arctic One. Both Matt and Bex, well I couldn't have asked to meet more genuine, warm and friendly people. The Arctic One Foundation was founded on 11/11/11 at 11:00 a.m. and became a registered charity in 2012; since then, it has done fantastic work raising much needed funds for many people. What is awesome about Arctic One, is that it really asks for nothing in return, other than to create awareness of the fantastic work they do via social media and word of mouth. Plus where people can assist in raising much needed funds, to keep the grant system running.

Now then this duathlon, as I couldn't run around the course I offered to take part in a relay. I would ride while Scott

Richardson, the P.R. guru for Pace Rehabilitation, would complete the running section. Scott is a below knee amputee, or as I like to call it a "minor flesh wound". This was following losing his leg in a motorcycle accident. Scott is also quite famous in his own right, as he played the character Quiggold in Star Wars Episode VII-The Force Awakens; he is a lovely bloke, with a fantastic dry sense of humour. Since the duathlon was more about having fun, I decided to complete the ride around the route on my Sandman fat bike. You can imagine everyone's surprise, when I rocked up on this fat tyred bicycle while everyone else was on road race bikes. I completed my loops and had a great time despite the challenging hills!

Fate decided to send me two more amazing friends in this year, Lee and Michelle. The story of how we met, I have tried to recount from what Lee and Michelle would go on to tell me. Lee is a very keen mountain biker, and one day, when both he and Michelle were up in Stanley, Lee spotted my rather unique Sandman Hoggar. The bike is quite unusual with its titanium frame, upside down forks and fat tyres. Lee immediately said to Michelle "Hey, have you seen that bike?" To which Michelle just thought, "Yeah, it's a bike with unusually big tyres". Lee went on to say, "He can't be from around here; no one has a bike like that in Stanley!" Then, as I rode past the pair of them, they noticed I was an amputee riding with this cool looking prosthetic leg. Lee and Michelle turned to one another, and from what they described, were then like, "Bloody hell, he only has one leg; that's mint, how he's riding his bike!" Going on to say, "Oh, I hope he didn't think we were staring at his leg". What a brilliant reaction! I loved it when Lee and Michelle recounted the tale.

Apparently, Lee couldn't stop talking about this kid with one leg and a "geet expensive fat bike". Lee is known for his research in anything he does, where bikes or bike packing equipment is concerned, if it's not super light and doesn't have the best reviews, it's not coming along. So, anyway, Lee started Googling. I hate to think what he was typing in while attempting to search. I'm sure he must have discovered some of my YouTube videos and my blog. He then started pestering poor Michelle again, saying, "I've found that lad; he lives in Stanley, nee way!" Michelle knew she would never hear the end of it, so she decided to be proactive, as she knew even though Lee was saying he was going to contact me, he wouldn't and was just making up excuses. Michelle obtained my email from my blog and sent me the most delightful and friendly message. Going on to tell me about her husband, and how he was a keen mountain biker and liked creating cycling videos of his adventures. Michelle explained how both she and Lee had seen me riding up at Stanley, and that Lee would love the opportunity to meet up and go for a ride sometime, if I was up for it. I read the message and immediately got back in touch, saying, of course, I was more than happy to meet Lee, and thanking Michelle for her kind words. Lee then sent me a message a day or so later, and we arranged a time and place to meet up, which just happened to be where my friends and I now affectionately call the "Famous Farmers Trail". It's only famous in our heads, as we often use that route during our cycling adventures. Lee and I got on like a house on fire, and not long after, I was introduced to Michelle. They are both what I would call salt of the earth kinds of people, and I think the world of them both.

Not long after meeting Lee and going on a few rides with him, I introduced him to John, and we affectionately named our wee band "The Three Amigos". Following a good few months of hanging around together, we all had a handle on each other's personalities, and would light heartedly tease one another. Lee's research became a running joke on adventures. "Oh, Lee have you researched this?" Then Lee would go on to tell us what he had been looking at. Lee is also very funny to go out on a ride with, as he has a somewhat dry sense of humour and a certain way with words to describe unsavoury characters, or when he is disgruntled at some stupid bylaws. John's party trick always appeared to be discovering dog shit, and then somehow not being able to avoid either riding through it or standing in it. He was a real dog poo magnet. Once John spotted the foul stuff, his bleating would begin, which always had Lee and me in stitches. John always started with "Awww Man". He would then have to stop and find an appropriate "Poo stick" to try and scrape off any doo doo.

On one outing with John, I recall we had a ride to the "Toon" (Newcastle). It was a really cold day, with patches of frost and the puddles all frozen over with ice. I digress a little here, but I love the sound of riding over the ice, particularly on my fat bikes and hearing the "Crunch" or riding through the woods in Autumn, when all the leaves have fallen to the ground, and hearing the susurrus sound of them beneath my tyres. I find it so satisfying. It's just the simplest things in life that can bring so much joy.

When John and I got into Newcastle, we rode over to Leazes Park, for a bit of a scout about, with the intention of also going to view the urban cows, which are sometimes located just up from the park or over on the Town Moor. I'm not sure what other folk think, but for me seeing all these cows in the built-up areas, always strikes me as unusual, but in a good way. In my mind's eye I see interesting photographs, especially in black & white, and I think I will revisit the cows to take some pictures in the near future. Back to John, and I heard that all too familiar "Aww man a've got dog shit all ower me shoe". Obviously when he had got of his bike he must have stepped in some. John then started searching for his favourite tool, a poo stick, and once he had found a suitable implement, began trying to scrape the horrible stuff from the sole of his shoe. Upon getting the majority of the brown sticky stuff off, John decided it would be a good idea to go to the edge of the lake, situated in the park, and try and wash the remainder off. So, there he was, right on the edge of the lake, trying to dip the bottom of his shoe into the water to give it a wash. This is when he slipped on the mossy side and almost fell into the lake. Fortunately, John was able to somewhat avoid disaster, alongside hypothermia, in a fashion, as he maintained his balance. It was only his foot that he had submerged in the icy water, up to his ankle. I was like, "What'yer deeing noo?" John replied, "Ah a've slipped, me bloody foots soak'un and the watter's freez'un." "Nee shit Sherlock." I mean, parts of the lake were frozen over, it was that cold. John immediately removed his shoe and began hopping around as he drained the water from it. He then removed his soaking wet sock, and stood on one leg looking totally dejected, muttering, "Aww man!" "He'or look'a, sit doon on that bench," I said, as I unclipped from my pedals and got off my bike. I propped my bike up against the bench, and took a seat next to John, whose foot had now turned a rather cold looking shade of blue. I then removed my shoe from my prosthetic foot, and took off my sock, which I handed to John. "There ye gan, sorted man" I said

The only time my prosthetic foot gets cold is when it's a phantom sensation in my head. Funnily enough, I have been out on freezing cold days, where my good foot feels like it's dropping off with the cold, and yet my amputated side can feel like it's in a nice warm bath. Obviously, when I get home and remove my socket and liner, my wee leg feels like a block of ice to the touch.

I don't know what my friends would say about me; you would have to ask them. What is my party trick, or what unique habits or intricacies do I have? Hopefully, they will say they enjoy my company, that I always bring a smile to their faces with my dark humour, and that I am a loyal and good friend who tries to make our time together memorable. I personally think one of the biggest compliments a friend can say is "I know you would be there if I really needed you", and *vice versa*.

We would go on to have some cracking banter on rides out, which was always fun filled, and you could guarantee something interesting, daft or bizarre would happen on each of our adventures. One of our favourite pastimes, when we were all out together, was spotting "scumbags" and joining in with Lee and putting the world to rights in a cheerful manner, such great fun and fond memories. Oh, and we didn't just spot scumbags; on the odd occasion, we came across what we politely called "Right Cocks". These are generally those types of people who are "Jobs Worths" or have a high opinion of themselves. I think the modern term is "a Karen or a Kevin". I can recall a ride the three of us had along by Tanfield railway. A gentleman was strolling along in front of us. As I went to pass him, I offered a polite "Hello", he then turned and started protesting about us riding on this particular route. Going on to say that there were notices informing cyclists, that they were not allowed, and by the sound of this overly irate man, "NOT WELCOME". I was near the gate we had just come through, having just crossed the railway line, and said, "Oh, do you mean this sign?", to which this gentleman angrily said, "Yes, yes, that's the one". I then replied back, "Oh well, you do know that is a disabled sign, and as you can see, I am disabled", to which this man aggressively came towards me and shouted, "What a load of crap". At this point, Lee got rather worked up while still mounted on his bike, came past me and went towards this bloke and shouted back at him, "What did you say, what did you say?" It's the most worked up I had ever seen Lee, and I thought he was going to have an aneurysm. The man and Lee then got into this brief to and fro exchange of words, as John and I looked on at one another with somewhat bemused expressions. Eventually, the bloke just toddled off, muttering under his breath, and we continued on with Lee commenting, 'I can't believe why some people have such a problem with cyclists, when they are being polite and not riding around like hooligans. It's like certain people just think they own the place".

Having met Michelle, she was to become an enormous source of support with various fundraising ideas to help Arctic One and myself. Unfortunately not long after meeting her, she was diagnosed with nasopharyngeal cancer. What a courageous lady she was. If you recall, I told you that when people say, "Oh, you have been through a lot; you are so brave", and how in reality you have no other real choice, you just have to try and muddle through. However, in Michelle's situation when she had to undergo things like having to get a nasal gastric tube (NG) inserted into her nose so that she could be fed, and it remained there for months, and then also having to undergo radiation therapy. I think I would have really struggled. The hospital had to make a custom mask, and this was bolted down during each radiotherapy session, to prevent any movement, targeting specific areas during the treatment. Man, even thinking about it totally freaks me out. I don't think I could do that. I had a meltdown when I had to go for an MRI, and they put a collar around my neck, to keep my head stable; it was awful, it felt so claustrophobic. It was also very embarrassing, a grown man having a panic attack in front of all the medical staff, who I have to say were very professional and caring.

Over the years, I have encountered some terrible panic attacks. Fortunately, they are rare and far between. They would mostly happen at night. However, I had experienced them during the day, when I had felt under a lot of stress. I could be fast asleep and then suddenly awake and have the most awful panic attack, alongside anxiety. Unless you have had them yourself, they are so difficult to explain. For me, I felt like I was going insane, and I just couldn't control my thoughts; my chest would become tight, and it would affect my breathing. I found it very difficult to process and rationalise any thoughts, to try and calm my mind. My poor dad has also suffered from similar attacks as he has gotten older. We have shared our experiences of them, and what they have felt like; however, it is very difficult to explain in words how panic and anxiety can consume you, and the sheer terror because that is what it presents as in your mind.

In August 2014, I participated in my first triathlon at Dorney Lake in Eton. Michelle, as mentioned, had been incredible in raising awareness, and much needed funds. I had to relearn how to swim to prepare for this challenge. It had been about twenty years since I last swam. This turned out to be more difficult than I had first anticipated, due to my amputation. My balance was all out of sync; if I tried to float on my back, I would slowly rotate and end up face down in the water. I had to compensate when swimming forward, as I would twist at my hips too far during my strokes. Bilateral breathing was also tricky because of my limb loss, which, again, had to do with weight distribution and rotating too far in the water. With continued practice, I eventually started to improve and was overjoyed when I completed my first mile in the indoor pool at Stanley's Louisa Centre. I went out and bought my first wetsuit, and proceeded to chop off the right leg, so that it wouldn't flop around and it just fit my stump snugly.

My next challenge was open water swimming, and I prepared for this by swimming in the lake at Druridge Bay. My old boss Dan from work, a keen swimmer, would meet me there and head out for a swim. I remember on one occasion when I was out in the deep part of the lake, suddenly, I got a really bad cramp. Dan saw that I was struggling and immediately swam over to assist me. He grabbed my good leg and began stretching it out, to try and alleviate the cramp. However, as he did so, he kept ducking me under the water, as I tried to float on my back. My dad would come along to Druridge Bay and either sit patiently on the sidelines or take Mr Hinks for a walk around the lake. Even John occasionally joined us, though he didn't venture into the water. Mr Hinks didn't like the water at all, so I was amazed as I was struggling to get out at the lake shore, attempting to get my one leg under me, that Mr Hinks thinking I was in trouble, jumped in and doggy paddled over to me. As if to say, "Hey dad I'm here, I will rescue you". John just happened to capture the image on his mobile phone, and I have to say it is one of my all-time favourite pictures and a very special memory indeed.

Arctic One went on to very kindly invite me to become a sporting ambassador, which was such an honour. I would blog and post whenever I had the opportunity and try to raise awareness of the fantastic job that everyone involved was doing. I enjoyed participating in the triathlon; however, when it came to the running section, I had to walk around as fast as possible, which left me feeling somewhat deflated. It can be very frustrating to be limited in what you can do, but as they say, it's the taking part that counts.

It's strange how, as an amputee, my life somehow became more fulfilling, and I felt unique, not special just unique. I was getting asked to participate in all sorts of things. Along the way I was being contacted to support fellow amputees, where I could provide tips, advice, and demonstrations related to being an amputee alongside my cycling. I was even asked to write a few articles in various disability magazines, and another related to my love of fat bikes. Later in my journey, I was excited to be featured in a popular mainstream magazine, *MBR UK Mountain Bike Rider*.

After completing and enjoying that first triathlon, I wanted to try another. The thing was, I really really wanted to be able to run the running section, not just walk around. I did a bit of research and discovered an organisation named the Challenged Athletes Foundation, who were based in America. I wrote to them and applied to see if I could get funding for a running blade. Each prosthetic part is expensive, but this would be the start, and if I got approved, I could take it from there. After waiting a few months, I received a reply from the Foundation apologising that they didn't support international athletes. I thought that was the end of it, so I put that particular dream to bed, concentrating on what I was able to do.

Imagine my surprise when, months and months later, quite out of the blue, Toby from Pace Rehabilitation got in touch, saying "Hey, I just got a message from this organisation called the Challenged Athletes Foundation, they've sent over a voucher for a running blade". I hadn't mentioned the application much to Toby, so he was as taken aback as I was. Now that I had been awarded this voucher, allowing Pace to obtain a running blade, I only needed to figure out how to get the other components to complete the prosthetic. This is where Arctic One stepped up. Matt, Bex, and the whole team at Arctic One supported me and raised enough money to fund my dream of getting a socket and sports specific knee, to go alongside the running blade. I could then have a go at learning to run or at least jog.

I was again invited to appear on BBC Radio Tees to discuss my upcoming triathlon and the sponsorship from Arctic One, the Challenged Athletes Foundation, and Pace Rehabilitation, who would go on to design and build the prosthesis. Pace Rehabilitation and the team recommend using a particular sports knee, an Otto Bock 3S80, and an Ossur Flex Run carbon blade. Work then began on my bespoke running limb. Toby went on to introduce me to another fantastic prosthetist named Paul Richardson. I loved Paul's attention to detail; he started working on my riding and running sockets. I have been so fortunate to have been looked after by everyone at Pace Rehabilitation. I would consider each of my relationships with the members of the team to be very special. Everyone at Pace had my back and always inspired me to push myself and keep moving forward. These people always made me feel special, and like I was their number one priority. My dad would come with me on each visit, and we always looked forward to catching up with everyone, as they had become friends as well as clinicians.

Paul went on to measure, cast and design a running socket for me, working very hard on its design. I remember that walking with the newly made limb was difficult, because it felt off kilter; the prosthetic limb needed to be slightly longer in its setup; this was to compensate for the impact of each stride. I could walk around with the knee locked out. However, when it was unlocked, it felt daunting at first. Taking that first stride outside of Pace's clinic on the grass was a real leap of faith, with Paul nearby to catch me if I stumbled. I think I caught him off guard because I just thought, "Sod it, let's go for it". Those first few strides were not pretty. It's counter intuitive, as usually, a hydraulic knee is locked out and stable when you are standing on your heel, and as you move your weight over your toes, the knee flexes. However, with a running blade, you have no heel. That along with the fact that all of your power as an above the knee amputee, has to come from your hip, which requires you to throw the prosthetic knee forward.

We decided to move from the small grassy area outside Pace's clinic to some nearby playing fields, where I could practise with a more extended area to run. My dad took some video footage, and I edited it to the theme tune of *The Six Million Dollar Man*. My first attempt at running must have looked like a lolloping buffoon, my arms flailing all over the shop, and a sort of staggered stride. That first attempt was exhausting, I only ran about the length of a football field, well, if you could even call it running at that point. After a few months of practice with Team Pace, that was Paul my prosthetist, who constantly worked on design tweaks and alignment, and the physios, I really picked up a more fluid running technique, and as my confidence grew, everything came together. My arms no longer flailed, and my stride was equal and more like a running gait, rather than a hop, skip and lollop.

Unfortunately, I started to encounter a major problem, experiencing severe pain in my quads each time I attempted to run, this was even when I attempted short distances. The pain was so bad that I could only manage a couple of hundred metres before my quads would swell up, and I'd have to stop because of a crushing sensation, down the back of my hamstring. It felt like I was going to tear the muscle from my femur. Paul had put a tremendous amount of work into my socket and alignment, but I couldn't get past the swelling and the excruciating pain, which prevented me from progressing. I was gutted and became depressed with feelings of frustration and extreme guilt. I felt like I had failed not only myself but also let down all the people who had raised money and supported me tirelessly. My running knee and blade now live in my wardrobe. Every time I see them, I sigh in frustration but keep thinking, "At some point, I'm going to revisit running.". It's the socket that causes the issues, along with the swelling in my leg. I know that I would have the technique down with a little practice. Paul and Pace agreed that the funds raised could be transferred into a cycling socket, so at least it wasn't a total loss, and my cycling continued.

Another memory from 2014, which at the time was not funny at all. However, John, Lee and I often reminisce and chuckle about it now. This happened around April of 2014. Lee suggested we go bike packing, basically camping while using our bikes to get to wherever we were going to camp. It was a bank holiday; Lee knew of a farm where we could camp over at Stocksfield. John and I were up for it, so the plan was set. John came down for me, and we rode to Lee's, where Michelle took a few photos. Then, we were off on our first overnighter together. It was a beautiful day.

We headed up the farmer's trail, which, as I have mentioned, is a regular route for us. Heading towards No Place. Then rode down and into Beamish, where there are several routes you can take depending on where you're going. On this occasion, as we were going to Stocksfield, Lee took us through Beamish, and past the entrance to Beamish Open Air Museum. Lee, being like the energiser bunny, led the way up the steep bank on the back road past the Black Horse at Red Row, and John and I ground our way up the bank to the top, almost coughing up a lung apiece. I had decided to take my fat bike, and what with all my stuff? It weighed a tonne. Obviously, I hadn't been researching the lightest gear, unlike Lee, the seasoned pro, a weight weenie, and someone who is like a bloody mountain goat. We rode past Tanfield railway and followed a route down the backside of Sunnyside and into Watergate Park, and from there found our way to Dunston. We eventually got to Stocksfield after having ridden along the Quayside at Newcastle and heading towards Wylam. Once at the farm, we paid the farmer for our overnighter, pitched our tents, and then headed to a local pub for a few drinks and a bite to eat. Upon returning to the farm and the field, a gentleman and his young son had pitched their tent just a short distance from ours. We were in a lovely corner of the field, and it was ever so peaceful, well that was, until this car came driving across the field in our direction. These people got out and decided to pitch their tent between ours and the other gentleman's. They had a much bigger tent than our small setups. Not long after they had gotten their tent up, they all jumped back into their car, and with music blaring, drove off. "Ahh peace once more".

As the evening drew in John, Lee, and I retired to our respective tents. I think John may have been sharing a tent with me, I can't remember. At about 11:15 p.m. or somewhere thereabouts, there was this commotion outside; I could see bright lights shining through the fabric of my tent. I then heard this loud irate voice shouting something along the lines of, "What the fuck do you think you're doing?" "You fucking idiot, you nearly ran over our tent." At this point, I opened the zipper on the tent door, and John and I peered outside to see what was happening. I noticed that Lee, who was just over from us was also awake and peeking out of his tent. That's when we saw this rather large ginger bearded bloke, standing in his Y-fronts, outside of his tent. It was the gentleman who had pitched his tent just across from ours with the young laddie. He was going wild, shouting at these folk, and with good reason, as the people in the car who had returned, had almost driven over his tent where both he and his young son were.

Thankfully, the driver had somehow managed to manoeuvre his car between our tents without squishing anyone, and then this lad and his fellow campers got out. As soon as he was out of his car, he began, "Calm doon, calm doon mate." speaking to the big fella. Well, that only wound the big man up even more. The lad then said, "Diven't worry mate we're from Scottsy (Scotswood area). A'll make ye brekkie in the mornin' like." "Ye like bacon n eggs' n that". "Just be canny man". "Howay man, we're from Scottsy, we diven't ge'r oot much like". With that, the big fella had a few more angry choice words and told this lad where to shove his bacon and eggs and then went back into his tent. These folks then made their way over to their tent, and we thought that was it. We closed our tent flaps and prepared to settle in for the night and go to sleep. Well, that was never going to happen. From the moment they returned to the campsite that evening, until around 6:45 a.m. It was like a mini-Glastonbury. They played music and raved the night away. I lost count of how many times I heard the name "Pickles" from across the way. It was Pickles this and Pickles that, Pickles must have been the name of this lad, who sounded like a real charmer. They were drinking, swearing, laughing, and having a right good time.

At some point I must have managed to drop off to sleep, don't ask me how. Only to be woken up by bloody John, in a scene reminiscent from the Blair Witch, he scared the shit out of me, as he was nudging me and saying my name, while shining this small torch. John had eyes like a fruit bat; he hadn't slept a wink. Then I got a whispered "Glenn, Glenn, I think those people are at Lee's tent." I was like, "What the fuck do you want me to do? Oh, I'll hop over there and sort them out." I mean, obviously, a visit from fucking Zebedee would really put the willy's up them and get them to behave. There I was with my leg off, as I don't sleep with it on, tired and angry. I then came over all guilty for snapping at John and just tried to reassure him that it would be okay, saying "John just try and get some sleep mate, it'll be alreet, they are just muppets, but a diven't think they are near Lee like." Poor John looked like a little boy who had just been told off. It was one long night.

The following morning when we opened our tent doors and looked out, "Dear me!", you'd think a tornado had hit the place. There were empty beer cans, and litter strewn all over. Many of the surrounding tree saplings had branches snapped off. They must have used them on a fire, or should I say fires, as there were scorch marks burned into the grass, dotted about in various locations. It was like a bomb site. Those people's tent and car were gone. Poor John, his eyes like piss holes in the snow, exclaimed, "There's nee way ah can ride yem; am absolutely knackered, plus I've got this spot on me arse that is geet sore like." I suggested I call Int-ERN-ational Rescue, yeah my dad, a term created by my cousin David, as he knows how much my dad has been out to rescue me and my mates over the years. My dad, bless him, drove through to pick John up without complaint. Lee and I set off riding home only after visiting the farmer to tell him what had happened. The farmer refunded our money and apologised, saying, "Well, that's the last time I allow camping on a bank holiday." The poor fellow had the whole area to clean up. I was absolutely exhausted on the ride home, and my mood didn't improve as I got a puncture. I tried to fix it but could only get a little way before my tyre went down again. On three separate occasions I attempted to fix the punctures. Tired and thoroughly miffed, I had to call The Ern once again. Lee was now on a solo mission to get home. I'd like to think the Cadbury's cream egg I gave him helped him on his return. Man, what an adventure that was. Of course, we laugh about it now, and will often bring up "PICKLES", and the obligatory "scumbag" moniker.

September of 2014 was also when we had to say goodbye to one of my best friends, dear Mr Hinks. I named Mr Hinks after the dog's original breeder, James Hinks, from way back in the 1860s. Mr Hinks was such a character. All my "Bullies" have been. I have owned five over the years, each with a different personality, all being friendly and not deserving of the bad reputation that ignorant people can give them. I believe a dog is only as good as how it is brought up and treated by its owner; I would never leave a child alone with any dog. I think where people go wrong with animals is that they "humanise them" and tend to believe an animal thinks on the same lines as we do, having the same values and standards. I love the breed, and now that we are without a dog, our house feels empty. I couldn't write this story without mentioning Tyson, Edwin, Gilbert, Mr Hinks, and Baxter. Sadly, Each one is missed, but the memories spent in their company live on. Dogs are fantastic companions; their only drawback is that they are not with us long enough.

Chapter 14

Moving into 2015, and July, a new addition to the family, my dad, Kyle, and I drove to Lockerbie to collect a puppy, which I would go on to call Baxter. I named him after a dog I had read about in a book years ago, the title of the book being "Baxter-A Novel of Inhuman Evil" by Jessica Hamilton. Our Baxter could not have been further from evil; he was so cute as a puppy. He was a white English bull Terrier who had a big black patch around his left eye, with a small bit of black and tan on his right ear.

Baxter, just like my previous Bullies, had the most amazing personality, and was a clever lad; I taught him lots of little tricks. He would bark on command and was very vocal if he wanted to let you know he was after something; Baxter could close a door, and boy, could he open one too, almost knocking it from its hinges. I would say the only thing he wasn't good at was recall. When he was out and doing his own thing, he developed selective hearing. It didn't matter if you had the tastiest treat; he would not come when called. Baxter disliked going for walks; this was down to his bad feet, which had developed what looked like awful corns, and he also had problems with his claws, which would require constant pedicures. He wouldn't let me anywhere near him with a pair of nail clippers, so I spent lots of time with a file and emery boards, while he lay on his back, patiently having his nails trimmed. My dad and I bought Baxter some little booties, which appeared to help when going out for a walk, particularly on his front paws. Watching him walk around the first few times, as he tried to get used to these weird things on his feet was hilarious. Baxter loved playing on the soft grass. He especially liked visiting the large field near the Black Path, where he would run about chasing his football, jumping and rolling in the longer grass and, of course, his favourite game, not coming when called when it was time for home, and then being chased.

In 2015, I applied for another part time job as a health trainer, this time with Durham & Darlington NHS Trust. It was only for 15 hours per week, so it fit alongside my physio assistant job, which was just over 18 hours per week. I completed various bits of training and obtained my level three health trainer certificate. Once again, I got to work with some dedicated and friendly people, focusing on what were classed as deprived areas of the local community, places like South Moor, where I used to live, and Quaking Houses. There were certain aspects of the job I really disliked, such as arriving at work to find myself inundated with emails and to do lists. There just wasn't enough time in the day to complete everything, and I found this stressful. However, I loved other parts of the job, like being out in the community, meeting people, signposting services, participating in healthy cooking lessons, and leading voluntary walks each week. My dad got involved in the walks and would bring Baxter, who everyone adored. The local people showed up weekly, and my dad and I built up some good rapport and friendships, which was very rewarding. I did my best to support everyone in their needs, and it was the face-to-face interactions that I really enjoyed about the job. After about three months, maybe a little longer, while working in the health trainer role, I began to develop some large lumps in my neck. These were called nodes. I also began experiencing some fatigue, so I went to see my haematology consultant, and it was decided that it may be time to start a course of chemotherapy, alongside some antibody treatment. This was around May 2015.

I had to go for a biopsy at Durham, and I can recall sitting in the waiting area with my dad; the doctor I was supposed to be seeing was running late. As we were sitting chatting, a gentleman came rushing down the corridor, the bottoms of his trousers all wet and muddy, along with his shoes. He quickly entered this nearby room, and then popped his head out just as quickly, ushering both myself and my dad in. A quick introduction was made, and I was then directed to a patient plinth and asked to "drop my drawers" and lie down. I was then given a quick inspection, with freezing cold hands on my abdomen, groin, under my arms, and around my neck, before being told to get redressed. When I got myself sorted and returned to the chair and desk where the doctor was sitting opposite, he said, "Right, okay, we'll sharp chop that out, no bother". That was the end of the consultation, now all I had to do was a wait until the day of the biopsy. Coming out of the doctor's office, I just said to my dad, "Well, that was short n sweet!" It didn't exactly fill me with confidence getting bits chopped out, but I liked the Doc's funny bedside manner, and both my dad and I had a joint chuckle as we left the hospital.

On the day of the biopsy I had gotten changed out of my clothing, and into a hospital gown and was awaiting what would happen next. I had been shown into a room, and asked to lie on a hospital surgical trolley, to await the anaesthetist. Not long after a gentleman who looked like a mad scientist, entered the room, and introduced himself. He was wearing small round spectacles, and had wiry blonde hair, that was sticking up like he had just been electrocuted. One of the first things he did upon entering the room was bang his head on the large, flexible patient surgical light. Then, while attempting to put a needle in my arm, I heard him say, "Oops." This didn't exactly fill me with confidence, so I just tried to look away and remain calm. Eventually, the needle was in, and once the anaesthetic was administered, I began counting backwards from ten. I love the feeling of the anaesthetic. I can remember the first time I had to have surgery and how scared I was; however, after that and having so many further surgeries, I wasn't worried. I mean if anything bad happened, I would be so far gone that I wouldn't know anything about it. I used to try and challenge myself to see how long I could resist the lure of the drugs before being forced into that deep slumber. That feeling of a heavy veil that drifts over you until you cannot resist it any longer, and then you're gone... Nothingness. Suddenly I am awake, having lost all sense of time, back to reality. It was all done, and I just had to hope the surgeon had removed the correct bit.

I'd had a biopsy some years before, it was taken from my abdomen when I was first diagnosed, probably around 2009. I still have a prominent four-inch scar running down my stomach; at the time, it was very uncomfortable and painful early on as it healed. I also had to undergo several endoscopies, the first of which I chose to be awake for. It was bloody awful, and I highly recommend being sedated for that procedure. Having an endoscopy is like the equivalent of having a garden hose stuffed down your throat, not very pleasant. Oh, and in my case, they took a sample when they were down there, it felt like someone had given me a couple of quick successive digs in the gut and winded me.

This new biopsy was down near my groin. Within a couple of days, I felt uncomfortable "downstairs", and things got progressively worse. I ended up looking like the character Buster Gonad from the *Viz* comics. My gait was already off due to my prosthetic limb; now, I was walking like John Wayne with a prosthetic leg. I had to visit the out of hours surgery at Shotley Bridge. At the front desk, I had to explain to the receptionist what was wrong. Some people might have found this embarrassing, but it was just par for the course after everything I had been through. I attempted to give a brief description while being as polite as possible. I mean I didn't want to say, "Man you would think I had had an overdose of Viagra, and I almost needed a wheelbarrow to carry my balls in".

Following a brief wait, a nurse called out my name, and I was invited into a small treatment room. The nurse asked what the problem was, so I told her about the biopsy, and the stitches I had "downstairs", and then went on to briefly describe this, "swelling and pain", which I thought might be due to an infection. We shared some light-hearted conversation with a bit of side humour while keeping things professional, which helped in what would normally be an embarrassing situation. Most people don't want to be visiting a hospital; it can be quite stressful and traumatic, especially when it's to do with your… "Errr Bits!" Having a good bedside manner and being able to judge your patient is a very useful skill to have in your toolbox. The nurse asked me if I wouldn't mind lying on the nearby plinth, and lowering my pants, which I did. The nurse then took a peek and exclaimed, "Ooh yeah, I think you may have an infection". "It's rather swollen down there". I was then invited to get up and get redressed. Just then, there was a knock at the door, and another nurse popped her head in, asking, "Do you need a hand at all?" The nurse who had just seen me chuckled and gave me a knowing look. She went on to prescribe some antibiotics. Now, some people may see that clinical interaction as unprofessional; however, it was perfect for me. The nurse did an excellent job of dealing with what could have been a potentially embarrassing situation, with a touch of humour and made me feel at ease while I was in a lot of discomfort. Over the years, I have been a fairly regular patient at Shotley Bridge, and everyone from the receptionists to the doctors and nurses have been fantastic. Oh, and by the way I was pretty much back to normal within a few days, thanks to the antibiotics and things had resumed their normal shape and size.

Unfortunately, I had to hand in my notice with Durham and Darlington, as I couldn't manage both jobs anymore; I felt like I was burning myself out. When it was time for treatment, I was scheduled for six months of chemotherapy, with a drug called Bendamustine, alongside an antibody drug called Rituximab. At first, the treatments didn't seem to have any adverse side effects. I went out riding my bikes during the course; it was like a sort of challenge to stick my middle finger up to cancer. I even walked home the eight miles or so after having a round of chemo. My dad had dropped me off at the hospital and wanted to return to pick me up. However, I said, "It's alreet am ganna walk yem along the cycle route". When I get a hair brained idea in my head, I am stubborn, and well, this was just another challenge. Mind you, I wish I had worn different shoes, as my good foot had blisters on it by the time I got home, and my lower back was killing me due to my prosthetic limb.

As time went on and I continued going in for infusions, it became clear that my white blood cell count was significantly dropping. It wasn't until one visit to hospital for a routine check-up, and my blood was taken that a nurse informed me that I was neutropenic. At the time I didn't understand what she was talking about. This nurse then went to get another nurse, and they both returned with hands over their faces, and remained at the door to the room, while they discussed my results. Then they went off again, and returned with yet another nurse, this time a sister. All three stood at the door, covering their faces, and asked various questions, ending in "what do you do for a job?" and "Where do you work?" I went on to describe my job and that I worked over at the Royal Victoria Infirmary. "Oh, you can't go back to work" I was told, "It's too risky". Basically, Neutropenia is when you don't have enough neutrophils, which are a type of white blood cell. Without these cells you can't fight off infections, especially those caused by bacteria. At this time, I was beginning to not to feel particularly well, very lethargic and fatigued. With everything that was going on, and the running blade having been a fail, I was not able to take part in the Arctic One triathlon that year. However, I did manage to attend the event, completed as many laps around the lake on my bike as I could, and raised some much-needed sponsorship to support Arctic One, which I was very proud to do.

After finishing the chemo, I was to have a further twenty cycles of Rituximab, meaning I had to go into hospital for infusions over the course of two years. That was a rough two years. My immunity was shot, and I constantly felt under the weather, catching various colds and chest infections. I eventually reached cycle nineteen and asked the consultant if I could stop, as I felt so tired, drained and unwell. I would say it took me a further two years to start feeling somewhat well again. To this day, my immunity is not that of a normal person. During the COVID-19 pandemic, I had to self-isolate for nine months due to being classed as being vulnerable. That period of isolation brought back memories of my previous limbo, and it was not a place I wanted to revisit.

I went for seven years from being diagnosed before requiring chemotherapy in 2015, alongside the antibody treatment. I have now been in remission since 2017, and to be honest, I don't even give the non-Hodgkin's the time of day. It is what it is and doesn't affect me. I tell myself, "It's gone; I have beaten it through sheer stubbornness and determination". I now only go for yearly check-ups, while being self-aware of any potential symptoms. Huge shout outs to the cancer specialist nurses who were, and by all accounts are fantastic. They are always at the end of the phone to support me if I need it. Oh, and I can't forget the auxiliary staff, who are all such lovely friendly and supportive people.

Looking back at my blog and its timeline, I started writing some poetry around 2015. I have a creative mind and love discovering and reading positive quotes. I find putting my thoughts down both enjoyable and at times, frustrating, especially when I experience a mental block. I even took to keeping a notepad and pen by my bedside, so that if I woke up in the middle of the night, I could jot down my thoughts and ideas. Nighttime is generally when I tend to do my best thinking or in some cases, overthinking. I never seem to be able to switch off; I have an overactive analytical mind. During periods of isolation, I would attempt to keep my mind focused, it's all too easy to start thinking negatively, when you give your thoughts free rein on the bad stuff in your life, those feelings of not moving forward, this can all to easily lead to a slippery slope, and at the end of that slope is the inevitable black hole, which gets increasingly more difficult to climb out of each time.

<u>Keep Keep Keeping On</u>

Born it begins, life's great race, a journey into the unknown.
We lie, then sit, crawl, then walk and finally learn to run.
Goals are set, targets are met, sometimes we fail to achieve.
Hurdles are jumped, turns are took, the meandering race of life.
Time for progress as we unrelent and do what our bodies allow.
Life can be hard, life can be cruel, a spanner in the works. But

the one thing that counts in large amounts is that we, Keep, Keep, Keep Keeping On.

Some of my poetry was weird and obscure. However, it made perfect sense to me, and it didn't always rhyme. It doesn't have to does it. Throughout this book you will discover some of my poems. They are about various things, a mixture of experiences. Some are dark, while others are fun filled and like I say some are just plain old nonsensical.

Thoughts of Riding Fat

Jersey and shorts selected,
got to look cool. Helmet
adjusted, non-protection is
for fools.

Gloves pulled over digits, flexed
to get a good fit. All the right
gear, now prepared, this is it.

Tunes selected, earphones in, not so
loud that it sounds like a din. Music to
ride by, to help with the flow, an
upbeat rhythm, nothing too slow.

Backpack laden with all the right gear.
Let's hit the trails and show no fear. Leg over
crossbar, right foot clips in place, a quick push off
with the left, a steady rallying pace.

Gathering momentum pumping hard on the cranks, praying
to the God of bikes as I give huge thanks.
The scenery goes by in the blink of an eye.
Today is a good day, not a cloud in the sky.

The great feeling of being outdoors, the wind in my face,
feeling so good to escape the rat race. Riding my fat bike
across mixed terrains, and when people see it coming,
they think it's insane.

With huge, big fat tyres, she eats up the trails,
Whenever I ride her, my smile never fails.
Adventure comes easy when I ride my fat bike, so
many memories created, and that's what I like.

Fat bike riders are awesome and now not so rare,
They discuss odd things like optimal tyre pressure and just how much air.
They welcome fellow riders into their fat bike groups, then invite them to visit and do a few local loops.

Chapter 15

As I told you earlier I was now fortunate enough to be working as a physiotherapy assistant at the Royal Victoria Infirmary in Newcastle. At this point, I didn't have a car, although I did have an "Ern", yes, my dear old dad. My dad would get up each morning without complaint and then take me to work, and once I was finished, come all the way back through to pick me up, before bringing me back home. I had not owned a car for about seven years, after selling my Mini Cooper S, which was my pride and joy at the time. My Mini had a manual gearbox, and as my leg became worse before my amputation, well, it was just like owning a very expensive paperweight. I bought the Mini new, and although I cannot remember the exact mileage when I sold it, I think in two years, I had only covered 2500 miles. Now that I was employed, I had been putting a little bit of money aside and saving. This would have gone towards yet another bike. However, while browsing the internet I somehow ended up on Autotrader, and I got my eyes on this small, bright orange Smart car, a limited-edition model called a Night Orange. "Ooh", I thought that would be the perfect car for work. It would give me more independence and allow my dad to have more lie ins; I mean he was retired at this point, so deserving of a few mornings where he could just stay in bed.

The following day, my dad and a friend of mine travelled down to Bradford to take a look at this tiny car. Upon seeing her, I instantly fell in love, so I bought her on the spot and even came up with her name, "Tango". I loved that wee car, and owned her for about seven years, before sadly having to say farewell, which I will describe a little later on.

I have three dream boards on my bedroom walls filled with pictures of houses, ideas, and written notes. I even have three £50 notes to remind me what they look like, and to focus on hopefully getting more. I have a cheque made out to myself, with a sum of money that keeps changing. I have pictures of famous people who I consider inspirational, along with some of their positive quotes; there is Nikola Tesla, Edgar Alan Poe, Walt Disney, Neville Goddard, Christopher Reeve, and Dr Martin Luther King Jr, to name but a few. Every now and again, I will add to my boards. It may be something I am aiming for, so I pin it up, and it helps me to focus and inspire me into action. One of the first houses I discovered online, which called out to me, was on the Isle of Mull. It was called Tor' Buan House. Obviously, I didn't have the money to purchase this house, however, that sense of sadness that washed over me when it was sold was a real feeling. It has happened many many times since, as I find each new property, and then imagine myself living there, only to see it sold and another dream come crashing to reality. That is the thing about dreams though, you can rebuild and start somewhere new. Another house I discovered was near the shore of Loch Ness. It was called Point Clare House and was designed by a ship's captain. The house was absolutely stunning, and I shared some images and wrote a blog about what I would do if I were ever fortunate enough to own such a house. I wrote about it becoming a retreat for creative writers and artists. I would have liked to invest in various mountain bikes and arrange guided bike tours with camping trips. Spending time looping around the loch over a few days. There could be water sports such as canoeing, sightseeing, crafts, and basically sharing the beauty of the area. Following the house sale, a lovely gentleman contacted me a few months later, informing me he had read my blog. Going on to say he had bought the house. He told me of his plans; they were similar to mine, and the house became a bespoke retreat. Amazing! I wished him the best of luck. Maybe my ideas and dreams aren't as bonkers as they seem. Hopefully the Universe will help me with let's say a win on the lottery, or possibly in writing a book that becomes a best seller, so that I can invest in my dream, see it come to fruition, and help it grow into something extraordinary, and then go on to share my vision with other people.

The thing is, money for me is not the be all and end all. It is just a vehicle to get me to where I want to be, as I always have other ideas floating around in my head, a lot of which involve other people's happiness and their own dreams. They say money makes the world go round, which is only partly true; in reality, it is people. Not your politicians or millionaires, but genuine salt of the earth, kind, and genuine folk. Sometimes, money cannot buy things that make a huge difference in someone's life. I saw a house just the other day, one of many, as it has become a hobby or pastime of mine, to look at houses online that I cannot afford "Yet!" The house was for sale in Oban and came with all the land, that set my mind racing in what I could do. The only cinema in Oban was also up for sale at about the same time. I believe Dame Judy Dench helped save the cinema some years ago; however, following COVID-19 and not as many people visiting the cinema, it had fallen into financial difficulties and had to close. My mind started ticking, and I was off in La La Land. How amazing would it be to buy both the house and the cinema? I would love to run the cinema, not only for the local people but also to have things like film festival screenings and possibly think of other uses for the space. Really, just give something back to the local community and make it a beacon of positivity. I enjoy daydreaming; it's free, and it's mine. In order for something to take shape, it must be first thought. I am not saying my dreams will ever come to fruition. "Hey, wait a moment, positive thinking Glenn!" Of course, they will! Just imagine. Yes, I am a dreamer.

We all have regrets some of which we cannot or could not have done anything about. One of my biggest regrets, and I guess it comes under the category, "You couldn't have done anything about it", is the fact that I have never been able to own my own house. Life has a funny way of disrupting your plans, and for me, encountering years of health issues meant I was unable to work; therefore, I couldn't get myself on the property ladder. It felt, or should I say feels like, another loss of being totally independent. That and a sense of shame and guilt that no matter what people say, resides within me. Especially when at fifty-six years old, and you have to tell someone, "Oh yeah, I still live at home with my dad". A lot of people don't get this or can be judgemental. This is why my dream house in Scotland holds so much importance in my thoughts; if I were to achieve that goal, I know I would have attained a certain kind of success.

This is a song or a poem (I say that because I don't claim to be either a songwriter or poet). It is about my dream of getting away, and how I envision the sights and sounds, smells and tastes, and how a house would speak to me.

<u>Dreams of Getting Away</u>

The grass lying dead under my
feet, all withered and turning to
dust. I live in the pure hope that
one day I will escape.

I allow my eyes to close shut,
and I drift off to sleep. sweet
surrender, as reality it just
fades away.

A seed planted so deep while I am in
my sleep, tended to with so much
love and care to bloom into life.

Wandering around in my mind,
filing cabinets that store my
dreams, only opened by me; that's
because I have a secret key.

A favourite dream is found,
stored where it's safe and
sound. In this place, my mind is
free; it is where I am most
happy.

I find myself beside a loch
shore. it's so calming,
tranquillity found there. It's
good for my soul.

Pebbles washed up on the shore, are carried
there by ebb and flow. Each one a special
dream, picked up and now treasured a
gratitude stone.

A Tartan land is where I really long to be, the
beautiful Munros the lochs, and all the trees. I
picture a wee house, my destiny
A special place where I'm supposed to be.

With no stresses or worries, there I rest my weary soul.
Inside my house, lying there on the couch, my hand
resting on the wooden floor; the house whispers,
"Welcome you're home".

A log fire burning warm and bright,
giving off a radiant soft light. With
flames that dance, as time goes by
I know that here my heart does lie

Now, I don't drink whisky,
but here sits a wee dram. It
came from a local distillery
right here in town.

A needle placed within a groove.
The speed it's set at forty-five.
A crackle, a hum, a memorable tune old
vinyl ghosts brought to life once more.

My own piece of heaven, I
carry it deep within.
Will this dream come to pass? Only
time will tell.

Tomorrow, I'll return and
play, out this same scene, in
the hope that one day my
dreams come to me.

Chapter 16

I am not entirely sure what made me think I could write poetry; maybe it was boredom. All I knew was I would get these thoughts in my head and then have to put pen to paper. Another one of my poems is dedicated to my "Buddy Christ", who is a little plastic bobble head, who stands on my bookshelf and watches over me. At this point, I do have to mention I am not religious. I am more agnostic, you know, one of those people who sits on the fence and doesn't particularly have a view one way or another about other people's beliefs, as long as they don't try and shove them down my throat. The Buddy Christ I have is from the *Jay and Silent Bob* movie. He is kept company with possibly the last Christmas gift I ever received from my mother; these are three wise monkeys made from a resin like material. Isn't it funny how some of our most prized possessions are so special, not because of their monetary value but because of who gave them to us, and their deeper emotional meaning?

Buddy Christ, My Little Plastic Friend

I'm not a religious fellow. I don't hold to any faith, just
preferring to live my life trusting in the fickle finger of fate.
Others may try to convince me and attempt to make me see
some sense.
I listen, learn, and respect their views; however, I sit upon my
fence.

I do have one special religious friend, who stands upon my shelf.
He is a good listener, watching over me, but doesn't offer much
advice.
He always greets me with a smile and never presumes to judge.
He points at me and gives me a thumbs up and doesn't hold a
grudge.

My little plastic buddy is so very, very cool.
When I am down, he cheers me up and offers a smile and a wink.
If he suddenly came alive, I wonder what he would say, and also
what he would think

Would he encourage me to follow a different path, or arm me with tips to survive?

I almost forgot he has a bobble head that wobbles upon a spring. One flick of this, and he wobbles with joy. He's so much more than just a toy.
I'd like to think he knows my thoughts and thinks I'm a "canny lad".
I know that when I am feeling down, and look at him, he helps me to not feel so sad.

My little friend is so special to me; I have had him for a while. I know he didn't arrive from heaven; he came from a shop online. Chances are he was produced in China or maybe Taiwan. This very special plastic toy, who is also a Holy man.

I've never asked him for fishes or loaves but have
asked for numbers to my dreams. A fortunate win
to help me along, with my slightly mad, chaotic
and mindful schemes

This is a short poem I wrote when I first started having chemotherapy. I made a few changes to the original verses while I was working on the book. You will read in a few of my words that I speak of "little white knights". How I imagine these are to be sort of like the healthy white blood cells that course through my body and go into combat with the bad things that may be there. I suppose not everyone will get it; in my mind, it works for me.

Dark Therapy

Vein located, sharp scratch, pierced skin.
Feel the needle sliding in.
Overactive sensations, phantom pain.
Drugs infused; it slowly creeps in.
Chemical assassins are released.
No remorse let's attack.
Imagined little white knights, In
protective armour.

Charging in on their horses.
Searching out the dark and evil forces.
Little monsters who are breeding.
They are multiplying, they are feeding.
Nowhere to hide and no redemption.
Eradicate all intruders with no exception.
Poison taken; now to wait.
Frozen veins capitulate.
Eternal cells will know their fate.
Fatigue hits hard; sleep can't wait.

    While looking through my blog for inspiration, I cannot even recall writing some of the stuff that I am now sharing with you. Some of the things I have discovered have really made me chuckle and given me pause for thought, "Where was my mind?" I can see that in certain parts; I was in a good place. I hope you enjoy the stuff I put in here as much as I am recounting it.

<u>People are Like bits of Lego.</u>

People are like bits of Lego, they range
in colour, shape, and size. Connections
are made together when they look into
one another's eyes.

People are like bits of Lego,
who work to a design, searching
for mutual passion and a place
together in time.

Not all people are like bits of Lego.
some come in different forms, like
Stickle Bricks or Meccano, jigsaws
or malleable play doh.

Some people like to stick on labels or
put you in a box.
If you don't fit their way of thinking, they'll
fit that box with locks.

Trying to accept all the other toys or puzzles.
It's a game which can be hard to do.
For instance, if you come across someone who is like a Rubix Cube
They are obviously fucked and possibly, so are you.

In 2016, I got my hands on a newly designed Bartlett Tendon Crossover, again supported within the industry. It was a real godsend. This knee was a new design, and its artificial tendons attached in a entirely different way. Now, I only needed a socket which remained designed for cycling. However, it didn't need the tendon receivers fixed in place on the socket, as the new design was all self-contained within the knee unit itself. I did bits and bobs of promotional work as a thank you, to those people and companies who continued to support me, one of which was a company in America called FabTech. I would demonstrate the knee in action, showing off the knees capabilities and kept up with my YouTube videos and blogging.

Not a great deal comes to mind about 2016 other than the usual cycling adventures. Oh, and I was dating for about a year. However, it was a "It's not you, it's me" kind of situation; honestly, the girl I was seeing was lovely. I don't know what to say; there was just something missing, other than my leg in our relationship, so I ended it. I still feel guilty; however, I would rather be alone than in a relationship where I have to pretend to be authentic and happy. That is just unfair and robbing someone else of happiness. I have now been single for seven or eight years.

Following a trip to Oban in 2016, I had the opportunity to travel to the Isle of Mull, and surrounding areas. Well, I just fell in love with Scotland. That trip was some nine years ago, and ever since I have had this desire, wish, dream, passion, infatuation call it what you will, that one day, miraculously, I will be living in my dream house in Scotland. I feel I have a certain affinity with Scotland; maybe it has something to do with my ancestry; after all, my surname, Johnstone, is associated with the area of Annandale, which is a strath (large valley) in Dumfries and Galloway. The Johnstone clan has its own tartan, crest and motto, which is Nunquam Non Paratus, which translates to "never unprepared". It was one of the most powerful border clans and unlike a lot of the other clans, only sought to raid England.

I have this picture in my head, of me living in Scotland. Having my own house and plot of land, and being quite eccentric, where I would take to wearing a Johnstone tartan kilt on occasion, while out and about exploring, whether on foot or on some cycling adventure. "Ahh the dream". I would also like to have enough land to pop say, some shepherd huts and run a small business. This would give me the opportunity to meet more friendly and interesting people, or if I felt like it remain in isolation. Of course, my dreams go much further, however in explaining them, I would probably have to attempt to write another book.

Chapter 17

I have been using my blog to remind me of some of the things I had done over the years. Upon checking it out, I discovered an interesting post I made in 2017. It was about cryptocurrency, and how I wish I had discovered it a lot earlier. This is taken from what I wrote that year.

"Around 2017, I got into investing in cryptocurrency. I didn't invest a great deal; it was just something interesting to do at the time and, like most people, I had the dream that I wouldn't have to do much work before becoming a millionaire. I invested a couple of hundred quid in various crypto and bought some Bitcoin, Stellar, Litecoin, and Ethereum. When I say bought, I don't mean whole coins, but small percentages of coins. Now, let me be clear I had no idea what I was doing. I had just heard about this thing called Bitcoin, which was created in 2009 by an unknown person, using the alias Satoshi Nakamoto, so by 2017, I was very late to the game."

"If only I had taken more notice when this new thing called "cryptocurrency" emerged. Bitcoin first hit the scene on January 3rd, 2009. Bitcoin began trading on the New Liberty Standard exchange at a value of $0.00076. So, let's say if I round it up that would be US $0.0008, it then climbed to US $0.09 by the month's end. That was the equivalent of £0.00058, moving up to £0.058. This was for one whole coin. Now, imagine buying 100 at £0.058; that would be £5.80; yes, that is right, £5.80. Now, go one step further and imagine buying 1000 coins at £0.058; that would have set you back £58.00. Okay, now I have checked to see what a single Bitcoin is trading for. It is £39,255.13 (at the time of my research 2017), so if we were to do our maths, that would mean your £58.00 would now be worth 1000 × £39,221.43 which would be £39,221,430 or thirty-nine million, two hundred and twenty-one thousand, four hundred and thirty pounds if my calculations are correct..."

In this year, "What are we in? Ahh, yes, 2017". I am sure I read a book about this guy who had picked up an ordinary looking pebble and then carried it around with him in his pocket. Using it as what he called a "gratitude stone". I thought it was a jolly good idea, so when I was out, I began searching for my very own pebble. I can't remember exactly where I discovered my "Perfect Pebble", but upon finding it, I popped it into my jacket pocket, and it became a constant companion. Each time I wore my jacket, I would take hold of this little stone and feel it in my hand. I would play with the pebble while thinking about what I was grateful for and give thanks to the Universe. Completing what you may call an affirmation. Of course, I did this in my head; I didn't want to be walking around looking like some raving loon, chanting some mantra to myself. When I was going to work, I would feel for the pebble and say a big thank you for things I was grateful for. This was a particularly beneficial exercise, especially if I had had a bad day, as it gave me the kick up the arse that sometimes we all need, in understanding that life could be so much worse, and that I should be grateful for the present moment. Having been in and out of hospital as a patient myself, I would think to myself things like, "How lucky am I to be going home, thank you" or "How fortunate I am to be able to do", and then whatever it was I was able to do. There is an old saying, which I am sure you will have heard many times, "There is always someone worse off", and while I agree with this in some respects, I also think that our own problems can be the biggest ones to deal with, this is because they are happening to us, and we feel their impact. So, in reality it doesn't matter if someone has say a corn or verruca; when compared to say someone with what appears to have a much more serious illness or disability, we should try not to judge and show kindness and compassion where we can.

It is scary how quickly we can all forget certain events as they fade from our memories and then become complacent in just taking things for granted. My little wee pebble was-is just a reminder to "say thank you". Now, I want you to imagine my heartbreak when I lost my little pebble, which happened to be not so long ago; I had had it for years. I bet you're thinking, "This guy isn't all there!" I was devastated; it was the perfect shape, weight, and colour; it fit into my hand just right, and to me, it was magical and priceless. The quest was now on to find a replacement; it took months to find the right one. However, I am pleased to say I did. I now play with my new gratitude pebble, just as I did with my old one. I continue to give thanks, and now I always make sure that my jacket pocket is zipped up when I don't have my pebble in the palm of my hand. Oh, and on my adventures, I have gone on to find some interesting pebbles at the beach. These are known as Hag stones, also known as adder stones. These stones have a naturally occurring hole through them. Hag stones were, and sometimes still are, believed to have magical properties. I have a little collection of them sitting on my bookshelf.

In 2017 while looking online at more "bike porn" I came across a bike; well, not literally, maybe I should rephrase that; okay, pretend you didn't read that last sentence. I don't want to come across as some completely weird pervert. Okay, let's try that again. While looking online, I saw this sweet looking ride on the internet. It was a carbon fibre framed, full suspension fat bike by a company called Silverback Bikes, who were based in Germany. I had never noticed the brand before or seen this particular bike; however, I fell in love with it. The bike in question was bright orange and really stood out, not only in its colour but also in its design. I immediately started researching the bike and the company. Following this, I fired off a positive message to Silverback Bikes, explaining my situation, how I loved the look of their bike, and being quite forward in presenting what I thought I could offer the company. I was over the moon when I received just as positive a response in return. Silverback Bikes invited me to become an ambassador for their brand, and agreed on a discount on the bike, in return for posting about my adventures while using their bike. It was a win win. I got to ride a bike I loved, and Silverback Bikes got some positive PR, especially as it also created disability awareness and that "can do attitude" of just getting out there.

Companies such as Sandman Bikes, and Silverback Bikes do so much for the cycling community because not only do they sponsor the elite pro riders, but they also care about the little man in the street; that "Joe Bloggs". For bike companies like this, it is all about the passion for cycling and creating inclusivity. I knew I could help promote the two companies in my own way, as I had a story to share. One which I hoped would capture people's imagination, and that would hopefully inspire others who may be going through a tough time. Silverback Bikes invited me to write a few articles and then asked me if I would do a Q&A video about why I loved my Silverback Synergy fat bike. I was only too happy. I still have both bikes from the two companies. The Sandman I've now owned for fourteen years, and the Silverback for eight. Both bikes have stood the test of time and are in good nick. I get as much pleasure riding them now as when I first got them.

It's funny how I could judge my feelings and mental state by looking at my blog. If I did not post much in a particular year, I knew it had been a bad year, either physically or mentally, as I didn't have anything inspiring going on. I can be quite the introvert and drop off the radar at the drop of a hat, before returning. Sometimes I just need to recharge. As you can tell, my passion is cycling in various forms, whether road, gravel, mountain bike, analogue or electric. When electric bikes hit the scene, I ventured into that area. It was around late 2018, early 2019, when I bought my Specialized Turbo Levo. As an above knee amputee, I use around 60 percent more energy, so an electric bike, while many people may consider them as cheating, I personally didn't.

I would set up my ebike and future ebikes to essentially give me my leg back. By that, I mean I would adjust the electric motor's power via the apps, to give me enough assistance so that I still had to work, however, I wasn't struggling by just using one leg to power my bike. The new electric mountain bike became a real game changer. I could now go out every day if I wanted, in the knowledge that I wouldn't have to beast myself, especially when riding with my non-disabled friends. Riding became even more pleasurable. Saying that the first ride I had out on my Specialised ebike was a complete nightmare. With the bike being new, I had not yet figured out how to set it up or use the app to help achieve a good range from the battery. I am one of those blokes that tends not to read instructions; no, I am more hands on, and if something doesn't work straight out of the box, well, obviously it's broken, or as they say in the Northeast, "It's Knackered Man".

Anyway, I headed off down to Sunderland on my new ride, experimenting with the various power modes. I intended to do a loop from Stanley down to the coast and back. So once down to Sunderland and Roker, I came along by the coast, heading through South Shields and made my way home following a route I knew well. It was at Birtley, just as I got on the C2C that my bike battery ran out of juice. Man, I hate that ride back up from there to home at the best of times. It's just a constant slog up an ever-increasing incline. However, now I had to get back home on a bike that probably weighed 40 to 50 pounds under my own steam. Did I mention I hate that ride from Birtley to home? Of course I did; it just feels never ending and goes on and on. Yet, another valuable lesson learnt, and another challenge completed, as I could have rung The Ern to come along and pick me up. I never made that mistake again, and I made sure to learn how to use the app, so I never encountered problems running out of power on any adventure again. To be fair, once the novelty of the "Turbo" mode wore off, I rarely used it, so this saved a lot of battery.

2018 was a special year, not just because I turned fifty. No, it was as if fate was at work. As I told you, I had bought a little orange Smart car to go back and forth to work with, which allowed me more independence. Well, this one day, while there was nothing particularly exciting to do, I was surfing the interwebs, and while looking upon Autotrader, I got my eyes on a new shape, Volkswagen Beetle. It was a model I didn't even know Volkswagen had produced, called a "GSR". "Gelb Schwarz

Renn sport," meaning Yellow Black Racing in German. There were only a few for sale, all of which had manual gearboxes.

As I began delving deeper into the history of the cars, I discovered that they had been offered in only one year of manufacture, 2013/2014 and that they had come with the option of either a manual or DSG gearbox (automatic), something I needed in order to drive. I decided to do a spot more research and found out that 3500 cars had been produced for worldwide sale. However, only one hundred had come to the UK. Of these, seventy were Yellow and Black, and the other thirty were Platinum Grey and Black, so obviously, these were pretty rare. I thought to myself, "What are the chances I would ever find a Platinum Grey and Black model with a DSG box?" Over the course of the next few days, I kind of forgot about the car. It wasn't until a few days later, again while browsing the internet, that I found myself on the Pistonheads website. Imagine my surprise when, suddenly, a Platinum Grey & Black VW Beetle GSR just popped up on my monitor. I couldn't believe it. I eagerly read the ad several times, taking in every detail, including the fact that this car had a DSG gearbox. Was the Universe trying to tell me something? Maybe along the lines of "Glenn, get yourself a bank loan, and go for it". I excitedly read the advert about another twenty times, looking at the images of the car from every angle, then excitedly went from my bedroom downstairs to where my dad was in his "dog end", his little den. I got him to pop the car up on his computer and asked his opinion. Now, my dad is old school and generally would say things like, "What do you need ten bikes for?" However, he knows once I am on a mission and get something into my head, there is no stopping me. Nowadays, he tends to be more like, "Here we go again, whatever". In fact, he is now an advocate for whatever makes me happy. It is a lesson we have both learnt, as life can be unpredictable. All we really have is "The Now". Anyway, in my head that sounded like approval from my dad, so I applied for a bank loan, got accepted online within minutes, and was on the phone with the car seller the very next day.

Now, I know you shouldn't really haggle over the phone and should thoroughly inspect a vehicle before purchasing it. However, I did the exact opposite, and I agreed on a price over the phone, and arranged a day for my dad and me to go down and view the car. We had to travel down to Oxfordshire, and upon arrival at the seller's house, practically as soon as the garage door was opened to look at the car, I knew, "Oh Yes, you will be mine". That was almost seven years ago. I still have "Grandma"; that is what I call my beautiful Bug. The reasoning is that she is a real wolf in Grandma's clothing, like from the Little Red Riding Hood tale. Grandma has a 2.0 litre turbocharged engine and is remapped, so pushing out almost 300 Bhp, and this is what makes her a bit of a "Big Bad Wolf".

My dad and I have done lots of various mods to the car, and I absolutely adore her.

I may have been having a midlife crisis, having bought a fast car and then trying to recapture my youth by deciding to buy a motorbike in 2018. My love affair with motorbikes started, much to the disapproval of my mother, when I was sixteen. My dad went out and bought me a little Yamaha TY 80 trials bike, and I got it on the road and rode it for a few months until I decided to strip it all down and paint it, and then it never got completely put back together again.

I can remember a hilarious incident with this bike. If you can recall earlier I mentioned I had been on a Youth Employment Scheme, working in my dad's garage on a placement, training to be a mechanic. I had stripped this bike down, and gone on to rebuild its engine, placing it back in its newly painted frame and now the half-built bike was sitting on a workbench without its forks or wheels attached. I informed my friend who was there at the time, "I think everything is back together as it should be", engine wise, so I suggested we pop a small amount of petrol into the carburettor and kick the bike over. This was to be the first time starting the bike since I had rebuilt the engine. My friend held on to the bikes frame to support it on the bench as I poured some fuel into the carburettor. I then replaced the top of the carb and held the frame with one hand while I used the other to kick the wee girl over. She didn't start on the first kick, nor the second; however, on the third, man, did she fire up, going from about nought to full toot in a second, with her throttle stuck fully open, "Whaaaaaaaaaaa!" "Oh shit, fuck", I shouted as I panicked. I thought she was going to blow up, as all 80cc of pure power screamed her head off. I didn't know what to do, then had a brain fart, and reached for the spark plug cap and pulled it off. What a numpty? I instantly got electrocuted, and so did my mate, as we were both holding on to the bikes frame. So, there we were with the bike "Whaaaaaaaaa'ing" away and the two of us screaming like little girls. Thank God it was only a little bit of petrol in the carburettor. I later discovered my error; I had placed the carburettor slide in the wrong way around... Oops!

Another memory that comes to mind again involving my love of motorcycles was when I was around 17. I used to go through to Westgate Road, where all the motorcycle shops were situated, without fail, every Saturday. This particular week, my mam and dad had decided to visit my uncle Eric and Aunty Doris in Ollerton, Nottingham. As I recall, they had been away a few days, and on the Friday evening, I was out tearing around on my Yamaha RD 125 LC, which sounded like a mad wasp with its Micron exhaust. What a bike that was; I loved it, for all it was just little, it could do a tonne. And so I was riding around on my wee bike, probably like a hooligan, when there was such a clatter from the engine. I ended up having to push my bike home in the dark as it was obviously very poorly.

Something had broken. In my teenage head, I thought, "Aww man, am ganna miss ganin te' the Toon the morra". I then had a cunning and devious plan and decided to take my bike indoors into our sitting room and start taking it to bits, to investigate the problem. Obviously, I put a big sheet down and used my mams washing up bowl to drain the oil. I got my tools out and began stripping down my bike's engine. After getting the engine's side cover off, I soon discovered that the clutch basket had exploded. There were fragments of clutch, mixed with broken bits of the clutch basket and the springs, just lying in the drained oil. There was nothing else I could do that night, so I retired for the evening with the next part of my plan in my head. One of my mates would take me through to Westgate Road early in the morning. I would buy the required parts to fix my bike, then have it sorted and ready to go before dinner time so that I could go to the Toon, and almost as importantly, have it "Oot the Hoose, afore me Ma got back yem".

Everything was going according to plan, apart from one major thing, my mam and dad arrived back early. "Oh Shit!" My mam went ballistic; while my dad, on the other hand, kept out of the way. I swear he had a smirk on his face and was thinking, "That's my boy". I tried to reason with my dear old mam, saying, "But Ma a've got te' get me bike fixed, ah need to get te' the Toon". My mam was having none of it. I got the look, along with a pointed finger directing me to our backyard, and I was forced to push "Elsie" outside (Oh that was the name of my bike, by the way). I now had to complete the rebuild in our yard. It was okay though as the weather wasn't too bad, and I could see what I was doing in the daylight. I got the job done in no time at all, after collecting the parts I needed, and I headed off to the Toon just in time to meet up with my mates.

And so, to my latest motorbike, which I bought probably trying to rediscover my youth at the grand old age of fifty. Yes, I have never really grown up. The bike in question was a Benelli TNT 125 monkey bike a little white and red model, which looked so cool. My dad and I modified the bike quite a bit so that I could ride it safely. We removed the rear foot brake, as I couldn't use it with my prosthetic foot, and we set the bike up a little bit like a mountain bike with the same handlebar setup. We fitted a stunt clutch and incorporated a rear brake lever on the bars. The front brake was left where it was. Of course, recapturing my youth, I also had to go out and buy a noisy exhaust. I could ride the bike but always felt slightly skewed when I sat on it due to my prosthetic socket, which dug into the side of the saddle. I had the bike for just over a year; it used to live at the bottom of our stairs and became more of a clothes horse than something you would associate with going out for a ride on. I just never felt comfortable riding the bike when it came to turning and leaning right, my amputated side. Planning a route where I only turned left didn't appear to make much sense, so I ended up putting the wee bike up for sale and moving on to my next idea of a thrill.

As mentioned earlier, a running theme over the years has been my mental health, sometimes good, sometimes really bad. So far, I have always been able to find a ladder and pull myself out of the darkest of holes. Of course, each time something bad occurs, it gets more and more difficult to find a rope, let alone a ladder. I consider myself non-religious. However, I often thank the Universe and believe in the power of positive mental thought. I started reading books on manifestation and mindfulness, and this really helped with my mindset and mental health. I tried to learn to live in the moment, figuring out that it is inevitable that when you are searching for a high and happiness, you will experience a low at some point, and all the things that come with that. It is called life.

In Buddhism, they speak of why people struggle with their emotions and feelings, and put simply as I understand it, it is because we all live with cravings. We crave happiness and then worry that that feeling will end. If we learn to relax, and this is where the meditation part comes in, we can then go on to learn to accept feelings for what they are, and live in the moment instead, of fantasising about how things could have, or should have been. I am not an authority on Buddhism, as you can tell by my interpretation. However, I find the concept of the teachings interesting. Mind you, I do not meditate for hours on end. Unfortunately, I have a very poor attention span and find it difficult to switch off. Even when I am trying to go to sleep, my mind is working at a million miles per hour, and very analytical, which can be so tiring in itself. I must practice more to calm my mind.

In 2019, Pace invited me to help with a presentation in Edinburgh. It was with a law firm and some associates. I was to demonstrate my various knees, both every day and sports, plus give a little feedback on the negative aspects of becoming an amputee and the positives of having a good support network, the importance of good rehabilitation, and being able to access the best available prosthetics, for each individual client/patient. The presentation went very well, followed by some fantastic feedback from the people attending, and then from Scott and Toby in an email a few weeks later. Obviously, I would love to be "normal", and have my own two legs; however, by becoming an amputee and being able to help people out, the very people who helped and supported me, it felt very rewarding. As if somehow, I had a purpose after all this adversity. I continue to make myself available to anyone who wants to talk, and I am always open to supporting various organisations. It is important to show that life can go on. It is about finding meaning, and that can be in the most unexpected of places.

I have always loved old Beetles since my dad bought me one when I was around ten or eleven years old. I can still remember the day he drove this old type-1 pale blue Volkswagen Beetle into the garage where he was working. Its little air-cooled engine happily ticking over. Anyone who knows the old, air-cooled engines will know exactly what I mean, that unmistakable sort of chirping from the wee twin peashooter exhausts. My dad had paid around £60 for the car. I used to sit in it, and imagine going for a drive, with the typical "broom, broom" noises. So, this was my first car, and I guess that is why I have an affinity with the model.

What the hell is wrong with me? In 2019, as if I did not have enough, with more bikes than I needed and two cars, I was bored and started looking for another project. This time, I got my eyes on a Type-1 Air Cooled VW Beetle, which reminded me of that old car that I just mentioned. The car had been restored and was in a garage. Unfortunately, it had been sold when I contacted the dealer, so I was gutted. I had jumped the gun a bit anyway, as I would not have been able to drive the car, as it was a four-speed manual. That did not stop me from looking and doing what I usually do when I have my mind on something, research. I discovered I could get what they call a "Duck clutch" or an "Infrared sensor clutch" retrofitted to make a manual gearbox into a semi-automatic. So, my hunt for an old VW Beetle began. It didn't take long to find an old 1965 model, which was on eBay. She was painted a lovely mango green colour and looked in good fettle. The car was up at Lockerbie. I arranged to go and view her with my dad. Upon viewing the car she spoke to me, so I purchased her there and then. We had to wait a few days before picking her up as the owner wanted to sort out a few little things before he handed her over. After a few days, we drove back up and collected the little Bug, which I affectionately named "Myrtle".

My dad had to drive her home from Lockerbie because I couldn't, due to her having the manual transmission. I was in Grandma, my new shape Bug, and followed my dad and wee

Myrtle all the way home; it was hilarious. Myrtle was only a 1200cc, so she would probably do 50 mph flat out; her heater wasn't working, so her windows were all steamed up, partly due to it also raining. Myrtle's windscreen wipers had a strange sort of speed, a little faster than pure stop. They would wipe, pause and have a little rest before having a jerk, then repeating the process. As I followed behind, I could see my dad furiously trying to clear the inside of the windscreen with his flat cap.

Myrtle had caused quite the tailback on the way home, around six cars and this big wagon. When there was a passing opportunity, and all the cars had got by, it was the wagon's turn. As the wagon passed the little car, she panicked, as did my dad, and began weaving all over the road, drifting towards the grass verge. I think the six-inch narrowed front beam, skinny tyres and being somewhat lowered had affected Myrtle's stability. Over the next four years, I lost count of the amount of money we threw at that little car in restoring her. I had Air Ride suspension fitted to her, which cost thousands, and got an Access to Work grant from the government to get a semi-automatic clutch fitted; this always glitched, probably my fault as the car was not driven enough.

Chapter 18

During the COVID-19 pandemic, I had to shield for nine months, due to being identified as having a compromised immune system. To relieve the boredom, when the weather was fine, my dad and I would spend hours working in our backyard and the fresh air on Myrtle. Those days spent with my father working on that little Bug remain so special to me. One of my underlying memories is my dad constantly bumping his head on Myrtle's bonnet while tinkering underneath her and then going on to mutter and swear. When most of the mechanical jobs were complete, I wanted to get Myrtle's bodywork sorted; this is when things became stressful. Taking her to various body shops to get quotes for the work to be done, it soon became apparent the cost was just way out of my league. I got quoted £15,000 at one place. Ownership became increasingly worrying, and I started having anxiety. You see, we didn't have a garage, and my poor little Myrtle was out in all the bad weather, just deteriorating each day. I decided the best thing was to put her up for sale and give someone else the chance to get her sorted. I took a considerable loss on the car in a money sense, but not from a memories point of view, these were priceless.

The start of the COVID-19 lockdown, occurred on 23rd March 2020, and there would be three lockdowns in total ending on April 12th, 2021. This period brought everything flooding back about being isolated. Things were to go on and get physically and mentally challenging in 2021, as I had no sooner gotten back to work from the COVID-19 shielding, when I found myself back off work, having to take sick leave, which was ironic, as I wasn't actually unwell. It was all to do with my prosthetic socket not fitting. The socket had been uncomfortable for some time; however, I had tried to just persevere, hoping my stump would change shape with exercise and diet. Although I had been cycling every day on my bike on an indoor turbo trainer during Covid, it wasn't the same as eating up the miles outside on the trails. Each day was a constant battle, and I developed various sore areas that broke down. I had what felt like a bruise on the end of my stump due to me bottoming out in my socket. This meant I was weight bearing on the end of my surgically cut femur, instead of my socket supporting me. I tried all sorts to take up the extra volume. Things like extra seals on my liner, stump socks, and I even resorted to trying Gaffa tape, to bodge some foam in place to make the socket fit. Each day, my leg would constantly drop off as the vacuum system was unable to keep its seal, and my stump was becoming more and more painful, which was also leading to additional phantom pain. I somewhat lost my Mojo during this period, "Here we go again", I thought. All I wanted to do was lead an everyday life, do normal things, go to work, have fun and be happy on my days off. "Fuck off, black dog. I can't even be bothered with you". I had to dig deep and use my wealth of experience from previous setbacks. I had to shut off those inner critical voices, the ones saying things like, "You are letting everyone down at work", "You will never get sorted, you are always going to fail"." This is it for you; you might as well just quit". I reverted to what had helped me in the past, took each day as it came, and treated this as a challenge. That old saying "It is what it is". I hadn't asked for any of this, and that attitude of "I feel sorry for myself". Well, where does that get anyone?

I was to be off work for four and a half months, and at that time, I visited the Disablement Services Centre, who tried their best to make me a new socket. The design of the new socket was called a BOA. It was an adjustable socket and looks wise, it was fantastic. There were panels with internal wires that could be loosened or tightened by a dial fitted to the top of the socket. It was a case of selecting whether I felt the socket was too loose or too tight and turning the dial. Unfortunately, when I received the design, it felt way too tight from the off. It reminded me of my attempts at running and the pain I had encountered. This new socket made me feel like my sciatic nerve was being crushed, even on its slackest setting, and it prevented me from walking more than a few metres at a time without having to stop and relieve the weight off my prosthetic side. Eventually, I would return to work wearing my old socket. I continued riding my bike on the turbo trainer, wearing my Bartlett Tendon Crossover knee, and attempted to up my miles. This helped build up my residual limb strength. Plus, I had been trying to eat healthily and maintain a good diet. While my old socket was still not a great fit, I had somehow managed to change my residual legs shape, and at least

I could sort of keep it from falling off, though I still had to wear two seals.

I think I have had my current sockets, for maybe eight or more years. The cycling socket was designed by my then prosthetist, Paul Richardson, over at Pace Rehabilitation. It was such a good fit that Paul took all the measurements and alignments, and provided me with a copy, which I then took along with a diagram to my then prosthetist at the NHS Disablement Service Centre in Newcastle, and a copy was made. This was to become my everyday socket. Over the years, I have changed shape, which is why these old sockets hadn't been fitting as well.

Moving into 2022, I had a few issues with Tango, my wee Smart car. I had now owned her for seven years, and while driving into work, I hit a huge pothole; Tango then started driving weirdly. When I got home that evening, my dad had a quick look and discovered she had broken a front spring. On my days off, we stripped down the front end of the car and removed broken and rusted components before ordering new ones. It came to just over £500 for springs and bushes, lower arms and whatnot; however, Tango was soon on the road again.

A month later, on the hottest day of the year, as I arrived back at home from finishing work, and parked outside our house I could smell burning oil. Upon getting out of my little car I could see that there was smoke coming from Tango's rear end, bless her. My dad came out to have a look, saying we should investigate the problem once she was cooled down. On that evening, when we checked on Tango, she wouldn't turn over; her engine had gone "Tight". "That's it", I said to Ern. "I'm not spending any more money on her". So, I came in, borrowed Ern's Facebook marketplace account, and put Tango up for sale for £1000 spares or repairs. Within about thirty minutes, eight people were asking about the car, and one guy said he would be through with a trailer to pick her up in the morning. I was at work, so Ern drove me in, then came back and waited for this gentleman to arrive, to buy my little car.

Upon returning home following work, I have to admit I was upset that my wee Smart car was gone.

I have some fond memories of Tango and some pretty embarrassing ones. One of which was when Tango broke down on the Redheugh Bridge's outside lane, near the traffic lights leading into Newcastle, as I was going into work. We held everyone up in the morning. I had to call the AA, and they informed the police, who arrived with their blue lights flashing. I then had to wait for a recovery truck, which seemed to take forever, and when it arrived, I was sat in Tango as she was winched up on to the truck. While that was happening, the local radio station was flying above in a helicopter, reporting about this little bright orange Smart car holding everyone up. Tango did get me up to Scotland and back with no issues, and it was amazing how much stuff was packed into her. Yes, good memories; I was sorry to see her go.

No sooner had I sold Tango, and I was on the hunt for another vehicle, more searching on Autotrader. I fancied something sporty, however small. An Abarth 595 Competizione appeared to fit the bill. So, there I was, researching the various models, and then I was off to a garage to have a look at an automatic Abarth 595 Competizione. The car was a beautiful grey colour, sounded awesome and drove perfectly, so I bought her, drove home and as usual started modding her. I never really had a pet name for the little 595; I couldn't think of what suited her. I held on to the 595 for just over a year, which isn't usually me.

I tend to fall in love with my cars and treat them like they have a personality. As I had not long sold Myrtle and had a little bit of money from her sale I decided to reinvest in another car. You see while searching for the 595, I had got my eyes on another Abarth. This was a 124 Spider, a convertible. At the time I thought it may have been a little impractical as a daily driver, however, me being me I convinced myself, "By Glenn you would look canny in one of those". I discovered that the 124's were going out of production, so I figured if I traded in my 595, and put the money I had got from Myrtle's sale, I could afford one before they got too old and had high mileages. The Abarth 124 Spider was, of course totally impractical, and it was more of a heart overhead purchase, than *vice versa*. If the car I wanted had been red, it could have definitely been considered a mid-life crisis. Funnily enough, I saw a red 124 Spider for sale locally and went to view it at a garage. It was a right dog, probably looking worse than it was, as it had not been cleaned either inside or out. I was invited to sit in the car and see how it felt. Honestly, it felt a little cramped. It was a nightmare to get in and out of, especially with my stupid fake leg, however, once I managed to figure out how to slide myself into the seat, it wasn't too bad. I returned home and started looking for more local vehicles. I got my eye on a blue one at Motorpoint, they had advertised on their website. At the time, blue was the only colour I didn't want. However, this particular car that was advertised was fully loaded. So, my dad and I visited Motorpoint, and I got and agreed valuation on my Abarth 595, and then paid the one hundred and fifty pounds to have the Abarth 124 Spider brought up from, I think it was, Derby.

      Around August 2023, was when I traded my 595 at Motorpoint in Birtley and got myself a beautiful metallic blue Abarth 124 Spider Automatic, which I named Lola (Loud, Obnoxious Little Abarth). Is she practical? No, not really. Is she cramped? Yes, especially with my prosthetic leg. Well, is she good on fuel? Definitely not, considering she is only a 1.4. I love this little car. I get mixed reactions from various people. The younger generation generally hurl abuse when I'm driving with the top down, or they will try to get past me aggressively. The older generation thinks I am a noisy hooligan, or if the car is parked up, they will sometimes stop and have a conversation about what sort of car she is. Of course, practically as soon as I got the car, I started modding her; it's my thing; I'm a petrolhead. Even my dad likes the Abarth Spider and takes great joy when I take him for a spin with the roof down. Mind you, like me, he struggles to get in and out of the car; my dad is an amazing man; he will be eighty-five this November and still tinkers with my vehicles. I recently discovered what I thought was a fun number plate for Lola, and my dad very kindly bought it for me, to pop on my car, it reads LE60 FFF; it looks like "Leg Off" and made us chuckle.

    I hope you are not getting bored at this point; some people reading what has gone on so far may think I have quite an active life, well the latter years at least. Those years from 1995 to 2007 have all merged into one long memory of "Turmoil". I'd like to think my creative side blossomed further when, around 2022, I decided I would like to learn to play the guitar. This must have triggered some creative ideas as I began writing some emotive lyrics and more poetry. I do have quite a bit of "downtime" and this is when I tend to lie on my bed and not exactly meditate, but I do drift off and daydream. I have always been a dreamer, with quite the imagination. Maybe because inside my head, although totally screwed up at times, it has been a far better place to live than in reality.

My wishful thinking would take me to that dream of living in that house in Scotland. Lying on my bed, looking at the three dream boards on my bedroom walls, various thoughts and ideas would spring to mind. I would often find an image online and then print it out to add to my wall, assisting me further in my imaginings, which helped with my positive mindset. After all, thinking and dreaming positive, and happy thoughts can only be good for your mental well-being.

I suppose I could be considered a funny sort of soul who is quite paradoxical. Maybe I just don't know what I want. Sometimes I want to be left all alone, or maybe I tell myself this as a defence against rejection. I guess the best defence being to reject everyone else and create an impenetrable bubble. I am happy in my own company; however, I suppose at times I do get lonely. I am getting on in years, and although I don't feel "disabled", I tend to think people who don't know me or are ignorant to the fact may think I need pushing around in a wheelchair, and require twenty-four-hour care. My son Kyle says, "You are too picky" when it comes to relationships, I just think I would rather be alone than be with the wrong person, and so far, I just haven't met anyone that I connect with, on a level where it is equal footing. I am not sure I made a pun there or not?

Another weird poem I wrote while lying on my bed and checking out my dream boards. Funnily enough, it is called.

<u>Lying on my bed</u>

Lying here my mind, it goes astray.
The world around me, it just falls away.

Lost in pictures that I have pinned in place. Colliding
thoughts I lovingly embrace.

Old pictures with their dog ears.
Worn and faded, each one tells a tale.
A story of where I can touch and feel.
A story of where I am supposed to be.

Three pieces of paper with famous faces. A
Queen that has passed, her reign now over,
and when turned, there is,
Alan Turing that mathematical genius and problem solver.

Superman looks on with words of wisdom.
He provides a plan to not become a victim.
Find the hero within yourself, all you can
do is try your best.

A special necklace of sapphire blue, an
old plastic ruler rescued from a fiend.
It's now retired, seen better days.
Pinned to my dream board, it now stays.

A cheque made out to pay myself.
The promise of imagined wealth.
Paw prints on paper from an old friend.
A special reminder hanging above my bed.

A Poem to remind me to dream by day.
Another is to believe things can come my way.
A guitar that, when played can sound so blue. I
really must learn to compose a happy tune.

Just a few things that I see each day.
Things that have meaning to me, in
a very special way.
Oh, and did I tell you about the geese?

    Hindsight is a wonderful thing; I have been learning to play the guitar for over two years. I generally get a one-hour lesson once per week, much of which is based on music theory. If only when I first took ill, and I was twiddling my thumbs, I had taken up the guitar. I may have gotten to a higher standard, and instead of being the way I currently am and just making a noise, I would actually have been able to play. That said, I am proud I have not quit. It's typical of me; I must have some addiction, as just like my bikes and cars, one guitar was never going to be enough. I now have seven and a Ukulele to boot. I love the aesthetics of these pretty pieces of wood, and when I do hit the correct notes, how much joy they bring me. I spend hours just messing around in my little world, especially as my fingers are now hardened and don't get as sore. Speaking of sore fingers, it reminds me of some famous lyrics from a song which I am sure many of you will be able to remember; it was by Bryan Adams recounting The Summer of 69.

As you will read, this poem/song is based on my experience of grief, which has featured quite a lot in my journey. I think after everything I have been through, learning to accept things has made me a stronger, more grounded person, and in some ways, losing my leg has had a positive impact on my life. Look at all the lovely people I have met over the years and the opportunities I have had.

Five Stages Denial
Everyone losing yesterday, all those memories of better days.
Time passes by so very slow, just waiting for the great unknown.
Denied reality, wishing things were back to how they were. Turn off the lights, just lock the doors, pretending that there isn't anyone home.

Anger
It feels like a really bad storm inside of my head. I'm so angry all of the time.
Emotions at breaking point, with a rage that leads the way.
A hurricane tearing at my thoughts I have no say.
I can't see through all of this red mist. So
much confusion I feel so lost.

Bargaining
Is there a deal that can be made?
With God in Heaven or the Devil in Hell?
Bargains are offered, but to what end? All my words fall on deaf ears.
Fate, it conspires at each turn, an unwritten contract I cannot burn.
Praying for change, all my dreams they turn to ash.

Depression
On those days that I'm feeling down, a black dog follows me all around.
Sometimes it's big, sometimes its small.
This sombre hound is no friend of mine at all.
The most dangerous human concepts that of hope and faith, both of which are lost upon my wretched soul.

Acceptance
Time the great healer, or so they say.
Searching for happiness, putting grief away.
Learning to accept the things we can't change.
Searching for answers, finding brighter days. Learning
to be honest with how I feel.
Looking to the future, embracing the change.

The following song/poem has a lyric, "Tilted screens are viewed; unconscious minds don't care to find the truth behind what they see". At the time, I was referring to how people are glued to their mobile phones. You know when people tilt their phones and check out "fake news?" Also, the line that goes, "In a room that is full, thoughts creep in, invisible, lost and lonely no one knows", reminds me of a time I was invited to a Ceilidh (a traditional Scottish dance). Everyone was dancing and having fun, and I just felt so isolated. It is hard to explain why I never feel more alone than when I am in a crowded room.

Beauty Lives in Scars

Beauty Lives in scars, fading in time, memories
live on, a story of who you are. Nature of your

thoughts, find happiness, where's it hiding?
Come out, and let's go play.

In a room that's full, the thoughts that creep in,
invisible, lost and lonely, no one knows. Tilted
screens are viewed, unconscious minds, don't
care to find the truth behind what they see.

A life not to plan, a compass that's broke, you can't find
your way, darkness drawing in all around. Sending up a
flare high in the sky, hoping someone sees, hoping
someone cares.

Mountains in your mind which appear to block your way.
They fill you with fear. They fill you with dread.
But positive thoughts soon make them disappear. Now
the path it becomes clear.

We all have our scars; some are on show, while others run so deep. All contain memories that are ours to keep. They tell a story of who you are, remember Beauty lives in Scars.

Chapter 19

On to an exciting bit, well at least for me. My apologies if I'm jumping around a little with events. As I have gone on to mention, probably overly so, I'm not a professional writer or editor, and as certain things spring to mind I think, "Ooh I will just add that bit; it might be interesting". Quite a number of people have commented on how I can go from one tangent to another in conversation, it's just me. I guess I can be a little like an over excited puppy.

    I often find I have no direction in life; by that I mean I don't really make plans. I am more of a spontaneous, play it by ear and wing it kind of guy. If anyone were to accuse me of being lazy, I think I would agree. Not so much in my work ethic, as I think I am dedicated in that area, but more so in general. Saying which if an opportunity comes along, nine times out of ten, I will take it. However, most of my time is, as I have mentioned before just spent daydreaming about I guess, you could say "Possibilities".

Well, In October of 2022, one of those unexpected opportunities was to come my way. Quite out of the blue I received an email from this Romanian gentleman named Dragos Mostenescu. I was to discover Dragos among other things was an actor, comedian, musician, screenwriter, and producer. Yes, he is a man of many talents. Dragos explained that he had discovered my blog and had taken great interest in my story. Dragos went on to tell me that he and a friend of his, also named Dragos, Dragos Teglas, had discovered the same online articles about me, and then discussed their ideas before getting in touch.

From this point, I will call the two Dragos, Dragos M and Dragos T, to avoid confusion.

Both Dragos were interested in making a short documentary about my journey. To be honest, at first, I thought, "This must be some kind of wind up. I mean, who would want to make a film about me?" I've never considered myself special; I just happen to ride bikes and have one leg. Dragos M passed on his details so I could check him out and confirm that he was who he said he was. A few weeks later, he got back in touch, and a video conference was arranged between the two Dragos and myself, to have a conversation about this project. Dragos T went on to give me some background and describe his production company, "This is Insomnia", then discuss his and Dragos M's vision. They were both very enthusiastic and passionate. The video call was very positive, and the two guys wanted to come up to Stanley, as soon as possible to make a start on the film. At the time, we were beginning to see the start of winter, so I suggested waiting until the warmer weather, explaining that the weather could be pretty harsh here in the Northeast during the winter months. Going on to say that the local trails would be, either be rock solid and frosty or a total mud fest. Both guys agreed it may be worthwhile holding off a few months and shooting the film the following year.

Those months before a date was arranged for the film to be shot were not wasted. I spoke and worked with Dragos T, providing him with things like my background, stories and photos. Dragos checked out the footage I had taken and put on YouTube and began creating a storyboard with ideas of how he was going to make his film come to life and tell the story of my journey.

Come the summer of the following year, 2023, Dragos T contacted me, saying he was all ready to come up to Stanley, with a small team and begin shooting the film. I had to explain that I had some rather bad news. Baxter had taken ill; it was just so unexpected; he had suffered kidney failure, and both my dad and I as you can imagine were devastated. There was nothing we could do. We had to arrange to have Baxter put to sleep. I explained to Dragos that only a week earlier, I could remember Baxter being in the field having so much fun, chasing his football around, and not wanting to come home. My dad had to go chasing after him, and Baxter dragged all the way back to our car. We lost Baxter on 17/05/2023. The vet gave me an imprint of his paws. They are pinned to one of my dream boards, just above my bed. I asked Dragos if he could give me a little time, just a few weeks, as losing Baxter had been such a big blow for both my dad and me. Dragos was very supportive and understanding and agreed that the film could be delayed for as long as I needed.

Two weeks flew over, and although I was still sad about the loss of my best friend, I was pleased I now had something positive to focus on. I had been back in touch with Dragos, and the day soon arrived where he and the small film crew came up to Stanley. My dad and I met them at Beamish, at a local pub, where they were enjoying lunch. We all spent a little time getting acquainted. There were the two Dragos, a camera assistant named Orwen, and a tech data guy named Cosmin. Following their meal and drinks, Dragos T, Orwen and I went for a ride around Beamish Woods. Dragos had brought along a couple of his YT Industries e-mountain bikes. Meanwhile, my dad took Dragos M and Cosmin for a little sight-seeing around the local area.

Having applied for the correct filming permissions from Durham County Council, we scouted various areas, looking for interesting places to ride for the upcoming shoot. I took Dragos and Orwen on multiple trails, and searched for an area where I knew local riders had built some drops and jumps, however, I couldn't find it. How I missed them, and we rode past, I will never know, as a couple of weeks later, while out for a walk with my dad, there they were. Ahh! never mind, it was fate. I think, or at least I hope, Dragos was more than happy with the trails and areas I showed him. He was able to get a sense of where he would like to begin, capturing me riding my bike. On the first day of filming, Dragos was trying to give my dad and I an idea of how his storyboard looked, and how he would like the film to begin. My dad suggested going up towards Consett, on the C2C at High Stables where the old lime kilns are situated. From there, Dragos could get a good backdrop over the valley with his drone. Upon driving up to the lime kilns and surveying the area, Dragos agreed this would make for an excellent place to shoot some footage. It was also a good place to complete some of the narrative contained within the film.

The second day, early in the morning when the guys arrived at our house to begin filming, as we were all in the sitting room having a morning's brew of coffee and tea, Dragos M quickly stepped out and then returned with this carrier bag that contained a wrapped-up box. He then handed this to me and said," There you go, this is for you, from us". I wasn't expecting anything, so it was quite a surprise. I was encouraged to open the gift as everyone looked on. Upon removing the wrapping paper, I discovered that the guys had gone out and bought me a brand-new GoPro 11, along with an extendable selfie stick. Dragos T said, "That is for you, so that you can continue to be the local hero". At that point, I felt a mixture of emotions, ranging from being very excited, to being a little overwhelmed by these people's generosity. Then, of course, me being me, I felt a sense of guilt in case I wasn't everything that they expected me to be.

Before I move on, here are two questions for you, "Do you ever feel enough?", and "Am I the only one who asks myself or thinks this way?"

The guys stayed for four days and shot over twenty terabytes of footage. We travelled locally, capturing various shots of the surrounding areas where I live. We visited Beamish, Quaking Houses, near the fell, the C2C, and what used to be called "The

Maze" at Leadgate, and we also went over to Burnhope on the back road near where the wind turbines are. I was very anxious about the film and cocking things up; after all, I am not an actor. Dragos T was very patient with me and walked me through the Q&A sessions. There were lots of takes to get things just right.

Dragos was always the professional, and not once did he push me to attempt anything I was not comfortable doing while upon my bike. I really respected him for this, as it can be challenging to do certain things that a normal rider may not even have to consider. During breaks in filming, when at home, I would chat with Dragos M; he would pick up my guitar and start strumming away; he is such a fun guy to hang out with, as he has a great sense of humour and is very talented. As we talked, I mentioned I had been attempting to write songs & poetry and invited him to read some of my stuff. Following reading a few bits and pieces, Dragos very kindly said, "I think some of this stuff would be great to have in the film", he then went to Dragos T and said, "Hey, I think we should include this in the film; it's part of Glenn". I was a little taken aback, that anyone would find the words I had written interesting. So for me it was like a "Wow!" moment.

I can recall sitting in our little shed, as Dragos filmed me while I read out one of my poems; it was chucking it down outside. That scene may not have made it into the film. However, some of my words did, and it's another of those little memories that sit in my filing cabinet of a mind, stored away. It's funny as the poem I read out aloud fitted perfectly with the miserable, gloomy, dark day. The poem being a one that I had written about my dark feelings of being ill, and how I had discovered a light in that darkness.

On the last day of filming, riding out of the saddle on that back road near Burnhope was tiring work. I was sprinting as my dad drove his car with Dragos either sitting in the back, with the tailgate open, or filming while sat on the back seat with the side door open. We went back and forth up the road as Dragos searched for the perfect shot.

Who would have thought that my dad and I would build up such a strong bond in only four days of meeting these amazing people? I feel so grateful that fate brought them into our lives. Following the guys heading home, Dragos T and I would stay in touch as he kept me updated on what stage the film was at. There was editing, colour correction, cleaning up, and adding background sound and music to be done. So much data had been taken, which would have to be condensed to make the short film. Hours and hours of footage had to be trawled through to create a relatable story that would catch the audience's attention. Dragos posted a microphone out to me, as he wanted more sound bites of me reading parts of my poem; he explained that he was looking for an emotional tone. I found this extremely difficult, recording many different takes of the words. I think the final result is what Dragos wanted. I guess the audience will decide.

A lot of hard work went into this creation, and when I saw the initial rough draft that Dragos sent to me, he asked, "What do you think?" I was blown away. It wasn't and has never been a kind of ego thing for me, you know, like, "Look at me; I'm a star in a film". This short film meant so much more; it allowed me to reflect on my journey and see myself as if I were watching someone else. A lot of what other people over the years had commented on, about my personality, drive, and fight I discovered was true. I always remember my prosthetist Toby Carlsson from Pace, responding to some email or another that I had sent to him, and Toby replying describing me as "Irrepressible". At the time, I didn't know the meaning of that word, so I had to look it up. It simply means "Full of energy and enthusiasm; impossible to stop." That one word from someone I respected so much, meant a great deal to me, and again got stored in the filing cabinet of my mind. Sometimes people don't have to do much to inspire one another. It can simply be just one word or sentence that enters another's thoughts and drives them on.

The film was also special to me, as it featured my dad, who had also been alongside me on this journey. It had captured a certain piece of him I had never seen or heard. He appeared to forget he was being filmed as he spoke openly, and this brought a lump to my throat and tears to my eyes. The film I must add I had no input in naming. It is called "Meet the Local Hero – Glenn Johnstone." I don't consider myself to be a hero. I'm just an ordinary lad who has been through some extraordinary circumstances and tried to deal with things the best way I can. I believe that out of every negative, if you look hard enough, you will find a positive, though in some cases it may be a difficult pill to swallow.

As the film went from the draft stage to the final edit and was then ready to be entered into various film festivals worldwide, I was so excited. That first message from Dragos saying, "Hey, we have won an award." What a great feeling. This soon turned into two, three, then four, and amazingly, it stands at six as I write this, all that in such a short space of time following the film's entry into the various festivals. Oh, and recently the film was voted as a favourite by the Audience in Amsterdam. I have to admit that each time I watch the film I get emotional. I have an enormous sense of how much my dad has gone through with me, and how amazing he is. It also makes me miss my mother and wish she could have seen how far I have come, as during her time, I was quite ill and none of the things I have gone on to achieve were thought of as possible.

I wrote this poem/song before I met my new friends and filmmakers. It is about a period of my life from 2006 to 2007 when I had a terribly painful, depressing, and very frightening year. I was in turmoil and felt completely alone, and trapped in time, neither moving forward nor back. I was just in limbo. This year was before my amputation when I thought I was losing my mind. Part of this poem is used in the film to convey some of the emotions, and as you will read in the last verse and come to understand, the light came from words from a lovely friendly and supportive nurse.

Thoughts So Dark

Thoughts so dark inside of my mind.
Questions of how did I end up here.
No escape. I'm so scared, locked in and trapped, inside
my head, it's a deathly tomb.

Imagination creates a barren wasteland, played
out in black & white.

I try to flick my inner switch to seek a corner and hide away.
Numb to the core, can't sleep, don't speak.

I think I'm losing my mind. A
dark chasm lies before me, an
abyss to steal all hope away.
Suddenly, I'm at its edge.

If I fall now, I'm forever lost.
The wind howls its wicked threats.
It tries to push, and I push back.
Ruinous shadows, malignant monsters, who reach out for me.

The call goes out to my inner white knights, to
gather forces and charge in on horses.
So much pain endured as this fight rages on. Thoughts
of survival, good versus evil.

Then I see a light in the darkness, it's
an epiphany that comes to me.
A light shines warm and kind.
It comes along to help me escape this place.

I wrote this next song or poem just after the guys left and based it on my time spent in Beamish Woods and shooting the film. It is simply called.

Ride

Warm golden sun on skin,
Radiant light reaching deep within.
Where should we go today?
Then, a beautiful place comes to mind,
A tranquil woodland, not far away, it's so magical.

Lost in thought, feeling free,
Searching for flowing lines between the trees.
Tyres bite, dust rises up.

With one foot down, drifting a bend.
With a mind so crystal clear, all stresses fade so far away.

Passing trees at an epic pace,
It feels so good to escape the daily rat race.
Dry fallen leaves scatter the ground, riding
through them, a susurrus sound. Blue skies
way up above, flared light through a
broken canopy.

A jump, a drop, skidding to a stop, the
chance to take in this Arcadian scene.
The songs of birds and their melodies,
carried on the warm, soft summer breeze.

A flowing stream, discovering its path, meandering
this way and that.
Nature doesn't need words; it speaks directly to your heart and
soul.

Chapter 20

A huge high; what with the film, it was inevitable I would now suffer a low. Recently, where my health had been concerned, things were more down than up, but hey, that is life. I had tried to learn to be more accepting of situations and just roll with the punches. I have to admit my resilience was being severely tested, not just physically but also mentally. I had a sense that an unwanted presence was waiting for an opportunity to creep up behind me and start following me around. At first, it was small, but it grew larger. My thoughts turned to "the black dog" and how I must avoid it at all costs. Life is never static, even though, at times, we feel like we are going nowhere, or a situation is never going to improve. Just like that nurse explained to me way back, we can get wrapped up in looking way off into our past and thinking, "Man, life was so good back then". Going on to then compare it to our "Now". Or the opposite, of getting ourselves all worked up about the future that we foretell ourselves. A future that is never going to happen. That negative mindset of our lives not improving, and us never being able to achieve even the smallest of our goals. How many of us, for instance, play the lottery, but in the next breath, say "Oh, I don't know why I bother putting it on; I'll never win"? Changing your thought process from a negative to a positive can be so difficult to do, especially when it just feels like the Universe is conspiring against you.

What you will discover is that when you are in a negative mindset, you somehow develop this amazing foresight, "I just knew that was going to happen to me!" and then go on to sort of congratulate yourself on the fact. When you think positively, you tend to see all the positives in life and become more grateful, thinking, "How lucky am I?" I am not saying bad things still don't happen. However, you can brush them off more easily and see them for what they are. I know I will encounter more opportunities and positive experiences; however, I also understand no doubt I will have to deal with just as many negative things. After all these years of facing various challenges. I do have a sense that I am better equipped for what life has to throw at me. Now then before I begin a more recent part of my story I am going to take you back just a little bit, this happened around

2023, and what I am about to recount, is a short story in itself. It is related to the older generation, and how they were brought up. My nana Johnstone, my dad's mother was a lovely lady. She like her mother and her mother before her, had been brought up not to waste things. So, for instance, with regards to food, when something was put down, before you to eat, well you couldn't turn your nose up at it, you had to eat everything on your plate. If bread had a little mould on it, then it would be cut off and removed, making the slice that little bit smaller, and you would receive the good bit. My dad being brought up in the same manner, well he is exactly the same. He is also a right hoarder, nothing gets "Hoyed Oot" (Thrown away).

So anyway, I had been shopping at Costco with "The Ern" (my dad). We had come across these beautiful looking Angus beef shepherds pies, and my dad decided he would buy four. We would have one each for our tea that evening, and he would freeze the other two for another day. A few weeks down the line, as I came in from a long day at work, my dad said "Oh, a've done ye one of them Sheep Herder Pies", well I was chuffed, and wolfed the hot meal down, and then just sat and relaxed in front of the telly. At about eight, eight thirty I was rushing upstairs, trying to get me kegs down as I went diving for the bog. Fortunately, our toilet is also right next to our sink, so there I was, now firing on all cylinders, from both ends. Explosive diarrhoea at one end, and at the other it was like a scene from the exorcist. I had the shivers, along with cold sweats which had soaked me through. As I looked in our small bathroom mirror, I appeared like "death warmed up".

I eventually managed to get back downstairs, telling my dad I hadn't been well. "Dee ye think it coulda been that shepherd's pie like?" I asked him. To which he replied "Nah, it shoulda been alreet, it's only been oot the freeza fower days." Going on to add "Then a just banged it in the oven like, for you comin' in." "Dear me! Ern…You've just nearly killed me," I exclaimed, "Am feeling proppa poorly ye knaa." My dad even went on to chuckle, the bloody cheek. It took me almost a week to recover and some time off work, as my dear old dad had poisoned me. Now I know what he would say in his defence… "Well, a didn't wanna waste it, like." See what I mean, old school and bloody dangerous.

It was sometime in the May of 2024 that I started feeling unwell while at work. I had a painful tummy and lower back. I then began with bad diarrhoea. Yep, this tale is warts and all. This time by now wary of my dad's cooking, I knew it couldn't be anything to do with him. So, I just thought I had picked up some bug or another; things didn't start improving, and the symptoms persisted into the following week. I had to take time off work and contacted my GP surgery to make an appointment. Upon visiting one of the practice nurses, I was provided with a course of antibiotics. Thinking I felt a tad better, I returned to work the following week; however, I only managed a day and a half before I had to go home ill.

At the time of writing, I had been off work for almost 5 months, and things were not improving. During this period, I had to go for various tests and investigations, some of which were very embarrassing. I mean, getting a finger up my rear end was most definitely not my idea of fun. I had to attend hospital, whereupon I had two separate colonoscopies, so more fingers as well as cameras up my hoop. These procedures were very uncomfortable, especially the second one, which was also painful. I thought the endoscopist was rummaging around looking for a winning lottery ticket; as he had been up there for so long. I do have to say, the worst part by far was the preparation for the procedures and trying to get the horrible laxative drink down; it was disgusting. The first colonoscopy required me to try and drink two litres of this terrible tasting mixture. The second I was informed I would need to try and drink four litres. "Fower litres, there's nee fucking way like", my internal voice cried out. Obviously, I was a bit more polite with the nurse. However, I was very anxious, telling her, "I diven't think a can manage all that horrible stuff." The nurse then went on to explain that I would also need to do this prep for five days, leading up to taking the horrible fluid… "Awww man what!"

The day arrived that I was dreading, "No not the camera up my rear end," I still had that to look forward to; no, it was the drinking of that foul stuff. I tried my best; however, towards the end I was gagging as I tried to get it down, it was just coming straight back up and coming out of my nose. I am not going to describe what was happening at the other end; once it kicked in, you don't need to be a rocket scientist to imagine; put it this way the stuff came out with more force than a high-pressure jet wash. What made things even more difficult was the fact that as I knew I was going to be going to the toilet regularly, I couldn't wear my prosthetic leg, so trying to rush to the toilet on elbow crutches made things, shall we say interesting.

Again, this is an honest bit of info. You see as an above knee amputee; I find it incredibly difficult to sit on a toilet when wearing my prosthetic limb. The socket gets in the way; as it extends up to the top of my thigh and fits under my sit bone, which is where the weight is supposed to be taken. It is not as many people think, something that only fits so far up what is left of my stump. When I attempt to keep my limb on while on the throne, I either slip off or, like on one occasion break the toilet seat. It's just one of the things people may not be aware of. I mean it's embarrassing and not exactly the sort of thing that comes up in polite conversation. I have also been asked, "Do you sleep with your leg on?" The simple answer is no; it is not practical and would be so uncomfortable.

Following the colonoscopies, I also had to go for an Ultrasound; these don't hurt; the worst part is that the gel is always cold. The good news was that I wasn't pregnant. However, the scan showed I had a polyp on my gallbladder. I don't even know what that means or what a gallbladder does, so fuck it, I don't care. I am not going to Google it and then cause myself more grief.

After the procedures were completed, I had a stressful period where I had to wait for a diagnosis. It turns out I have been diagnosed with ulcerative colitis. Well, I think, that is what the hospital is saying. The consultant has been a little ambiguous with the results, so I require further tests. I am still not entirely sure what's going on, or the end game. I just want to start feeling well. Following reading a little bit on trusted websites, I learnt that the disease is caused by the immune system not working correctly, the story of my life. The IBD nurse provided me with a link to a good Crohn's and Colitis website: crohnsandcolitis.org.uk. Following the colonoscopies I then had to go for two sigmoidoscopes, "Oh my God I am not sure how much more my little corn hole can take" I thought, as the Johnny Cash and his song Ring of Fire sprang to mind. Another MRI and yet another major melt down, as I was in the machine, where I began shouting, "You will have to get me out of here, I can't do it." The radiographer was brilliant, sliding me back out immediately, reassuring me and giving me time to settle. He then suggested placing me in the machine upside down, saying, "Let's try it this way, as you will be able to see out of the bottom of the machine." All scans done, with pictures of my various tubes and pipes and the results of bloods and poo samples. "So, what do I have… Errr and how is it going to be fixed?" Well, my scans and whatnot don't coincide with my symptoms so… I haven't a clue. My mindset, using my years of experience with health-related things just tells me "Take each day as it comes".

To try and combat the inflammation, I was placed on two months of steroids, starting on eight tablets per day. Then, I had to reduce these by one tablet per week until the course was finished. The steroids began working within days and improved my symptoms. However, as I reduced them, I started feeling unwell again. As I write this today, man I am not feeling great.

The clinic I am under decided to put me on a drug called "Octasa", it contains "mesalazine". "Oh my God", after only being on this three days I was out of my tree. I was lying awake at night and could hear this high-pitched ringing. My thoughts, and then I can even recall talking to myself saying "where the fuck is that coming from?" After some intense searching and more talking to myself. Desperately trying to discover this annoying sound, that was driving me up the wall. I eventually thought the noise was coming from the socket extension for my computer in my bedroom, so turned this off. The drug made me feel paranoid for some reason, and how the hell I managed to drive both into work, before being sent home I do not know. My work colleagues later commented they thought I looked ghastly, and as if I was on "speed". I was just insistently talking, however not making much sense.

Following this I got placed on another drug, called Salofalk granules, unfortunately this drug which also contains mesalazine, had some serious side effects too. At first I didn't recognise anything was wrong. I actually started feeling a tad better, where the ulcerative colitis was concerned. However, after being on the stuff for about 4 months, and having terrible cold and flu-like symptoms, with blocked sinuses. Going on to have numerous courses of antibiotics, and a steroid spray for up my snout. Well, I just felt generally unwell, so I stopped taking the Salofalk, after reading of its side effects on the NHS website.

Funnily enough, during this period that I was taking this drug, I started encountering bad, and I mean horrific panic attacks. I know I have mentioned them earlier on in my story, where I would get them now and again, so I do have a history. But these new episodes were every night, then started during the day. Something as simple as hearing a song, and then not being able to remember the artist or title would set me off. It could be anything, a film, a puzzle I couldn't solve, a word that dropped out of my head, a note I couldn't find on my guitar. I would end up Googling things and then panic if I couldn't find the answer. None of us have the answers to every single question, so try and imagine, when things just popped into my head and I didn't have the answer, I would panic. Now that I can rationalise that thought, it makes sense, however at the time of these episodes, all I had were thoughts coming from every direction and attacking my senses.

Any little thing would set me off. I would have to sleep with my bedroom window wide open, so that I could feel the cold night air and be able to breathe. I would go for a walk or jump in my car at stupid o'clock in the…well I am not sure if you would call it night or early morning, knowing I had to go to work in a few hours. No amount of anyone talking to me could bring me round when the attacks struck, it was like I felt I was going insane. Fortunately, now I have come off the medication, although I am not feeling great, from a colitis point of view, the panic attacks have gone, and it is such a huge relief. I read about how magnesium can aid with the mind, muscles, relaxation and support energy levels, so decided to give them a go, purchasing some 3-in-1 capsules. Now I don't know if it's a case of just being like a placebo effect, however I have been sleeping a lot better, no panic attacks and I feel more refreshed upon a morning.

Upon reflection in my mind, I can honestly say I think all the years I have been on various antibiotics and painkillers, plus a whole host of other medications, they have severely compromised my natural ability to fend off bugs and whatnot. It's ironic that my own body is attacking itself. I can't lay the blame on any one particular treatment. Everything I have been given, I guess, was in my best interests at the time. I just want to be well and not have to rely on drugs to maintain my health.

This poem is rather sad. I wrote it on one of my down days. It explains that sometimes I get down and feel all alone. I then have to give myself a good talking to and understand that there are people out there who love and care for me, and I am not broken.

When You Are All Alone

When you're all alone, and the only hand to hold is your own, when it feels like no one cares, and you build your walls so high.
Questioning their real purpose, is it to protect your heart or save your soul?
Don't want to be part of the rat race; rather, be alone and do your own thing.
Just like an old toy that's worn, torn, threadbare and rejected.
Maybe lost an eye or has a missing limb.
Lying in a dark place, all alone, questions in your head, will it be okay?
Always feeling lost, like you don't fit in.
Trapped inside your mind, why so critical?
You have to stop. You have to learn to love yourself.
To value who you are, we're not all the same.
You're the only one.

Life can be a funny old game, so there I am, and I would say for the first time, after everything else I had been through, asking, "Why me?" have I not had my fair share of ill health? Without now being diagnosed with another long-term illness. I was on a super low, trying to avoid that deep dark hole and having that damn black dog for company.

I had been spending a lot of time lying on my bed, feeling thoroughly wiped out and sorry for myself. This one particular day was no different. As I was on my bed, my phone "beeped". I reached down to put my glasses on and saw that it was a WhatsApp message from my friend Dragos, the director and filmmaker of our short film. The first message read, "Have you been learning your Spanish?", followed by another "beep" and "did you get your passport sorted?" I replied, "What are you on about?" and "Err... No," informing Dragos that I had been feeling poorly over the last few months. Dragos then sent me a link and info on getting an urgent UK passport, going on to invite me over to Spain. He then started arranging an itinerary. It all happened so fast. Dragos explaining that our film was going to be screened in Barcelona, and that we had been invited to the Love & Hope Film Festival.

Everything which was done next is a blur. I forced myself from my bed and got dressed. I then headed to the local post office to get my I.D. picture taken. Returning home, I logged on to the government website using the link Dragos had sent me, and I completed the application for an urgent passport. I was amazed that the photograph I had taken at the post office had been sent through to the government website, and I could view it online and then use it for my application. I was then offered an appointment in two days' time at the Durham passport office. Dragos booked my flights to Spain, flying into Alicante airport and their return... Even though I was not in top form, I told myself I could not miss this opportunity. I contacted my employer, as I didn't want to be seen as being off work and then just jetting away on some trip, and I explained that I aimed to return to work, so that was one less stress. I returned to work on a phased return, still on medication; however, as I had further reduced the steroids, the symptoms were returning and getting worse. So I contacted my GP and explained about the unexpected trip and kindly asked his advice about possibly upping my dose of steroids for five extra days while I was away; I mean, I didn't want any unexpected accidents on the plane, "Parp!.. Excuse me madam", or when I was visiting friends.

On the ulcerative colitis front, I have to say it is one of the most debilitating things I have encountered. It is embarrassing and painful and has had me totally floored. It is also very stressful.

Over the last couple of years, support has somewhat dropped off regarding my prosthetics. This may be due to me not being as proactive and putting myself out there, coming off social media, and the like. It may also be because I am getting older, and people think I am past it. Pace Rehabilitation became part of the Otto Bock family alongside Dorset Orthopaedic. With the change, I understood that they may not be able to offer me the same support. Of course, I remain friends with everyone who used to work there, and I still chat with them now and again, always offering my services should they need me. I am eternally grateful to all those people and companies who have been part of my journey, and I owe them a huge debt. When I think back to all those years ago, I can honestly say if I had not been very kindly pointed in the right direction, and discovered Jamie, Pace Rehabilitation, plus Brian and his unique knee design, I probably wouldn't have had the same passion for riding or pushing myself to do the things I have. I don't think I would have had "purpose", and may have just resigned myself to a life of being disabled. Once you change your mindset and find your path, it can give you purpose and drive, along with a totally different outlook on life. Part of moving forward is having the courage to ask for help, whether that be physically or mentally.

Personally, I now had some choices to make, either to think to myself, "Ahh, you have had a good run and quit!" To give up cycling, as my old knee was done, or swallow my pride and ask total strangers, "Hey, would you like to support me in my journey?" I cannot bear the thought of revisiting over a decade of not being active and cycling, so there was only one choice. I decided to start saving and set up a Go Fund Me page. "I needed a new knee so that I could continue." I thought the lovely people at BBC Radio Tees might be interested in my further adventures, so I contacted them, and they were only too happy to feature me on their show. So today, that is where my dad and I have been. We arrived very early, were introduced to a few people, and then one of the presenters recorded my interview, which would be edited and aired later in the week. I hope I came across okay. "Dammit", I forgot to mention the two most important bits, the title of the film, and my Go Fund Me page, which was the whole purpose of the interview. What a "Muppet". I also decided to rejoin Facebook to put myself out there. I thought I needed to be a little more proactive, as it might help me in moving forward. Plus, if there was anyone I could help out at the same time, well, that could only be a good thing.

When I rejoined Facebook, I reconnected with Matt from Arctic One; he encouraged me to apply for an Arctic One Forward Motion Grant to help with the cost of a new G3 Infinity Knee. I was so grateful when I was awarded £500 towards my target, plus Matt informed me that potentially, dependent on fundraising, further money might be added. In total, I received £900, which would certainly go on to help me out with the purchase of a refurbished knee. Look at me, banging on about this knee, and yet I bet most of you reading are thinking, "What the hell is so special about it?"

Well, the Bartlett Tendon G3 Infinity Knee is an advanced "Hybrid" design, which can go from a walking mode to a highly responsive sports orientated knee in a matter of minutes. It can operate in all environments, being what is known as a "dirty design"; it is constructed to take a beating and continue performing. The knee features a light 6061 aircraft aluminium frame, which houses a Rock Shox hydraulic shocker, just like what you would see on a mountain bike. Part of the intuitive design is the "Tendon CAM System," which delivers smooth energy absorption and is designed to mimic natural body movement. I have ridden on all of the past production incarnations of the Bartlett Tendon, and they have enabled me to take my riding further in a more natural riding position, being able to tackle rough trails while riding foot over foot out of the saddle. I can stand out of the saddle with my cranks level to avoid pedal strikes, plus also complete jumps and drop off's. I found all the things I have just mentioned very frustrating/ impossible while using a regular everyday hydraulic knee, it just didn't offer the same level of ability in its design. So, as you will have read, I am pretty passionate about getting my hands, or should I say leg, on one of these awesome bits of kit.

You may ask, "Why can't you just go and get one from the NHS?" Well, that is the thing, although the NHS and my local Disablement Service Centre in Newcastle can provide me with an "Everyday leg", there is no provision for what they class as a "sporting prosthetic". The real shame here is that children are encouraged to participate in activities and are provided with sporting prostheses, such as running blades; however, as soon as they reach the age of eighteen, the provision of sporting prosthetics ends. It must be incredibly difficult and frustrating for a youngster to go from being active to being told, "Sorry, we can no longer support you". They then potentially have to give up on their active lifestyle and any hobbies or interests that they may have been involved in, or, like in my case, go cap in hand to try and get much needed support, or if they have the finances, self-fund their own equipment.

It is true what they say, you only really miss something once it is gone. I dare say that even after reading this, the next time you go for a walk, a run, climb a hill, or even march up the stairs on an evening to go to bed, you will not stop to think, "How amazing is my body?" I think working as a rehabilitation assistant on a busy stroke unit, it has most definitely made me more self-aware. I tend to stop and think to myself about all the things I am able to do, the sensations I can feel, and the range of movements I possess. Simple things like the opposition of my digits, where I can gently touch my thumb to each of the tips of my fingers, and in some cases my attention is brought to the various pains and niggles that arise from getting older. Have you ever tried to prepare a slice of toast, by using only one hand? Keeping the slice of toast from moving away, while attempting to spread the butter, followed by the jam. How about going one step further, and only using your non dominant hand, it really is a challenge. Again, the human body is amazing in how it can adapt, and it does this throughout our lives, both mentally and physically. As we go through life it sometimes becomes more about the things we can do, rather than getting caught up in the stresses, of what we are no longer able to do. It is about what brings us joy, peace, happiness and a sense of achievement.

So, as we are approaching the final chapters, I hope you have enjoyed going from destination to destination with me. I am sure many more adventures and experiences will come along my way, as in your own lives. Fingers crossed, I haven't traumatised you too much or made you cry, unless it is with tears of laughter.

Hopefully, you can see that I have discovered some light in the darkest of places, and that although I was lost, with the support of some caring people, I was able to rediscover myself and become found. Yes, from time to time, I still have to get my flashlight out to help find my way.

Moving forward, learn to be open to new opportunities and grab them while you can. Even a negative experience is an experience, and you will either think to yourself, "Fuck that, I am not going to do that again", or "Mmmmm! I think I will do things differently". If things start getting you down, think of three positives to combat those negatives. If you are trying to solve a problem, take a piece of paper and make two lists, one for negatives and one for positives. I guarantee that when you start doing this practice, if you are in a negative frame of mind, your negative list will far outweigh your positive; however, as you turn things around and become proactive, your list will change. Start doing little things to empower yourself with changes for the better and be kind to yourself. At times, we are our own worst enemies. Learn to tell that internal, self-critical voice to "Fuck Off!"; just do it under your breath; otherwise, people may think you are "Cuckoo!"

When I visit with patients in my care, I tend to use an analogy, saying, "Everyone wants to get to the top of the mountain, and they want to do it in one big leap. In reality, none of us can make that one big jump; we have to take small steps to achieve our goals, which can be hard work. Some days, we may go up one step, and then the following day, we find we are knocked back down two." The key is to keep going, one important steady step at a time" and not to be overly critical of our progress". Your best is enough. This philosophy reminds me of a quote by Dr Martin Luther King Jr, which I have pinned to one of my dream boards and goes. "Faith is taking the first step, even when you don't see the whole staircase."

I really must end this book here. I have discovered that it is difficult to decide where to stop. It has also been challenging to configure the book so that you, the reader, can keep track of events as I jump back and forth in time from years gone by.

As my life is ongoing, and I am still on my journey, and I hadn't finished the final draft, when I returned from Spain, I thought, "Oh, I will just add this bit." So before I say farewell, I must tell you about my trip to Spain, and the Love & Hope International Film Festival.

Chapter 21

The trip to Spain was fantastic. The only other time I have been outside the country was when I told you about my visit to America in 2013. Although Newcastle airport is small compared to some other international airports, it was still a little daunting, what with where to go and whatnot. I have learnt that anxiety and stress, alongside those butterfly sensations, can sometimes be mistaken for another emotion, which is excitement. Understanding the difference can help you transform one set of what would appear to be negative feelings, into something much more positive and beneficial. So refocusing that energy and calling it what it really is, "excitement", can really empower you, along with boosting your confidence and drive.

With a little help from the man at the Bureau de Change and his initial directions, I eventually found which way to go. Going through customs, I was stopped and asked to open my backpack and empty everything out. While I was doing this, my suitcase was also being opened and checked. The X-ray machine had picked up my Bartlett Tendon Knee, which was in my backpack, and there was also an item in my suitcase that the customs personnel wanted to inspect, it was a small spray bottle of "Malibu" sun protection oil. Upon removing my knee from my backpack and offering this to the customs lady, she examined it and said, "Well, that's the first time I have seen one of those." Checks were complete. I was invited to repack my backpack; with some advice that the sun spray I had brought along sometimes failed the spray test and wouldn't be allowed on board the plane. On this occasion, it was okay, and I was allowed to go on my way.

I walked through the duty-free area and arrived at a little seated area, where I could keep an eye on the boarding screens and await to see which gate I would board at. I sat for roughly thirty minutes, intermittently looking up from the book I had brought along, Eckhart Tolle's The Power of Now. After a short while, my gate number appeared on the overhead boarding screen, and I picked up my backpack and began wheeling my case down the corridor to the boarding area. After about fifteen or so minutes of waiting, it was time to head off to board the plane. This required me to head down a set of stairs, which was a little tricky, as I was carrying my backpack slung over my shoulder, the wheeled case and a pair of elbow crutches I had brought along. Stepping out onto the tarmac, the Easy Jet plane awaited me. I can remember thinking, "Wow, that plane is much smaller than I expected." My underlying memory was of a big aircraft when I flew to America, but that said, it was an international trip and not like some stop over flight. Once on the plane, one of the helpful cabin crew assisted me in stowing my small suitcase and sticks in the overhead locker. Then, I found my seat, which was next to a window at the front of the plane. I settled myself in with the other passengers and waited to taxi to the runway and take off.

As we got onto the runway, we were running about thirty minutes late. The plane began accelerating and then took off, rattling and shaking as it did so. Rather than look out of the window to see if the wing on my side was still attached, I closed my eyes and tried to calm my mind. Finally, up in the air, the plane was very loud, and as I looked out of the window, it felt like we were not moving forward at all, as if fighting against a stiff headwind, and the wind was winning. Obviously, we were moving, as some 2 hours or so later we approached Spain, and as I looked out of the window of the plane, I could see the most amazing lightning storm off in the distance, which was sporadically illuminating the sky, making clouds come to life and reveal their shapes. Arriving at Alicante airport and having gotten off the plane, it didn't take long to get through customs. I was initially stopped at the first checkpoint and then directed to a small kiosk, where I had to hand over my passport, and a customs official carefully inspected my details. The customs officer looked me up and down and then, happy with who I appeared to be, pointed to some lifts so that I could head down to the floor below and find my way out.

Dragos had been messaging me while my phone was on aeroplane mode, and as soon as I switched it back on, I read a message letting me know that he was outside near the airport car park waiting for me. I made a quick phone call to let Dragos know that I had arrived, and then I asked a friendly lady at the Easy Jet counter which way to go to get out to the car park. I discovered Dragos waiting outside and received a warm welcome with a "Hey, Glenn," followed by a big friendly hug. Dragos directed me to his car, and the journey from Alicante to Alzira began.

The journey would take us around two hours, so plenty of time to catch up on the drive. Dragos and his partner Ana, had only recently relocated to Spain a few months earlier, so it was interesting to hear about Spain, it's people and culture and how both Dragos and Ana were settling in. We shared lots more general chit chat, which included how proud we were of our film. Dragos went on to explain that he was feeling proper stressed at the moment, as he had just bought a second-hand BMW 330 estate, which he had only driven a few hundred kilometres before the engine had broken. Going on to explain that he was in the middle of trying to deal with both the seller for a resolution, and the BMW dealer in Alzira, where his car currently was. Eventually, after the long drive, we arrived in Alzira, turning off the highway on to what appeared to be an unadopted road, which was more like a trail that was strewn with potholes and rough as hell. This beaten-up roadway would lead us to the gated driveway that in turn, led to Dragos's villa. After a short bumpy ride, where I thought I would lose some fillings, we were at the gates to Dragos villa; he got out and opened the gates, which were on squeaky hinges, then drove through. Dragos then got back out of his car and returned to the gates to close them. The gates have to remain closed as there are wild boars in the region, and given the opportunity, these boars would enter the grounds and go on to destroy all the orange trees in the nearby fields. They can also be aggressive and dangerous.

Continuing up the drive in the pitch-black darkness, we arrived at the villa, which sat in an elevated position, amongst all these trees. Due to the time of the night, there was no natural light, it being around 2:00 a.m. in the morning so it was difficult to get a sense of the surroundings. Dragos went to open the villa door, and upon doing so Joy, his small collie came running out barking; she wasn't sure about this new guest coming to visit her. Joy then recognised me as I put my hand down for her to sniff; realising it was her friend, Glenn, she began running around excitedly. Dragos very kindly invited me in and then gave me a quick tour of the ground floor of the villa and showed me to my room where I would be staying. It was late, so we wished each other a "goodnight", and after a bit of unpacking and retrieving a pair of shorts and a T-shirt to sleep in, I got settled in for the night.

The following morning, I discovered Dragos in his kitchen, and not long after, his partner, Ana, came along and greeted me with yet another friendly hug. Just like Dragos, Ana is such a lovely, giving person, and so easy to get along with. We spent the morning having some breakfast along with some very enjoyable conversation, and Dragos took great delight in showing me around his villa and the surrounding grounds. Now that we were in the daylight, I could get a better view and appreciate the beautiful location. As the afternoon approached, Dragos suggested how would I like to go and explore a trail he had in mind on some bikes. The trail started just at the end of Dragos's drive on that bumpy road we had driven along the previous night. It would take us up into the foothills of the mountains on a winding combination of initial trail, then to tarmac and then back to a loose rock and gravel surface. I think Dragos was as excited as I was, as he had not yet explored the area where we were going to be riding. There had been mention we might get the opportunity to have a ride during our back-and-forth messaging, so that is why I had brought my Bartlett Tendon Knee and some cycling gear along.

Swapping out the pedals on the ebike for a pair of my own SPD's, also known as clipless, which I had brought along. I have to use a clipless system to help keep my prosthetic foot on my pedal. You see the Bartlett Tendon Knee has a lot of resistance due to the artificial tendons, the knee wanting to be in full extension at rest. Giving both of our bikes a once over, we were good to go. Already with Joy accompanying us, I soon discovered what an excellent trail dog she was within the first mile or so. Weather wise, it was fantastic, as it was around twenty-two degrees. There were so many beautiful sights that I attempted to take in as we rode along. Orange trees row after row; scenery that was awe inspiring, just getting better and better as we rode further up the trail. Turning from the rough trail on to a section of road, which was tarmacked, Dragos stopped to point out a variety of oranges overhanging a farmer's wall. He picked two ripe oranges, handing one to me to sample. Dragos explained that these oranges were a combination of lemon and orange, a hybrid, and that the oranges tasted wonderful; he wasn't wrong. The orange was soft, succulent, and sweet, and it indeed tasted wonderful. As we set off again, heading up a short steep bank to get to the next level of the trail. I fell over. I was still clipped in on my prosthetic side, and as I went to push off with my sound leg, I didn't get enough momentum due to the incline. Inevitably, I fell over, you see, I cannot stop myself from falling on this side, as I cannot unclip quickly enough to get my prosthetic leg down.

After recovering from the slightly embarrassing fall, Dragos and I continued on our adventure. Apart from a few scuffs to my Bartlett Tendon, there was no real damage. I just had to stop a little further on, to readjust my foot, as when I had fallen it had knocked it out of alignment. As we rode further, gaining altitude, we would stop now and again to catch our breath and take on fluids, also, importantly giving Joy a well-earned and essential drink, as after all, she was running alongside us and needed to keep hydrated in the warm weather. Stopping we had the opportunity to look back across at the mountains and valleys. What a beautiful vista! We could see the trail we had just ridden along, winding this way and that, cutting through the landscape, part of which appeared like some scene from an old Spaghetti Western, with a kind of desert type terrain, while also having so much greenery in other areas. Even Dragos was taken aback by the spectacular views, as he was new to this area. The sun's radiance, the sky with its beautiful blue hue and fluffy white clouds. At that moment, words could not do justice to the scene's beauty and being there with my newly found friend. Sometimes, you have to just stop, take a breath, say nothing, and then take in the memory, a memory you can bring to mind that brings you great joy in the future. Of course, a few quick photos also needed to be taken.

We rode a good few miles and eventually decided to have a little sit down, a well-earned snack and take on more fluids before turning around and heading back along the same trail. It's funny. One of my other underlying memories of that ride was when I commented to Dragos, "Hey, that is the first puddle I have seen all day". I know that may sound like a funny thing to think back on, but I am from the Northeast of England, and generally, all we have are "Geet big puddles".

While out on the trail, if I fell behind, Joy, bless her, would track back to make sure I was okay, and patiently run at my side; she had boundless energy and was very protective, intelligent, and loving. On the way back from our ride, we pulled into the car park area of what I think was a restaurant or possibly some bar that was being renovated. There were some wooden benches and tables, and sitting on one of these was a fellow cyclist. Both Dragos and I greeted him with a "Hola". I may possibly have fallen into my native dialect and said "Alreet". As we chatted, we discovered that this lad was called Victor, a local of Alzira. There was an instant connection between Victor and ourselves. We began chatting with each other about various adventures, experiences, and interests, which included Victor telling us a little more about the area. Victor went on to offer to show Dragos around any time, and we all exchanged details so that we could keep in touch. Victor told us about working at his family restaurant and invited us along one evening while I was in town. We agreed to take him up on his offer, and then, following a little more friendly banter, we bid farewell. Dragos and I headed back onto the trail, and as we were going down the bank, Victor passed us with a smile and a wave of his hand.

Upon reaching the trail that would lead us back to Dragos's villa, Dragos asked if I would like to have a look at the derelict property which resided next to his. I agreed, and we went along the lane to the entrance and driveway of the property. There was no gate, just a rusty old chain strewn across the entranceway. We left our bikes at the entrance to the drive and walked about maybe five hundred metres up towards the derelict buildings. On each side of the rough dirt track, there were orange trees. It was sad to see that many of these trees were desperate for water; they had not been tended to for so long and that their fruits had begun to fall to the ground and rot. The buildings were also in a sorry state of repair; however, as Dragos said, if someone were to purchase the property, and invest in some time and money, this place could make a beautiful home with amazing grounds.

Yet more wonderful memories created and stored away. I felt so fortunate and extremely grateful. While staying with Dragos and Ana, I was inspired to write this.

The House on the Hill. Now I know that sounds more like a horror story title, but it was quite the opposite. Hopefully I can set the scene and do it justice and maybe think of a more appropriate title.

Closed gates that stand guard; rusty sighs are heard when opened wide.
A long and winding drive with many beautiful trees.
Those sentinels standing to attention, that line the route.
With whispered words brought forth from the leaves. Floating on a warm, soft, melodic breeze.

Welcome, welcome is the sound, an invitation has been extended and can be found.
Open up your mind along with your senses.
Bask in the beauty of all that is around.
Create magical memories that become embedded within,
Colourful internal photographs that capture the scene.

A picturesque villa that stands upon a hill,
sunlight dancing between a canopy of trees. A warm golden glow cast upon the walls, Vines that cover the house in nature's embrace as if offering protection in loving arms,

Close your eyes and listen closely.
Water flowing, it's so relaxing.
A life source meandering to aid with growth.
Moving freely across red tinged earth.
Nourishing water to give rise to new birth.

Fields that go on as far as the eye can see.
With row on row of orange trees.
Each one tended to with love and care.
Bright, vibrant fruit growing everywhere.

A memory stored within my mind
I just have to close my eyes, and it is easy to find.
There with friends who mean the world to me. Each
of them holding a special key.

    The day had arrived for us to head to Barcelona for the screening of our film at the Love & Hope International Film Festival, at Cinema Malda. Dragos had a spot of work to do at home before we could head off, which meant we were a little late getting away. Dragos and I packed our overnight gear into the car, and Ana passed us some sandwiches she had very kindly prepared for the journey. Dragos then drove from Alzira to Barcelona, a trip of about four hours. This gave us plenty of time to talk about many things. As I asked Dragos questions to keep us entertained, I commented, "Hey, this is a bit like a Q&A session; we should have recorded it". One of the questions I put to Dragos was, "What does success mean to you?" It's a very interesting question, and everyone has a different view. Dragos's answer was to follow his passion and related to creativity, loving what he does, as a film maker among other things. However, he described it more eloquently than I ever could. Dragos returned the question to me, and I found it difficult to respond and give a response. I was good at coming up with failures in my life, the fact I have never owned my own home or that I couldn't pursue my goal of running, even though I had a good go at it. I stated, "I guess success for me would be my dream house in Scotland. That would give me the sense of independence I feel I have been missing and bring that dream alive in what I think I would like to do". It's all in my head, and my plans change from day to day. Sometimes, I want to be alone in my house, and at other times, I would like to be surrounded by lots of people. People I could bounce off and share life's experiences and memories. In my imagination, I see a large campfire, with lots of people sitting on makeshift seats, all just having a good time with laughter and song. We also joked about what we would do if we won big on the lottery. Dragos's ideas are a lot bigger than mine; he would like to live in Hawaii for a year or so and have the opportunity to ride next to this big active volcano". Depending on the sum, I'd like to think I would find it rewarding to help other people's dreams become a reality in some way. I think in an ideal world, I would like to setup a non-profit organisation, or some way to subsidise people, so that they could get away for breaks. Offering them an escape from the stresses of life, even if it was just for a short time. I guess this is where my idea of carrying out mountain bike excursions, or doing something creative to do with art or the crafts comes in. After all, money can only buy you so much happiness, and there is not much point if you can't share that happiness.

The traffic was decent on the way, and I enjoyed the conversation and looking out the window at this country's beautiful scenery, which was new to me. As we arrived on the outskirts of Barcelona and approached the city, it became stressful. We began running even later as the traffic started to back up. It was horrendous. The traffic was at a standstill at certain points, with vehicles bumper to bumper. Driving in Spain is an entirely different experience than driving in the UK. I mean not just because they drive on completely the wrong side of the road, but also because of their mentality. The Spanish don't appear to use indicators; they drive bumper to bumper, won't flash you in, and love the sound of their own horns. Oh, and don't even get me started on motorcycles, or worse still scooter riders, who are bonkers, weaving in and out of gaps with absolutely no apparent concerns over their own safety or the highway code, if there even is one in Spain.

As we got deeper into the city, Dragos asked me to check Google Maps to see if we could find a parking spot near the hotel where we were booked. This proved to be a lot more difficult than I had anticipated. Google Maps directed us to turn down this road, and as we did so, we were presented with one of those barriers that had two large posts that sank into the ground, and that could just as easily shoot up again; I was concerned as if we were not allowed to go that way, the posts would shoot back up and cause a lot of damage. I told Dragos, "Hey, I don't think we should go down there; what if those posts come up under your car and we get stuck or worse still, it wrecks your car?" By now, we were both stressed, and it didn't help that we now had a taxi to one side of us and slightly in front and one to our rear, who was constantly beeping his bloody horn.

Dragos quickly got out of his car and checked out the barrier signpost, which was also like a metre thing. However, he was still trying to figure out what to do as he couldn't read or speak Spanish that well. I just said, "Let's try and find another way". So Dragos got back in his car and attempted reversing so that we could carry on; however, both taxi drivers refused to move and kept insistently beeping their horns. I will never know how Dragos kept his cool. We quickly had another scan on Google Maps and discovered an underground car park not far away, so we headed straight for it. Upon finding the car park, Dragos retrieved a ticket from the machine, found a spot, and then the pair of us quickly jumped out of the car, grabbed our "film festival attire", then proceeded to get undressed in the car park and get changed. A speedy walk followed using Google Maps once again, and we eventually arrived at Cinema Malda with only about five minutes to spare.

Dragos M was at the cinema to meet us, and the poor bloke was so stressed, as he thought we wouldn't make it. We all hurriedly went through the cinema doors to find some seats. It was pitch black in the cinema, so much so I couldn't see where the hell I was going. A film was already playing, and we didn't want to disturb the audience. The two Dragos were ushering me to take a seat; however, as I couldn't see, I was afraid I would fall down a flight of stairs. There I was, trying to feel my way around with my one good foot; I mean, the other one is plastic, so I couldn't feel what that one was placed on. Eventually, I figured out where there was a nearby seat by reaching out in front of me with my hands and trying to discern which way it was facing. I selected the nearest one, then slid myself into position, thankfully avoiding a fall or sitting on someone's lap. I am pleased we sat at the back because, every time I watch our film, I have to try and contain myself; I always fail and then end up tearful, so yes, it is best to be at the back; this film is so emotional for me. We had arrived just in time as our film was next to be shown, and following it's twenty-two minutes screening it received a huge round of applause from the members of the audience. At that moment I felt very proud.

There was one more film shown after ours, and then there was a short Q&A session where everyone involved in the making of the films were invited to the front of the cinema, and the audience in turn were invited to ask questions. A question was presented to Dragos, and his response was very touching. He said, "Although the film is called Meet the Local Hero – Glenn Johnstone, the actual hero is Glenn's dad. This is because of his unrelenting support of Glenn and just the man he is". I was very touched by those kind words, and I know them to come from Dragos's heart, as whenever we speak, he doesn't call my dad by his first name, Ernie or Ern; he always asks, "How is Dad?"

At the end of the Q&A, everyone went downstairs to network and discuss the various films. The two Dragos went out for a smoke, and I remained in the foyer, in my somewhat introverted mode. I was very surprised when people started coming over to me, reaching out to shake my hand, and offering congratulations on such an inspirational and moving story. I received some lovely comments about my dear old dad, and some people even asked if they could have their photograph taken with me. It felt like some kind of alternative reality. I am not used to such attention. I was blown away by the wonderfully kind comments from people within the independent film industry, following the screening. I didn't expect to have people coming up to me, asking me various questions, and taking such a genuine interest in myself or my dad, plus commenting on the fantastic editing and cinematography of our film. The film is a short documentary, and is just over 22 minutes long, so when I wrote my blog, I called it "22 Minutes of Fame in Spain". There is a quote by Andy Warhol, which goes "In the future, everyone will be world famous for fifteen minutes." I'm not sure this would be classed as my fifteen minutes of fame, but if it were, I would have possibly stolen an extra seven minutes. Nevertheless, what a fantastic experience. Given the opportunity, after having enjoyed attending the film festival I would love to be able to go to more, and travel around seeing these unique and inspiring stories, presented by independent film makers.

There was to be an after show get together in town, so before heading to this, the two Dragos and I used Google Maps, and we set about trying to find the hotel that Dragos T and I would be staying in. Once we found the hotel and checked in, deciding to leave all our gear in the car until the following morning, we searched for somewhere to get a drink and have a bite to eat. As we walked through the busy, narrow streets of Barcelona, we discovered what appeared to be a nice-looking place, as we peered through its window. We decided to head in and spoke to one of the staff, then we were shown to a table. As we had walked past one of the restaurant-bar counters, some of the most amazing looking tapas were on display. Taking a seat at our table, we ordered drinks. Then, I went to view what was on offer placed on the after mentioned counters and behind the glass display units. Each of us got some of those tapas, while our main was being prepared, the main being these delicious looking and tasting burgers.

"Wow!" The food was amazing. Once we had finished the tapas and our mains, we shared three desserts between us; these went down a treat. The friendly waitress then gave brief instructions on finding a taxi rank, and we headed off. Man, this is when I got my eyes opened. Walking through Barcelona, which was very busy, Dragos T spotted this sort of small bright light. The light drifted up into the air some twenty feet or so, clear against the night sky. "That is someone selling drugs!", Dragos exclaimed. Sure enough, as we crossed the street, this dodgy looking character came right up to us and, as cool as you like, asked straight out, "You want some Charlie, best in all of Barcelona". Even though I am pretty naive, I knew he wasn't trying to sell us "A can of Coke or a Pepsi Cola". We all politely declined and walked on.

A little further on, while looking for the taxi rank, this other guy came up to us, and this one had even more patter; not only did he offer us the "Best Charlie in all of Barcelona", amongst other drugs, he must have been like a walking pharmacy. This friendly chap also wanted to introduce us to some… "Errr!", how to put it "Ladies of the night", who he went on to describe did some wonderful things. "No thanks; I think I'll pass." This guy was quite helpful as he directed us to a nearby taxi rank, with a parting word." "I will see you when you come back this way." I'm sure this was followed by a "Muhahahahaaa", and when we got out of earshot, Dragos T commented, "Man, that guy is the Devil." We discovered the taxi rank and got a taxi to the party venue. Once inside, it was very nice to have the opportunity to talk to some fascinating people, and when the evening was about to wrap up, Dragos M left to go to his hotel as he had an early flight home the following morning. Dragos T and I caught a taxi back towards our hotel, grabbing a drink in a bar and getting a few bottles of water to take back to our hotel rooms. The room I was staying in was absolutely tiny. It had a single bed, no bathroom, and a small table with an electric fan placed on top, and that was about it. By now, both my phone and prosthetic knee were just about out of charge, and as we had left our gear in Dragos's car, I couldn't charge either of them.

The following morning, I went to Dragos's room, knocked on his door, and he was just about ready for the off. We handed in our keys at the reception desk and headed off in search of a coffee shop to have a spot of breakfast and a coffee. The only place open was a Starbucks, so we went in there. Upon finishing up in Starbucks and stepping outside, I recognised the plaza and knew it was close to where the car park was. As we walked towards the car park, Dragos reached into his wallet to retrieve the parking ticket and then, exclaimed, "Oh fuck I've lost the parking ticket", "You're joking!" I said. No, he wasn't. He couldn't find the ticket anywhere. I popped my positive head on and just reassured him it would be okay, and we continued to the car park. Dragos had to use the ticket machine call button, and a friendly parking attendant replied. I don't know why, but I was expecting to hear Manuel from Barcelona, played by Andrew Sachs, you know from the old TV show, Fawlty Towers? Imagining Dragos trying to explain the lost ticket, and the attendant just saying "Que". Anyway, the attendants English was quite good, and as Dragos explained the situation, the attendant sorted everything out. As I recall, the ticket cost fifty-four Euros, and as we went to go through the barrier at the exit, the barrier wouldn't go up. This required more trying to communicate with another Spanish parking attendant at the exit. Unfortunately, he didn't speak any English at all, and the phrase "Que", which means "What" in Spanish sprang to mind, maybe I had discovered Manuel after all. Dragos ended up trying to use a combination of broken Spanish, with bits of English, a few "Fucking Hells" and some gestures. "Ticket'o, paid for'o, barrier up'o." Never mind, he eventually managed to get his message across, and we escaped the car park.

Dragos informed me he still had a little work to catch up on, so he suggested we find a coffee shop near Gaudi's cathedral. I could walk down to the cathedral and have a look around while he finished some work on his laptop. As I mentioned earlier, my old phone, whose battery wasn't great, had gone down to five percent. Oh, and my knee was just about out of juice and had decided to beep and vibrate every now and again. For some reason, I later discovered my prosthetic leg didn't like Spanish electricity, so it wouldn't charge. It was more likely to be the charger. Anyway, I now had a flat phone and a flat leg. So I had to lock my knee out and walk around like some soldier doing half a goose step.

Gaudi's cathedral looked terrific from the outside. Unfortunately, there were huge queues, and I thought, "Aww my phone is flat, so I am not going to get any pictures", so I returned to Dragos, but not before buying the obligatory fridge magnets for our fridge at home. Soon, we were returning to Alzira, where I would spend one more night with Dragos and Ana, before flying home. What an awesome experience, spending time with Dragos and Ana, and meeting up with Dragos M. Enjoying the beautiful scenery, riding in Alzira, viewing our film, hearing the positive feedback and comments, and, of course, meeting all those lovely people.

On our way home from Barcelona, Dragos was extremely stressed; it was all down to that second hand car that I mentioned earlier. Throughout my visit, Dragos had been trying to get his car sorted and repaired, and well, things just weren't happening. In Spain, things move differently. Time is not of the essence, shall we say. Upon that drive home, I was trying to reassure Dragos and help him translate English into Spanish using Chat GPT so that he could speak to the BMW garage and arrange for his car to be transported to another garage to see if it could be repaired. I'd like to think I helped Dragos when he needed me most. Allowing him to see that there can be positive resolutions; it's just that sometimes we have to calm our minds and give situations a little time. Things worked out with the car, kind of, as when we got back to Alzira, Dragos had managed to arrange transport to take the car, which was undriveable, from the BMW main dealer to a garage that would look at its engine and then be able to provide a cost for repairs. Although there was still a way to go in getting the car sorted, I could tell Dragos was feeling a little less stressed, as at least now something was happening.

Upon returning to Dragos and Ana's home, we chilled for a while. Dragos had managed to find an old charger, and he was able to solder a cable to it that would fit my knee. We plugged it in, and it worked, allowing my knee to charge up. As the evening drew in, Ana suggested we took Victor up on his offer of visiting his family restaurant, so we had a drive down to Alzira town centre, where Dragos, Ana and I met up with Victor, who was extremely busy yet made time for us. We had a wonderful evening, with delicious food and a few drinks, engaging in fun filled conversation with lots of laughter, and the atmosphere outside of the restaurant was friendly and full of life.

Upon our return to Dragos and Ana's villa, we spent the remainder of the evening chatting about some of our favourite things. We discussed music and listened to some songs. We talked about culture and films, and Dragos went on to show me some of his early work, and fantastic creations, explaining where he took inspiration from. It was a lovely, relaxed evening, and I just felt so at home in the presence of these two wonderful and interesting people, both of whom have had a far wider reaching perspective of life than myself.

The following morning, as I packed my stuff. Ana made me a lovely breakfast, and the three of us just relaxed on the porch until around lunchtime. The time had flown over, and my stay was now at its end. It was time for me to head back to Alicante and my return flight home. Another two-hour drive from Alzira to Alicante, this time in the daylight, another beautiful day with Dragos and Ana. The conversation never dried up during my visit and was always pleasant and very interesting. I couldn't have asked for better hosts, and I know I have found lifelong friends. I feel incredibly grateful, whichever way you look at it, fate the Universe, or just sheer good luck.

Upon arrival at Alicante, I said farewell to Dragos, who remained outside with the car. Ana accompanied me into the airport and helped me find my way to where I was supposed to go. It was time to say goodbye to Ana and thank her for looking after me. Then, I was on my way back home.

Chapter 22

My old, infected leg played a massive role in me being stuck in limbo. Having it removed allowed me to experience things I probably would never have gotten to see or do, had I remained with both of my legs, which sounds bizarre. I just never really had the drive, imagination, or any real purpose. I have now gone on to meet some wonderful and amazing people upon my journey. I have been spurred on to become more adventurous; it has given me more fight and changed my way of thinking. I am human and will always want more in my life; however, I am very grateful for what I have right now.

My dad has a little sign hanging in our kitchen that reads.

"Never let the things you want make you forget the things you have".

It is a very important and meaningful message.

As we draw near to the end of this book, I do hope you have enjoyed it, and that you can take something away from my experiences, yes even the negative ones. Whether that be to look at life in a slightly different way and appreciate not only all the amazing things that you have in your life, but also the small things that can mean so much to someone else. Like taking the opportunity to say "Thank You" or "I love you" to a loved one, asking questions of yourself, and being honest when you do so. Take an interest in others and try not to judge them, for if you do, be prepared to be judged by your own standards. Make more time to be in the moment, as all that worrying gets you nowhere, and time spent stressing over what has passed or what you think may lie ahead makes what is important, "The Now", redundant. Don't rob yourself of valuable time. Try to be the best version of yourself you can be. We are all a work in progress.

So, what now for the next chapter in my life? Well, that is the thing about life. Although we think we may be in control of our destinies, none of us really know what direction we are headed in, and what may be in store. I would like to think of life as more of an adventure, and just going with the flow, allowing past experiences and knowledge to help me find a path through the unknown. Short term goals include getting a new Bartlett Knee, alongside a nice shiny bike to inspire me to new heights. Oh, and of course, I want to get this ulcerative colitis or whatever it is under control. In the long term, I tend not to make plans; that is not to say I don't dream of things like "my house in Scotland", along with the idea of some sort of "paying it forward" type of deal. Something I know I would find very rewarding. Hopefully, I will also be able to get a lot more involved with the Arctic One Foundation, completing challenges on their behalf. I believe Arctic One are in the process of arranging a two-day tour of the Isle of Wight, which I would like to take part in; it would be an excellent excuse to purchase another specific type of bike to aid in my adventure. I will also continue to blog, writing in my own unique style, never really worrying if anyone reads my stuff, as I quite often write for self-reflection. That said, I do hope that by sharing my thoughts and words, I can have a positive impact, possibly if someone is struggling.

I will practice with my guitar, which I am not entirely sure I will ever get any better at, but hey, it brings me joy and allows me to calm my mind. Oh, and I am seriously considering getting another dog. The pain of losing Baxter still resides within me, however I can also look back upon some very fond memories and know that the time spent with him was very special. I would like to think I could offer the same level of care and love to a new furry friend. I am considering a very different breed, perhaps a Border Terrier, as upon reading about them I think our personalities would match. I even have a name picked out, Neville, after one of my favourite authors.

Now, I know that little summary doesn't sound too exciting; however, like I said earlier, you don't know what is meant for you. I mean, I never expected to be in a small independent film, featured on the news, radio, or in magazines, write articles, travel, or return to work in a completely different role, a role which would never have occurred to me unless I had taken ill.

What can appear to be a negative situation in some cases can lead to very positive outcomes. I guess our mindsets and how we deal with our personal experiences can make or break us.

I thought I would end with a poem I wrote just recently. As you will read it has a lot to do with something we all encounter, and that is "Just not knowing", with all those questions that rattle around inside our heads. You will see, my words end in a positive tone. I think this is down to me becoming more mindful over the years. Understanding I have so much to be grateful for, and just saying a simple yet heartfelt, "Thank you".

It's ironic to think

It's ironic to think that whilst I love myself, my body is in chaos destroying its health.
It doesn't appear to know right from wrong; I'm suffering from internal conflict which is doing me harm.

Drugs that are meant to treat symptoms, have Ill effects. My body and soul they choose to reject. Panic attacks, anxiety and fear, these strange feelings of I'm going slightly insane. Questions of how much longer can I tolerate this pain?

My thoughts of which I have many all based upon Why. Some of which can cause me to want to burst out and cry. Those Penrose stairs, those impossible steps. Always trying to move forward, whilst glancing back.

Vicious circles, though locked in a box, clinging to a lottery ticket, that really should be a key to a lock. Relying on numbers, will they open a door, stepping from a daydream to discover what's in-store.

Scrolling through the wishful pages of a broken dream. Searching through so many memories of places I've never been.
Feelings of being lost and never being found.
Whispering voices inside my mind going around and around.

Searching for answers though the questions aren't clear. Battling inner demons showing no fear. Bringing forth light into darkness, chasing dark moods away. Practicing mindfulness, offering gratitude each day.

Chapter 23

Finally, in closing, I would like to thank you for purchasing this book. In doing so, you will become part of my journey. You will be with me upon each bike ride and new adventure. You may even be part of my dream and that wee house in Scotland.

About the Author

Hi I'm Glenn.

Things took a rather unexpected turn for me around June 1995. I was twenty-seven years old when I was diagnosed with a giant cell tumour in my right leg. That diagnosis marked the beginning of a very difficult 12-year journey, which was filled with surgeries, infections, and some of the most excruciating pain you could ever imagine.

In 1996, I underwent surgery to have a Kotz prosthesis implanted into my leg to replace my diseased bone. The prosthesis remained in place for over a decade, until September 2007, when I made the difficult decision to have an above-knee amputation. Surprisingly, that choice brought a new sense of freedom and the beginning of a new chapter in my life. It gave me the chance to rebuild and pursue things I never imagined possible.

Re-learning how to ride a bike—something I once took for granted, wasn't easy, and I had many moments of frustration and self-doubt. But with determination, hard work, and a positive attitude, I pushed through. I was incredibly fortunate to have the support of the amazing team at Pace Rehabilitation, who believed in me and helped me along the way. I also owe a lot to inspiring individuals such as Brian Bartlett, the creator of the Bartlett Tendon, and to Arctic ONE, an incredible foundation that offered me friendship and support.

Life has never been static for me. I've faced many challenges that have tested my resilience, both physically and mentally. However, through it all, I've learned to take one day at a time, understanding that every challenge has shaped me into who I am today, and I'm grateful for the strength I've found along the way.

Hopefully my story will inspire others to the power of perseverance, proving that with a change in mindset, (and as you will have discovered mine has not always been the best) with the right support, you can go on to push yourself to new limits, embracing life's adventures, no matter the challenges.

https://kotz68.blogspot.com
https://www.facebook.com/profile.php?id=61565724050937